To John Wooden,
and
To the memory of
Arthur Summers

ACKNOWLEDGMENTS

If the test of a basketball program is the young men it graduates, then what was seen as the demise of UCLA basketball never happened. As a group, the Bruins are some of the most gracious and articulate people one could hope to meet.

My thanks to them and everyone else who was gracious enough to be interviewed: Kareem Abdul-Jabbar, Toby Bailey, Pat Barrett, Keith Bean, Joe Bryant, Mitchell Butler, Jim Calhoun, Norman Chad, Jackie Ciunci, James Cotton, Schea Cotton, Denny Crum, Cameron Dollar, Tyus Edney, Bud Furillo, Craig Francis, Jack Haley, Roy Hamilton, Michael Holton, Roy Hamilton, Steve Hartman, Marques Johnson, David Kahn, Bobby Kortsen, Don MacLean, Gerald Madkins, Rick Majerus, Jeff Marx, Nigel Miguel, Reggie Miller, Victor Neil, Keith Owens, Al McGuire, Ed O'Bannon, Michael Pasano, Pooh Richardson, Steve Samms, Sonny Vacarro, Dick Vertlieb, Donnie Walsh, Bill Walton, and Jerry West. A special thank-you to Kenny Miller, the Los Angeles *Sentinel* reporter who was sucked into the John Williams recruiting mess. He got his story the hard way; he got run over for it.

My thanks to the coaches, past and present, who were similarly gracious: John Wooden, Gene Bartow, Gary Cunningham, Larry Brown, Walt Hazzard, and Jim Harrick. I was unable to reach Larry Farmer who was in Kuwait when I was researching this book, obliging me to use second-hand sources for his quotes.

I am indebted to *Sports Illustrated*, especially Bill Brubaker, Armen Keteyian, Curry Kirkpatrick, Gary Smith, and Alex Wolff, and the Los Angeles *Times*, especially Jim Murray, Tommy Bonk, Tracy Dodds, Jerry Crowe, and Tim Kawakami; to Kawakami, who did the interviews of O'Bannon, Bailey, and Edney; to Richard Justice of the Washington *Post* who interviewed MacLean and Butler; to Lyle Spencer of the Riverside *Press Enterprise*, Ron Rapoport and Mark Alesia of the Los Angeles *Daily News*, Frank Burlison of the Long Beach *Press-Telegram*, and Bob Padecky of the Santa Rosa *Press Democrat*.

There is a remarkable and growing body of work that bears witness to the mercenary pressures on youth basketball: the movie "Hoop Dreams," directed by Peter Gilbert, Steve James, and Fredrick Marx; the books *Raw Recruits* by Wolff and Keteyian; *Caught in the Net* by Tates Locke and Bob Ibach; and *The Last Shot* by Darcy Frey.

I am also indebted to John Wooden and Jack Tobin's *They Call Me Coach*, to Abdul-Jabbar's *Giant Steps*, to Reggie Miller and Gene Wojciechowksi's *I Enjoy Being the Enemy*, to Joe Gergen's *The Final Four*, and Dick Vitale and Kirkpatrick's *Time Out, Baby!* Also to Marx and Michael York for their series on the Kentucky program in the Lexington *Herald-Leader* and to Alan Greenberg and Mike Littwin for their series on Sam Gilbert in the Los Angeles *Times*.

My thanks to the UCLA sports information office, especially Marc Dellins, Bill Bennett, and John Dolak for their help.

Thanks to my editor, Jeanine Bucek, my agent, Steve Delsohn, and my friend, Littwin, for helping me think it through.

And as always, my thanks to my wonderful Loretta for everything.

—Northridge, Calif.

January, 1996

Contents

When I first approached Marques Johnson, he was sitting at the press table in Pauley Pavilion getting ready to announce that night's game. He asked what kind of book I was writing. I said it was something about college basketball's loss of innocence since John Wooden.

He laughed.

OK, so it was never really innocent. Not in the '70s when Sam Gilbert was watching out for Johnson and his teammates, or the '40s when John Wooden arrived in Westwood and the first big betting scandals hit, or even the '20s when Wooden was playing at Purdue and that West Lafayette physician offered to pay his expenses.

Today, however, the game has become commercialized beyond recognition. The parents of a high school player may pay $300 to a firm like The Next Level of West Chester, Pennsylvania, where coaches will assess their son's strengths and weaknesses. For $600, Collegiate Scouting Service offers parents its "professional exposure system to help you gain the advantage needed in today's college recruiting and admissions process."

The stars don't have to shell out; they have only to sort between offers of merchandise, trips, et al., from competing summer camps, AAU teams and, of course, high schools until they start the big dance: choosing colleges. If they're good enough, like Kevin Garnett, they can skip apprenticeship and go right into private practice. Indeed, a year after Garnett hopped from Chicago's Admiral Farragut Academy to the NBA, top preps like Tim Thomas and Kobe Bryant were delaying their choice of college, reportedly to see if the pros were interested in more teens.

For better and worse, it was the NCAA Tournament that made the game big time and UCLA that put the tournament on the marquee. Before Wooden's run started in 1964, it was a cult phenomenon; when he finished in 1975, it was on its way to today's mass audience.

The 1979 game between Magic Johnson's Michigan State and Larry Bird's Indiana State inspired not only collegiate prosperity but the NBA renaissance. In 1995 rookie Grant Hill would out-poll all the established stars for the All-Star Game. Hill's exposure had been relatively modest except for one event: His Duke teams had played in three Final Fours.

If college basketball has earned its premier niche, it has a dark side getting darker.

Campuses, which are supposed to be shelters for free inquiry, are now venues for what are essentially major league franchises honeycombed with a deceit born of the tension between amateur ideals and bottom-line reality.

The programs are deeply entrenched. The money the athletic department makes is only the start. Successful teams bind alumni to schools, a requisite for the ongoing fund raising that is more important in an age of tightening budgets.

Worse, it's out of control.

Debates on reforms are endless and pointless. Pay athletes? Which athletes? Those from revenue-producing sports? How much? More to the point, is anyone naive enough to believe that will stop the cheating?

OK, how about a salary cap?

History suggests conflicts between the commercial and the ideal are fraught with peril for all concerned. When presidents like Kentucky's David Roselle and UNLV's Robert Maxson placed themselves athwart their powerful basketball programs, the presidents wound up leaving.

This is not something that bad people like Jerry Tarkanian do because he isn't good like Dean Smith. At the core, they're all just basketball coaches, grateful at the chance to earn a living at a game. They just had different starting points. Smith, himself, has said things might have been different if he'd gotten his first job somewhere farther down the line, which is where Tark started.

The problem is systemic. No one wants to hurt anyone. Everyone—players, coaches, alums bearing $100 bills, camp organizers, street agents, wheeler dealers, press people, fans—just wants to be part of it.

Interestingly, UCLA players were unanimous on one point: even if it was a pressure cooker, they loved being there. "It's not a hard place to play," said Reggie Miller, "it's a hard place to coach."

Of course, not everyone gets a four-year scholarship at a fine school on a beautiful campus, which is the real problem. The universities have become a stop on the way to the NBA—and most of the pilgrims become casualties of the competition, like William Gates and Arthur Agee in "Hoop Dreams."

For better and worse, this is college basketball, colorful and corrupt, exciting, and philosophically more tenuous than ever.

Sometimes when you win, you really lose. And sometimes when you lose, you really win. And sometimes when you win or lose, you actually tie. And sometimes when you tie, you actually win or lose.
Winning or losing is like all one big organic globule, from which one extracts what one needs.

GLORIA IN "WHITE MEN CAN'T JUMP," WRITTEN BY RON SHELTON

They ought to hire me. Why ruin two lives?

KENTUCKY COACH JOE B. HALL, WHO SUCCEEDED THE LEGENDARY ADOLPH RUPP, ON THE HIRING OF LARRY FARMER, THE FOURTH COACH IN SIX YEARS SINCE JOHN WOODEN RETIRED

CHAPTER ONE

PARADISE MISPLACED

Yeah, we heard about it an awful lot. The John Wooden legacy was there. All those banners hanging in the rafters every day in practice. You never can get out from under that shadow, teams trying to live up to that, which is never going to happen again.

But the pressure was there. Everyone expected you to win and to perform at a certain level and succeed at a certain level. The other teams would definitely get up for UCLA, wanted to knock UCLA off, even that freshman year when we were a middle-of-the-barrel team.

Didn't matter. You've got UCLA across your chest so everyone's gunning for you.

—KEITH OWENS, CLASS OF 1991

In the spring of 1995, as if to announce a change of season, John Wooden returns to the NCAA finals.

It's eleven years since he's been to one of these. The last one was 1984 before his wife Nell died. He did go back to Indianapolis on Final Four weekend in 1991 to accept an award, but he stayed away from the games. Instead, he went to the church where he and Nell were baptized.

But this is another time and a different UCLA team, too, businesslike, unselfish, and full of a joy the players communicate to everyone around them. Could it have been only a year ago they did their usual number, when Ed O'Bannon said he didn't know that first-round opponent Tulsa was in Oklahoma, shortly before Tulsa waxed them?

This has already been an incredible tournament for them, what with Tyus Edney's last-second, end-to-end dash to beat Missouri in the second round. Wooden, 84 years old, decides to attend, even if it means flying home from a high school all-star game in St. Louis and grabbing a flight to Seattle early the next morning.

He's lucky there aren't camera crews at the airport to meet him.

In his time it was just a basketball tournament, but now the Final Four is one of the premier events on the calendar. An air of commerce hangs over it like gold dust over a boom town and a frenzy over the huge press corps, which wants to know if Wooden will address the Bruins. Does he still come around? How well do the players know him?

No, he won't address the team. Yes, he attends home games, sitting two rows in back of the UCLA bench with his daughter, Nan. Jim Harrick comes over for breakfast every month or so at a Cocos near Wooden's home in the San Fernando Valley. The players?

They think he's a nice man who did something special at UCLA a long time ago—sometime after they built the pyramids but before they had video games—and now nobody will let them forget it.

"They don't know him very well," Harrick says. "They've never spent much time with him at all.

"And really, young people aren't real history buffs. It could have been 800 years ago for all my guys care. In the 1960s and '70s—that's so long ago, I mean, you can't even believe that.

"Young people, you'll find out, are enthralled with the moment."

This is some moment, too, the climax of a month of excitement known as March Madness: national spectacle, merchandise-moving vehicle, and ratings engine rolled into one. CBS is charging $500,000 for 30 seconds of commercial time, almost double the 1995 World Series' $275,000 per minute. The basketball television contract provides 75 percent of the NCAA's entire $190 million operating budget.

With UCLA back, there's some serious front-running going on, too.

Famed Laker fan Jack Nicholson has attached himself to the program. Even Harrick can't believe that one; he calls him "our new-found friend." Nicholson's people claim he bought his tickets, but the Seattle *Post-Intelligencer* reports Smilin' Jack showed up in a network trailer and, according to a CBS official, "demanded credentials for himself and six of his friends thirty minutes before game time. And he got them."

CBS loves shots of celebrities in the stands, even if it has to comp the celebs itself. Jack, however, is bounced out of the press room by a guard who hasn't been briefed on the handling of movie stars.

Kevin Costner's here. He and friends go to the University of Washington on the off-day to play, but the courts are full. A UW official asks the guys playing at one basket how long they'll be. They say Costner's team can play winners. He leaves, instead.

Wooden appears on CBS's pre-game show. The Final Four having assumed the importance of a world summit, the NCAA transcribes and distributes his brief remarks.

3

Q: When did you last speak with UCLA Coach Jim Harrick?

Wooden: I speak with him quite often and not always about basketball. We've talked several times during the tournament. I called him to congratulate the team on a fine season.

Q: What do you think is going through Coach Harrick's mind entering the game?

Wooden: I think he is more concerned with his guard's health than anything else. I'm sure he's not thinking about the past or my teams at UCLA. He is concentrating on the game tonight.

Wooden takes his seat at mid-court in the mammoth Kingdome, sitting with his trademark pose, first finger on pursed lips. He watches as Harrick's guard—Edney—who has carried the team on his little shoulders, leaves in the opening minutes with a sprained wrist and the fearsome Arkansas press strips his replacement, Cameron Dollar, the first time he touches the ball.

Wooden remembers thinking, "This is going to be difficult."

This is not an ordinary man.

How unfortunate it is that time has shrunk Wooden into an icon; "winner." How ironic that his dynasty would launch college basketball from campus sport into entertainment industry, shot through with irreconcilable contradictions.

Winning, as he would tell you, is a shallow value compared to more important ones like doing one's best and being part of a team. There's so much luck involved. Anything can happen in one game, like the '63 first-round loss when the same Bruins who'd start the dynasty a year later were blown out by a torrid Arizona State team.

He had a 14–12 team he enjoyed as much as some of his champions, especially the talent-loaded squads in the years he had to remind his players they had to go out and play, or deny them permission to smoke dope for their aching knees, or threaten to suspend them if they missed practice due to an arrest for lying down on Wilshire Boulevard during a protest.

He always knew there was more to life than winning and losing. He was always secure enough to remember it when no one else seemed to.

He wasn't just a throwback to a simpler time. He was old-fashioned when he arrived at UCLA in 1948, a straightlaced Hoosier in this sun-splashed land that care forgot, a departure for writers who preferred wisecracking coaches who'd take a drink. The teetotaling Wooden was like their grade-school teachers.

Wooden did love his lessons and parables and diagrams like the Pyramid of Success that still hangs on a wall in his den: 25 virtues like Friendship and Loyalty, piled atop one another to form a pinnacle of Success ("... peace of mind which is a direct result of self-satisfaction in knowing you did your best....")

Actually, he was his own best example: a giant of a man in an unremarkable frame, principled, consistent and blessed with that rare gift, proportion.

He wasn't afraid to lose and, indeed, never talked to his players about it, freeing them to do their best and see where it took them.

"It was paradise," says Bill Walton. "I thought that the whole world was like this. It was one of the problems I had with my life. I grew up in a perfect family. John Wooden shows up and says, will you play for us?

"The first game I ever saw in Pauley Pavilion was [Lew] Alcindor's last game. I go in there and the place is jam-packed, the band is cranking up, the cheerleaders are dancing all around. I'm this 16-year-old kid from San Diego. I said, 'Yeah, this is what I want!'

"And then I got to UCLA and everything was perfect. In college, that's the greatest time in the world. On a basketball scholarship? At UCLA? With John Wooden as your coach? What more could you ask for?

"We wanted to be like those other great ones. We wanted to be like Hazzard and Goodrich and Erickson and Slaughter and Goss, Abdul-Jabbar and Warren and Lucius Allen and Shackleford and Wicks and Rowe and Heitz and Patterson and Vallely. We wanted to be like all those guys. We wanted to be the champions. We thought it was a sacred gift that was passed on to us, that, 'Hey, you're the ones John Wooden has chosen to come and keep this thing going!'

"It was like an elite society and a tremendous responsibility, like 'You'd better win.' We felt that and we liked that.

"You win all your games there, you join the NBA ... and I said, 'What's this?'"

Winning is fun but illusory. After Wooden bowed out, with ten titles in his final twelve years, there wasn't much proportion left in Westwood.

"One of the funniest things," Wooden says, "and this is funny to me, not upsetting, funny—one of our alumni, after we won the last championship in San Diego, immediately after the game, he's so happy: 'We did it, we did it, we did it. You let us down last year [the semifinal loss to North Carolina State] but we got 'em this year.'

"Very fine supporter, helps UCLA in every area, the athletic, the academic. Very wealthy man."

After that, the chuckles came harder. It has been twenty years since Wooden retired and his six successors have spent their tenures, however brief, looking out the window for villagers carrying torches.

Gene Bartow went 52–9 and fled after two years to take a job at a school that didn't have a team yet.

Gary Cunningham went 50–8, left after two years and became athletic director at a tiny school named Western Oregon State College, although it, at least, existed.

Larry Brown was a blur, taking the Bruins back to the NCAA finals his first season, abandoning them a year later. He told friends leaving was "the worst mistake of my life" and pined for Westwood until the Bruins rehired him in 1988—whereupon he promptly changed his mind and left again.

Larry Farmer, a deer on the expectations freeway, lasted three years, at the end of which he was a withdrawn, burned-out shell and left to pursue his craft in Utah and Kuwait.

Walt Hazzard, who vowed never to quit, didn't. He was fired after an unhappy four-year dissension-filled struggle.

The last seven years have been devoted to torturing Jim Harrick, the little guy they hired in 1988 after all the big guys turned them down. He's won 20 games every season but the NCAA Tournament has turned into Pratfall City, capped by the '94 swan dive against Tulsa.

Harrick is a ritual target on talk radio and has a virtual section of his own in the weekly letters to the Los Angeles *Times* where readers work him over, borrowing the style of columnist Jim Murray:

HARRICK BEING OUTCOACHED HAS BECOME ANNUAL EVENT

Although it's a new year, some things never change: The weather was beautiful for the Rose Parade; there is a disagreement over who is No. 1 in college football; and another Jim Harrick-coached Bruin team, with an overwhelming superiority in talent, was outplayed, outhustled and totally outcoached by lowly Oregon. Bring on Tulsa!   —*Leonard Levine*,

Tarzana

This appeared after a loss at Oregon—the Bruins' first of the 1994–95 season in which they were never ranked lower than No. 4. When they finished No. 1 and the catcalls died down, Harrick joked they were only "in remission."

Now, he's in Seattle for the game he's been waiting all his life for, with his point guard out and a sophomore in his place who has just been turned over and shaken like a piggy bank by the dread Arkansas press.

Harrick, who has been dreading this scenario all day, remembers thinking, "We're in doomsville now...."

At home in Huntington Beach, a high school sophomore named Schea Cotton, the player of his generation, so far, watches Edney leave the game on TV and draws the same conclusion.

"I thought," Schea says later, "they were kind of dead in the hole."

Schea's brother plays at Long Beach State, and Schea has been more into the 49ers. Shea's got his own career. This is the Next Generation in person with a lifestyle that shows how much the game has progressed, or degenerated.

7

He has already been profiled in *Sports Illustrated,* where his 6-5, 210-pound frame was compared to Michelangelo's David. He plays all winter and summers, too, on the AAU circuit, hawked by college coaches, scouting "gurus" and well-wishers, many of whom would love to help shepherd him through the hectic decisions to come.

His parents, James and Gaynell, are hardworking, down-to-earth people but they're involved, too. They've heard Schea will command big money and it may not be long, either. He's been in high school two years and has transferred twice.

Top players now evaluate high schools by several criteria: rapport with the coach, style of play, exposure, level of competition. Academics are incidental. Kevin Garnett, a hot stick from South Carolina, got tight with Chicago Farragut Academy's Ronnie Fields at Nike's summer camp, transferred up for his senior year, failed to make a test score that would qualify him for a college scholarship and went right into the NBA draft.

Garnett was the fifth pick. Now all the kids are restless as jumping beans.

"Yeah," says Schea, "you hear it a lot because nowadays, I think, a lot of people are in it more for the money than for the love of the game.

"I don't look at it like that. I look at it, when I stop having fun, then I just stop playing so until then, I'll remain in school."

Actually, Schea has told his parents he'd like to hop to the pros, too. Kids these days grow up knowing how to say the right thing to the press. Everyone will Stay in School and Get My Degree. It's a mantra. Why aren't there more degrees then? The latest NCAA statistics show 58 percent of college basketball players didn't graduate, up from 54 percent the year before.

Schea has boosters and detractors. He has a budding career. When it doesn't interfere, he has a childhood.

It is a peculiar kind of amateurism, in which the schools make millions, the coaches hundred of thousands and the players get educational opportunities they may not want.

It's a peculiar time.

At Connecticut, where the men's and women's basketball teams were once simultaneously ranked No. 1, Coaches Jim Calhoun and Gene Auriemma are reportedly feuding.

The parents of Chris Street, an Iowa junior killed in an auto crash with a snowplow, sue the county. CBS commentator, Billy Packer, and NBA scout, Marty Blake, testify Street could have earned more than twenty million in an 8-to-12-year NBA career. The county calls former Iowa star Al (the Vanilla Gorilla) Lorenzen, who didn't make it in the NBA, to testify just how hard it is. "Maybe he would have made it," says Lorenzen, "and maybe he wouldn't." The jury finds Street was at fault in the crash.

A member of the Fresno State athletic board, which is seeking a new coach, receives a threatening phone call from a fan, supporting the candidacy of Jerry Tarkanian.

Art Long, a burly University of Cincinnati forward, is charged with intoxication and disorderly conduct after local police allege he punched one of their horses; Long's lawyer says his client was "petting" the horse.

The University of Hawaii fines football coach Bob Wagner, citing "declining ticket sales." At a press conference UH basketball coach Riley Wallace confronts his boss, Athletic Director Hugh Yoshida, asking if he has to win to keep his job. Yoshida says this isn't the time to discuss it.

Coaches Mike Krzyzewski, Tim Grgurich and Gary Williams all miss parts of the 1994–95 seasons with diagnoses that include "exhaustion."

Of course, UCLA is where they invented exhaustion and these days, it's harder than it ever was. Gary Cunningham, now athletic director at UC Santa Barbara, says the pressure on his old assistant, Harrick, dwarfs anything he had to deal with. UCLA is still special—America's team, Larry Brown suggested once—with high standards, colorful letter writers and unreconstructed romantics. Even Wooden argues another dynasty is possible.

"Absolutely!" he says, "It's just as possible today as it was then. It was impossible then in the eyes of everyone, including myself. It wouldn't be logical, for example, to say, 'This happened in this particular period. It was impossible before. It was impossible afterward. It was just that time.'

"If that were true, I was sure lucky that I was right there at that particular time.

No. A very improbable thing. Improbable then. But not impossible at all."

"Sure it can be done again," says Walton. "You just need someone who's willing to stay there and be a humble leader. Someone who's a giving person, not someone who wants to take.

"You've got to create an atmosphere like it was then, where people don't want to leave. Because in college basketball today the minute you have a good game, everybody's looking to go right to the NBA. Whereas at UCLA, we had the best players, but nobody even gave it a thought about leaving.

"The quality of my life went downhill when I left UCLA and I joined the NBA. And I became the highest-paid player in the history of pro sports."

You might need a time machine as much as a humble leader. Ask Jim Harrick, watching gloomily as Arkansas' Clint McDaniel scores on a layup off Dollar's turnover—this stuff ain't easy.

CHAPTER TWO

THE WOODEN YEARS: CALIFORNIA GOTHIC

... There sits a statesman,
Strong, unbiased, wise ...
And there a doctor,
Whose quick, steady hand
Can mend a bone....
And later I may say
"I knew the lad,
And he was strong,
Or weak or kind or proud,
Or bold or gay.
I knew him once,
But then he was a boy."

They ask me why I teach,
and I reply,
"Where else could I find
such splendid company?"

—GLENNICE L. HARMON,
"THEY ASK ME WHY I TEACH," ONE OF
JOHN WOODEN'S FAVORITE POEMS

In the beginning, it was paradise.

It was Southern California in the '40s, beautiful and unspoiled as in all the period movies with the familiar shots: the palm trees; the propeller plane touching down at the airport; the men in fedoras; the boxy cars.

John and Nell Wooden, lifelong Hoosiers, arrived in the summer of 1948, with their kids jammed into the back of their old Mercury, having stopped off at the Grand Canyon and Carlsbad Caverns, en route to Dad's first big-time job.

Actually, UCLA was a new school with a second-rate basketball program and scant concern about it. The campus was beautiful and spacious. USC, the traditional finishing school for Los Angeles' power elite, sat downtown in the middle of what would be increasing blight, but UCLA nestled in Westwood at the base of the Santa Monica Mountains, bordered by Beverly Hills on the east, Bel Air on the north, Brentwood on the west.

The beach was five miles from campus, down Sunset Boulevard, and the onshore breeze kept the village cool in summer, warm in winter. Students strolled to class in shorts and sandals. They had year-round tans. People always said they looked like Hollywood extras in a movie about college life.

It would take Wooden sixteen seasons to launch the UCLA dynasty, but nobody suffered in the meantime. This was California in the '50s and '60s. There was still an available American Dream and this was it.

In nearby Torrance, the Beach Boys would soon be cranking out the string of hits that would paint California's azure skies on the brain pans of a generation. Psychedelia was coming, and the Summer of Love. Two UCLA students named Jim Morrison and Ray Manzarek would soon form The Doors and start playing high school proms in the San Fernando Valley.

Westwood would grow into a cross between a campus town and Rodeo Drive, with rents so high businesses would go bust as fast as oil wildcatters. In 1963, it was still Westwood Village. There were no skyscrapers with faux-French names on the Wilshire Corridor, no multimillion-dollar condos.

Wooden ate breakfast at Hollis Johnson's drugstore on Westwood Boulevard, a block from the campus gates. The village awoke slowly. The breakfast crowd was small. The pace was leisurely. Life was as good as it could be.

Jerry West, the Laker star, was another Hollis Johnson's regular. "Like a calm sea" is how West remembers Wooden. "One of the greatest men I've ever met in my life.

"Forget his accomplishments. He's a great man."

Wooden's early life could have come out of a movie, or more appropriately, since he was an avid reader and amateur poet, a book, say Mark Twain's *Adventures of Tom Sawyer*.

He was born October 14, 1910, one of four sons of Joshua Wooden, an Indiana tenant farmer. John's childhood was packed with turn-of-the-century Heartland images: the house without electricity, the three-holer outhouse, the chores, the tomato basket with the bottom knocked out that was his first basketball hoop, the carnival where he first set eyes on pert Nellie Riley, the park where they attended band concerts, the hayrides, square dances, county fairs.

Mythology notwithstanding, farming was already declining as a way of life. The Woodens got a little 60-acre spread near Martinsville, but lost it in the panic of 1924. Joshua moved his family into the town of about 5,000 and got a job in a bath house, giving massages. He was a gentle, religious man who read the Bible daily and never swore. The worst thing his kids ever heard him say was "Goodness gracious sakes alive!"

Joshua read poetry aloud to his sons, too. John called those times "some of the happiest memories of my childhood."

John became a basketball star at Martinsville High. The game had only been invented in 1892 (it still had a center jump after every basket), but it already dominated Indiana community life. High school gyms often held more people than the town had, since fans from outlying areas had to be accommodated. Districts consolidated for bigger schools and better teams.

Martinsville won the state title in John's junior year. The towns-people gave the players silver Hamilton pocket watches. Wooden still has his under a glass bell, and it still runs.

Recruited by the major colleges in Indiana, Wooden chose Purdue because Coach Piggie Lambert played the daring, new fast break instead of the conventional pattern ball. There were no schol-arships; a school only promised an athlete a job to help him pay his own way. That was before student-athletes were hired to watch the automatic sprinkler system water the football field or wind the electric clocks. Wooden washed dishes in a fraternity house and sold programs at football games.

Of course, things were changing.

When he was a sophomore, Lambert told him a West Lafayette doctor had offered to pay for his housing and tuition. In Wooden's book, *They Call Me Coach*, he recounts the conversation.

"Are you going to take it, John?" [Lambert asks].

"What do you mean?" [Wooden answers].

"I just wonder how you're going to pay him back."

"Coach," I said, "I thought you just told me he wanted to do it."

"That's right, John, he does. Remember, though, that I told you that when you came to Purdue, you would work hard but you would get through and wouldn't owe me or anyone else a cent. You will have earned your way. Now if you accept this doctor's offer, even though he doesn't expect to be repaid, I think you're the kind of person who wouldn't feel right about it unless you did.

"Think about it, John," he said, "and in a day or two, I'll talk to you again."

A couple of days later, I went by to see him, "I decided not to take the doctor's offer."

"I really didn't think you would, John," he said, "after you thought about it."

They didn't have the word then, but Wooden was a superstar, a three-time All-American, college player of the year as a senior. He was nicknamed the "Indiana Rubber Man." Before he ever won an NCAA title as a coach, he'd be inducted into the Basketball Hall of Fame as a player.

He had an offer to barnstorm with the original New York Celtics, which was professional basketball in those days. The pay was a princely $5,000 a year, but Lambert didn't think Wooden was that kind of person, either.

"What did you come to Purdue for?" Wooden remembers Lambert asking in *They Call Me Coach.*

"To get an education," I told him.

"Did you get one?"

"I think so."

"You're not going to use it?" he asked.

"I hope to."

"Well, you won't be using it barnstorming around the country playing basketball. You're not that type of person."

Instead, Wooden took a job as basketball coach, football coach, track coach, athletic director, and P.E. and English teacher at a high school in Dayton, Kentucky, for $1,800 a year.

He and Nell were married in a small ceremony in Indianapolis. They had dinner at the Bamboo Inn and went to the Circle Theater to hear the Mills Brothers who sang encore after encore and became John's favorite group for all time.

In thirteen years, he worked his way from Dayton to South Bend, Indiana, Central High to Indiana State, where he coached an NAIA runner-up in his second season.

The year before, he had turned down an NAIA bid because reserve Clarence Walker, who was black, couldn't participate. He accepted the next season when the tournament moved from Kansas City to New York's Madison Square Garden. There were coaches, like Piggie Lambert, who thought college teams had no business playing in any off-campus arena as if they were professionals or vaudevillians. Lambert had refused to take his Purdue teams there and was disappointed when Wooden took Indiana State.

At South Bend Central, Wooden had thought of himself, not unhappily, as a high school coach for life, but now he hoped to move up the ladder, assuming that meant the Big Ten. Indeed, Minnesota was interested. He also had an invitation to interview with a West Coast school—UCLA—where he'd been recommended by an old Hoosier friend, Bob Kelley, who'd become the radio voice of the Los Angeles Rams.

Wooden wanted to go to Minnesota. It was a huge school with good facilities. UCLA was pretty but as far as basketball went, primitive.

However, Minnesota wanted Wooden to keep the old coach as his assistant. Wooden wanted his own man. Minnesota said it had to talk it over; an official promised to call that night at 6. When he didn't call and UCLA did, Wooden accepted the UCLA job.

An hour later the Minnesota official called, explaining he'd been delayed by a snowstorm. Wooden said he'd taken another job.

The Minnesota official asked Wooden if he could call UCLA back and say he wasn't coming. Wooden said he couldn't.

And so Caesar came to Rome.

Rome was a little rustic in 1948.

If there was nothing on the West Coast to equal Hoosier Hysteria, there was still interest. There were famous coaches and a talent pool. Howard Hopson's "Tall Firs" of Oregon had won the first two NCAA titles. Stanford's Hank Luisetti had invented the jump shot. A young man from Oakland named Bill Russell would lead USF to back-to-back titles in the '50s and Pete Newell's California Bears would win in 1959.

Los Angeles, however, was no hotbed. The glamour sports were Rams football, USC football and track. The city would go head over heels for the Dodgers but would barely notice the Lakers' arrival.

UCLA was largely a commuter school with scant athletic tradition. Originally a teacher's college downtown on Vermont Avenue, it had become part of the University of California at Berkeley and had been named the Southern Branch of the University of California. It didn't move to Westwood until 1929. Its mascot was the Bruin, befitting the offspring of Berkeley's Bears. Until 1985 when Bill Conti, the Oscar-winning composer who wrote the theme from "Rocky," provided a replacement, the UCLA fight song, "Hail the Sons of Westwood," had the same melody as Cal's "Hail the Sons of California."

The Bruins had basketball players of note—Jackie Robinson; Don Barksdale, the first black to play in an NBA All-Star Game; Dr. Ralph Bunche, the U.N. diplomat who won the Nobel peace prize; Knick star Willie Naulls—but they were no power. Their record when Wooden arrived was 281–281. They once lost 42 games in a row to USC.

They played on a musty court on the second floor of the Men's Old Gymnasium, nicknamed the "B. O. Barn." It held only 2,400 fans with pullout bleachers; it wasn't a problem because 2,400 rarely showed up.

The Barn would have fit into one of the big Indiana high school plants several times. Nor was the team that Wooden found up to Indiana standards.

"The level of interest was very, very poor," says Wooden. "I was most discouraged when I first came.

"I probably would not have come. I was led to believe we'd have a nice place to play on campus by the end of my three-year contract. I was promised that. We got it in seventeen years. Had I realized the situation, I'm quite certain I wouldn't have come."

"We'd carry in bleachers they had stored somewhere and we'd seat around 2,400. I believe it was after the third year, the fire department stepped in and said there could only be 1,100 in there.

"And from that time on, we played—I'm not sure of all of them—at Santa Monica Junior College, Long Beach City College, Long

Beach Auditorium, Pan-Pacific Auditorium, Olympic Auditorium. And then when the Sports Arena [on the USC campus] came along we started playing there, but always doubleheaders with USC. One time we couldn't get any place, and we went to Bakersfield to play a game....

"We practiced there [Men's Old Gym] for my first seventeen years at UCLA. While we had practice there, gymnasts were practicing along the side. Wrestling was at the end. And there were trampolines on the other side. It was a three- or four-ring circus.

"It was just as hard for the other coaches, you know. The gymnastic coach, he's just as interested in gymnastics as I am in basketball, and our wrestling coach, too. It was tough for all of us and because of that, those two coaches became two of my very dearest friends because we were sharing adversity, in a sense.

"Before we practiced every day, for seventeen years mind you, I had the Buildings and Grounds people make me 10-foot brooms, a couple of those, and then 10-foot wide mops. Before we practiced, because there was a lot of physical education in there and the dust would accumulate, we would sweep it, I and the managers. We took towels and dampened them. I'd walk along in front—I took the easy job—with a pail of water, like feeding chickens. Every day for seventeen years I did that.

"To me the most amazing thing of all our championships was those first two that we won under those conditions. No private dressing rooms. No private showers for either coaches or players."

Wooden thought he'd stay a couple of years. By then, however, his kids were Californians through and through and they never left.

Wooden's Indiana-style fast break began turning the program around. His first team, picked to finish last in the Pacific Coast Conference, broke the UCLA record by winning 22 games and captured the first of four division titles in a row.

The NCAA Tournament, however, was something else. In national competition, the Bruins always ran into someone better. Wooden began wondering what he was doing wrong. In 1953, his boyhood friend, Branch McCracken, won an NCAA title with Indiana's Hurryin' Hoosiers. Wooden jumped into his arms after the game and later confided to McCracken his doubts of ever matching him.

After a 14–12 season in 1959–60, his worst record, Wooden began reevaluating everything he was doing. He says he never figured it out.

Actually, it was easy.

The game, as Wooden understood it, was to find some able young men who wanted to attend your school and turn them into the best possible team. This did not mean searching far and wide for the best players. Wooden didn't believe in that.

"I refused to do that," he says. "I made that clear when I came here. My family comes first. I would not go away to scout. I would not be away from home. I refused to do that, and I didn't have assistants do that.

"Now Southern California, yes, I'd go see some players but normally it was assistants—after I got some full-time assistants. I didn't have any for several years. It wasn't proper for an assistant coach, either."

Nor was he slick about the recruiting he did.

Denny Crum, a young player at Pierce Junior College in the San Fernando Valley, remembers his tour of the campus with Wooden in 1958: past a row of garbage cans behind Kerkhoff Hall where the training table was, in the back door, through the kitchen, then after they had eaten, being asked abruptly, "Well, are you coming or aren't you?"

"He preferred to have local kids," says Crum. "And if you talked to him about a kid who you were trying to sell and would he call him, he'd say, 'If he's not interested enough to pursue us, then forget him. I'd rather coach someone that wants to be here.'

"Coach Wooden was very good at talking to kids and stuff once they came to campus, but he wasn't one to go out to see them. So Jerry Norman, when they hired him as a full-time assistant, he started going out and looking at kids and determining who to recruit and then recruiting them. Well, in the past UCLA had never done that.

"It was amazing to me that they ever won as many games as they did on the basis of how they ran the program in those days."

Call it luck, call it fate, call it overdue, but things began to change.

In 1961, Naulls told Wooden about a flashy young high school guard from Philadelphia named Walt Hazzard, whom he'd seen in a preliminary game.

Wooden never saw Hazzard and couldn't even offer him a scholarship because his grades weren't good enough. Hazzard had played on an Overbrook powerhouse with future pros Wally Jones and Wayne Hightower and had an array of choices but was so taken with UCLA, he came west, even though he had to first attend Santa Monica College.

In Hazzard's first season at UCLA, the Bruins reached the NCAA semifinals. They were tied, 70–70, with eventual champion Cincinnati when Hazzard was called for charging. UC's Tom Thacker then hit a a long jumper with :03 left to win the game.

Midway through the next season, Wooden, who used to exchange poems with a former player, Pete Blackman, wrote one about his team:

... At Washington we lost a pair,

We were quite cold, as was the air,

No one could hit and Fred was flat,

And played more like "Sir Fred of Fat."

... Sir Mil of Wee now feels that he

A starter evermore should be,

But young soph Gail of fingers long,

Cannot agree, he knows that's wrong....

Sir Fred just called to say that he

And Gail at practice could not be;

In the morn at eight they have an exam

For which today they wish to cram,

They know for this I can't say "No,"

And I'd be wrong if I did so;

Miss practice—for study! I'll always agree,

But they've had no exams in the past days—three!

It was expected and it came,

Jack's knee is sore, in fact he's lame,

He cannot practice on this day,

But is sure this weekend he can play,

He called along with Chuck and Keith,

From practice they all seek relief....

However, Pete, there's optimism

Beneath my valid criticism,

I want to say—yes, I'll foretell,

Eventually this team will jell,

And when they do, they will be great,

A championship could be their fate,

With every starter coming back,

Yes, Walt and Gail and Keith and Jack

And Fred and Freddie and some more,

We could be champs in sixty-four.

The burly Fred Slaughter—"Sir Fred of Fat"—was their tallest starter, at 6-5.

Keith was 6-5 forward Keith Erickson, a free-spirited beach boy who was good at basketball but better at volleyball.

Jack was 6-3 forward Jack Hirsch, a transplanted New Yorker with a motormouth and a street-wise game, a rich kid who used to call Wooden "JW" and later described himself as "just a screw-off" and "the odd Jew-boy on the team."

Gail was Gail Goodrich, a stumpy guard who had only recently spurted to a height of 5-11 and had just beaten out Jim Milhorn— "Sir Mil of Wee"—for a starting job.

All but Hazzard were second-echelon prospects. Three were junior college transfers. But they were quick, smart, and played together. They would proclaim an undying respect for Wooden, if only in retrospect. "He was a wise man, a great man," Erickson once told *Sports Illustrated's* Frank Deford. "Of course, I didn't know that at the time. He wasn't any big deal to me. I didn't listen to anything he said."

Hazzard, who revered Wooden, almost left as the straight-arrow coach tried to break him of playground nuances like behind-the-back passes.

"I didn't agree with the way he approached me, as opposed to the way he approached Gail," says Hazzard. "He would come at me with a heavy hand. He would go to Gail with kid gloves.

"I was raised in the schoolyards of Philadelphia by Guy Rodgers and there was no better ballhandler or passer. He taught me how to pass the ball and dribble it. Coach had to learn to live with it. The main thing was to make the play. I mean, I didn't do it just to show off. It was always to create the play. And sometimes your imagination takes you beyond where you should be....

"Coach was complaining. I was getting ready to leave. I had missed a pre-game meal, not intentionally. I had tried to help a friend. We got caught in a time problem and by the time I showed up for the pre-game meal, it was over. By the time I got to the Sports Arena to play the game and tried to explain what happened, he didn't want to talk to me.

"So he benched me. It was against Ohio State—Jerry Lucas and John Havlicek. It was a big game, my sophomore year. It was just a big, big game.

"He didn't start me. OK, I'll take my punishment. I missed the pre-game meal, that's fine. Puts me in the game, we make a run, we almost have a chance to win the game.

"The next night, we come back against Utah and he benches me again but at the same time, he's screaming and yelling at me. I didn't like anyone yelling at me. I'm as sensitive as anyone. We lose again.

"So I called home and told my parents, 'I'm coming home.' And my father says, 'No, you have to stick it out. You made a commitment. You have to stay there and the coach will work with you.' "

Hazzard stayed. Wooden, realizing he'd gone as far as he could, eased up. The Bruins went 20–9 in 1962–63 and brought their starting team back, now highly rated despite its lack of size, which Wooden made up for by pressing full-court all game.

Wooden had pressed under Piggie Lambert and had coached a press at Indiana State but had only dabbled with it at UCLA. Pressing was then considered a desperation tactic that wouldn't bother the sophisticated player of the day over the long haul. The game was infatuated with size and strength as athletic big men replaced the old lumbering giants. Teams like Michigan piled hulks on top of each other, even if Cazzie Russell, their 6-5, 220-pound guard had to dribble hunched over with one arm out to ward off defenders.

UCLA was about to rock traditional notions of defense. It didn't have to sit back and react. It could force the offense out of its patterns. It could be a weapon, not a shield.

The little Bruins took to the press like ugly ducklings to water and opponents never knew what hit them.

"It was unheard of," says Hazzard. "Totally unheard of. When we first hit with it, it was an innovation that just shocked people. It was a surprise element, and it had a tremendous psychological effect on other teams.

"They spent a lot of time working on it, figuring out a way to break the pressure. Now today with videotape and all the technology that's available in basketball, a press is still effective as a surprise element but you can't use it as your primary weapon. Everybody knows how to attack it. It's not a psychological thing any more. And the ball-handling skills, you have players that use both hands better than they did back in that day.

"I mean, you could see teams worrying about the pressure, trying to control the tempo of the game, trying to break the press. I mean, it was a big accomplishment for them to get the ball across half-court. And then to see that over the course of the game that you could wear them down, to see the energy draining from their bodies.... It would never fail. At some point in the game, it would be a blitz."

Teams dropped into black holes against the Bruins, committing turnover after turnover, giving UCLA layup after layup. The Bruins became famous for their game-breaking bursts. They went into the NCAA tournament 26–0 but were written off again as a curiosity, an afterthought to semifinalists Michigan and Duke. *Sports Illustrated* predicted the Bruins wouldn't win "because only two teams in history have ever gone undefeated up to and through the tournament."

The Bruins had only escaped Seattle, 95–90, and USF, 76–72, in the West regional. In the semifinals at Kansas City, they trailed Kansas State, 75–70, with 7:28 left when their cheerleaders, whose plane had been delayed by bad weather, rushed in waving their pompoms.

Coincidentally or not, the Bruins went on an 11–0 run and won, 91–84.

Underdogs still, they played Duke, who had beaten Michigan. The well-drilled Blue Devils, the pride of the rising Atlantic Coast Conference, had two 6-10 starters and an All-American forward, Jeff Mullins. The Bruins were five inches smaller per man. When Wooden was asked how he looked at the Blue Devils, he answered, "Up."

The Dukies led, 30–27, when the press got them, too. The Bruins ended the first half with a 16–0 run. In the second half, a reserve UCLA forward named Kenny Washington started hitting long baseline jumpers, one after another. As improbable as any of the Bruins, Washington was from Beaufort, South Carolina, and had been recommended by Hazzard who claimed he was 6-5. It wasn't until Washington climbed off a bus, which he'd ridden 2,400 miles cross-country, that Wooden learned he was more like 6-2.

Washington went 11 for 16 that night and scored 26 points. The Blue Devils didn't mount a serious threat in the second half. The Bruins won, 98–83, their largest margin of victory in the tournament.

They sat atop the basketball world and decided they liked the view.

In later years, Wooden would say that he'd like all his friends in coaching to win an NCAA championship.

And those he wasn't as fond of, he'd add with that old JW twinkle, he'd like them to win more than one.

Not that anyone thought he was in great danger of repeating. Graduation had taken Hazzard, Hirsch, and Slaughter. In the 1964–65 season opener at Illinois they were demolished, 110–83.

UCLA made it back to the NCAA finals, all but unnoticed in the hype around the Michigan–Princeton rematch of their Holiday Classic shootout in Madison Square Garden, in which the Tigers' Bill Bradley had scored 41 points before fouling out.

Princeton and Michigan met in the NCAA semifinals at Portland. Bradley scored 29 points but fouled out again, and Michigan won, 93–76.

The tournament was then played Friday and Saturday, a problem for Michigan coming off its emotional victory. The Wolverines jumped into an early lead again but fell into another of those black holes. UCLA led by 20 points in the second half as Goodrich, who had been and would be underrated so many times, scored an amazing 42 points. Kenny Washington came off the bench to get 17.

"I guess if we can make it to the finals," mused Wooden, "Washington will take care of us."

In retirement, Wooden would discount the difficulty of winning 10 titles, but his first two champions would have a special place in his heart, reserved for the runty players who climbed those stairs every day to that dusty, little gym.

"There were only two championships that amazed me," Wooden says. "The very first two, under the conditions that we won, I still think that's the remarkable thing."

Without them, none of what followed—blue chippers everywhere facing west and bowing, the greatest dynasty the college game would ever know—would have happened. It was improbable, exhilarating and, best of all, real.

Years later, Arkansas Coach Nolan Richardson, who had his own point to make about the stereotyping of black coaches as recruiting specialists, would ascribe the dynasty to, of all things, salesmanship.

"The game has changed so much from the days when coaches brought their kids in and ran their little offense," Richardson said. "It was perceived as an 'intelligent' game. My offense will try to outwit your defense. Then John Wooden changed the game. John *recruited*."

This was a great irony: Wooden, who so disdained the practice, painted as a pioneer in the process.

Wooden had been a token recruiter before winning two titles and after them, he no longer had to worry about it. Now, he *harvested*.

UCLA was suddenly the center of the basketball universe. The beautiful school, the grandfatherly coach, the golden state, the aggressive, up-tempo style, the new arena going up on campus all added up to one thing: blue-chip prospects recruiting themselves in droves.

It started the summer after the first title when Wooden, in Valley Forge, Pennsylvania, for a clinic, was asked by a New York City high school coach if he'd have an interest in his young center.

It was Lew Alcindor.

The 7-1 Alcindor, who'd later change his name to Kareem Abdul-Jabbar, was a once-in-a-generation prospect, the greatest big man since Wilt Chamberlain. Wooden said he was quite interested, goodness gracious sakes alive, and asked one favor: Could the young man save his visit to UCLA for last?

Abdul-Jabbar wasn't an easy mark. Shy and self-conscious, he was also smart and skeptical. He was getting a big rush from the adults and he had an inkling it wasn't just because they liked him.

He was a New Yorker, through and through. If St. John's hadn't forced Coach Joe Lapchick to retire, he would have gone there. He had known Lapchick for years and was friendly with his son, Rich.

Now St. John's was just one of the finalists, along with Michigan. It was a horse race until Abdul-Jabbar saw Westwood: the campus, the green grass, the sunshine, the women! Like most teens, he'd been dying to come to California since Disneyland opened. Seeing the campus, he wondered couldn't he just stay? Did he have to go back home?

He met Wooden in the coach's little office. Wooden was correct, as always. He called Abdul-Jabbar "Lewis." He didn't act like a used car salesman. Abdul-Jabbar liked the sound of "Lewis," and appreciated not being jollied along.

Abdul-Jabbar walked into Wooden's office uncommitted and left a Bruin.

He got the whole Hollywood trip, too. Producer Mike Frankovich, a UCLA alum, got him a cushy messenger job at Columbia Pictures, delivering a few memos at a leisurely pace and otherwise watching the movie biz at work at $125 a week.

Moving west, or anywhere, was an adjustment, though. He later wrote that he was so homesick, he didn't unpack for a week. However, he made friends and started living the college life, with all that entailed.

The Free Speech Movement had been born at Berkeley. An inter-campus mobilization in 1967 protested the Vietnam War. Students shut down campuses nationwide. Even the insular world of college sport was politicized and radicalized. Whole teams were going off line as black student-athletes staged strikes.

A counterculture was busy being born. In his book, *Giant Steps*, Abdul-Jabbar details adventures of all sorts, smoking marijuana and taking LSD, late-night road trips listening to Wolfman Jack broadcasting out of Mexico with advertisements for roach clips and hash pipes.

This was Abdul-Jabbar's description of one LSD escapade:

That Saturday we dropped a whole tab each and got crazy. We called another compadre and he came with his car and chaperoned us up into the mountains. There were jet-stream trails behind everything that moved—my hand, my friend's whole body, cars that passed us on the road—and we rushed and tripped and somehow found more than an earthly significance to it all.

We sat on rocks high above Los Angeles and wondered aloud among ourselves about where the sun came from, what life really meant.... We talked about race, the difference between black and white, cosmic realities, cosmic myths. We were 19 and I loved it.

When Wooden was younger, he'd throw players off the team for smoking cigarettes. Now he had a young guard named Lucius Allen who was arrested twice for possessing marijuana.

Despite UCLA's image in a world that romanticized winning, they weren't Boy Scouts on an outing. There were always players sneaking girls in after curfew, players ready to bolt, players chafing at Wooden's tight rein, players upset they weren't playing, players who lived to test their coach.

But it never got out of control. In Wooden's bearing and his word was an authority his players were obliged to accept.

"A lot of coaches have a hard time with that," says Denny Crum, "because they're dealing with stars, so to speak, and it's hard to say no to them. They have never had no said to them.

"And Coach was very good at that."

Of course, everyone knew what was coming with Abdul-Jabbar: three more titles.

Abdul-Jabbar wasted no time proving his superstardom. In the opening of Pauley Pavilion, in a game televised locally, he scored 31 points, took 21 rebounds and led the freshman team, known as the Brubabes, to a 75–60 romp over the varsity, the two-time defending national champions.

"All I remember is they couldn't press us and we were faster than they were," says Abdul-Jabbar. "We broke the press real easy. They'd pass it to me and I'd come up by our free throw line in the backcourt there and I'd just hit guys cutting left or right and they beat them down the court.

"That was an easy game for us."

The varsity, beset by injuries, went 18–8 but Bruin fans relaxed, secure in the knowledge their freshman, not yet allowed to compete, could have beaten anyone. In the 1966 NCAA finals, an all-black Texas Western team beat an all-white Kentucky team in a landmark title game that was memorable for another reason: It was the last one anyone but UCLA would win for eight years.

In Abdul-Jabbar's first varsity game, he scored 56 points against USC. The next time the archrivals met, Trojan Coach Bob Boyd held the ball all game.

The Bruins went 26–0, outscoring opponents by 26 points a game. They swept through the NCAA tournament, drilling four opponents by an average of 21 points. In the finals, the crowd in Freedom Hall booed UCLA's Kenny Heitz for knocking Dayton star Don May to the floor with an accidental elbow.

They couldn't have picked a more unlikely villain. Heitz was a pale, slight, 6-3 forward who wore glasses. Said Heitz, afterward: "We're not very popular, are we?"

No they weren't. It was the only thing they didn't have.

"It was fun because of the success," says Abdul-Jabbar. "It was a great challenge because of the success. I don't know if everybody would have liked dealing with those type of challenges. They could be pretty daunting, but we managed to have fun doing it.

"The lows had to do with going up against the expectations because it removed any sense of discovery for us. There was nothing for us to achieve. If we won the NC2A, everybody expected that. If we didn't, then we were failures, so it was difficult to get that whole positive feeling back on it.

"After we won it the first time, they changed the rule about dunking. That actually helped us because it was more like us against everybody. It made for more cohesiveness."

Nobody may love Goliath, as Wilt Chamberlain lamented, but everyone is interested in seeing him fall. As the Bruins cemented their reign, the college game began to change from regional phenomenon to national pursuit.

In 1965, when they won their second title, the game wasn't on network TV and wasn't shown in many parts of the country. In 1968, when they played Houston in a regular-season game, a hastily arranged syndicate of 150 TV stations carried the game in 49 states.

The UCLA–Houston "rivalry" consisted of the previous spring's one-sided meeting in the NCAA semifinals and Cougar star Elvin Hayes's sneer at Abdul-Jabbar. But anticipation ran so high in Houston, the game was booked into the mammoth Astrodome, which billed itself as "The Eighth Wonder of the World."

The Eighth Wonder had been built for baseball and football and didn't remotely resemble a basketball arena, but the Cougars sold every seat plus 4,000 standing room for a total attendance of 52,693. The portable floor—shipped in pieces from the Los Angeles Sports Arena—was placed over second base, far from the stands. The players may not have known they were part of history, but they could tell they were part of something strange.

"The whole physical aspect of it was weird," says Abdul-Jabbar, "playing out at second base in a baseball stadium. The closest people to the court were like 60, 70 yards away."

The Bruins had more problems than ambiance. Abdul-Jabbar had had an eyeball scratched against Cal, had sat out two games and still had blurred vision. He missed 14 of his 18 shots. Hayes scored 39 points with 15 rebounds and eight blocked shots, and Houston won, 71–69, ending UCLA's 47-game winning streak and Abdul-Jabbar's perfect record.

Afterward Hayes dismissed Abdul-Jabbar's eye injury as a factor. "Last year when they beat us in the tournament, I didn't make any excuses," he said.

Sports Illustrated's cover the next issue was a photo from that game, under the headline, "Big EEEE Over Big Lew."

"I took that cover," says Abdul-Jabbar, "and taped it up in my locker."

Fate was kind. It served the Cougars up to the Bruins in the NCAA semifinals in the L.A. Sports Arena. In a rare gimmick that suggested how eager he was, too, Wooden put forward Lynn Shackelford on Hayes, arrayed the rest of the Bruins in a diamond-and-one zone defense and watched them dismember the disbelievers.

UCLA led by 44 points, cruised to a 101–69 victory, and broke out huge smiles. Noted point guard Mike Warren who'd go on to star in TV's "Hill Street Blues," "We're a very vindictive team."

In a title game that was almost an afterthought—the crowd of 14,438 was more than 1,000 under a sellout—the Bruins made mincemeat out of Dean Smith's "Four Corners" stall and routed North Carolina, 78–55, the biggest margin of victory in an NCAA final.

Abdul-Jabbar's senior year was strictly mop-up duty. He was controversial now, after announcing his support for the 1968 Olympic boycott. The actor Kirk Douglas called him to urge him to reconsider. On "Today," Abdul-Jabbar blurted out that this was "not really my country," and host Joe Garagiola asked why he didn't move.

The Bruins were loaded to the point of embarrassment. Lucius Allen had flunked out, but there were three three-year starters and two hot sophomores, Sidney Wicks and Curtis Rowe. Wicks had talent coming out of every pore and defiance, too, and Wooden tethered him to the bench to get his attention.

Try as Wooden might to keep them student-athletes, they were becoming stars. There were more requests for interviews, greater demands on their time. Wooden kept his dressing room closed after games and brought out a star player or two. He didn't like the spectacle of the writers gathered around one player, ignoring the others. Friction was inevitable. In Abdul-Jabbar's senior year, *Sports Illustrated* sent out its crack writer, Curry Kirkpatrick, to profile the Bruins, but Wooden nixed his interview requests. The players didn't like it. Heitz and two others met Kirkpatrick secretly off campus. In the coming years, Kirkpatrick would hold more such meetings, including one with Bill Walton and Greg Lee in a broom closet in Hollis Johnson's drugstore.

If the Bruins were awesome, they weren't as happy or as efficient. They found themselves in a struggle in the NCAA semifinals with little Drake, which scored eight straight points to cut their lead to 83–82 with :09 left. With a chance at the unthinkable, Drake turned the ball over and the Bruins hung on.

They then ripped Purdue, 97–72, with Abdul-Jabbar scoring 37 points with 20 rebounds in his college farewell.

"I'll just say it feels nice," he said afterward, restrained as usual. "Everything was up in my throat all week. I could see to the end, but there was apprehension and fear. Fear of losing. I don't know why but it was there. Before the other two tournaments, it didn't feel this way."

"It was not as easy an era as it might have seemed to outsiders," said Wooden. "But it's been a tremendous era, I think."

Abdul-Jabbar's era was over, but UCLA's was not.

The squad that reported in 1969 was a power but no longer overpowering. Expectations diminished, the Bruins breathed a sigh of relief. They went back to pressing.

"I remember our 1969 championship," said guard John Vallely, who'd started on that team, "and a lot of guys didn't feel anything about it because they didn't think they had contributed. And they hadn't. It was all so easy. But now everyone is helping each other a lot more, not just saying, 'Too damn bad' if another guy makes a mistake."

Even Wooden seemed happy at the difference. "Now I feel like I have something to do," he said. "I feel more alive. It's been a long time."

The Bruins reached the NCAA finals at College Park, Maryland, but as underdogs. The favorite was Jacksonville, who had sprung from nowhere behind a flashy coach named Joe Williams who favored white three-piece suits like a singer in a Las Vegas lounge act. Williams's 7-2 center, Artis Gilmore, and his 6-5 forward, Rex Morgan, were known as "Batman and Robin." Unlike Wooden, Williams had no problems with promotion.

Williams started another 7-footer named Pembrook Burrows III, just to scare opponents. The Dolphins averaged 100 points a game and towered over the Bruins' 6-9, 6-8, 6-6 front line. Wooden had to find a volunteer to guard the massive Gilmore.

In a surprise, he decided on the 6-8 Wicks. Sidney picked up two fast fouls while JU dashed to a 14–6 lead, forcing Wooden to call a rare time-out and think of something else. Instead of fronting Gilmore, Wicks would stay behind him and the other Bruins would sag.

Then something funny happened: Wicks took over the game.

Shortly after play resumed, Gilmore went up for a short jump shot and Wicks blocked it. He blocked four more of Gilmore's shots while Williams pogoed up and down the sideline, claiming goaltending. Gilmore fouled out late in the game, having gone scoreless for 16 minutes in one stretch. UCLA won, 80–69.

Winning, however, was no longer a cure-all in Westwood.

At that spring's team banquet, a reserve forward named Bill Seibert got up and complained of a "lack of communication" and a "double standard." Wooden met individually with players to find out if more were unhappy. He told them he understood how they felt, but if they felt, they had to leave, he'd understand that, too. Coincidentally or not, his players sent President Richard Nixon a telegram protesting the National Guard's slaying of four students at Kent State. Wooden was uncomfortable with protest and they knew it.

The NCAA was in turmoil, too, with the upstart American Basketball Association signing players wherever and whenever they were ready. Two of the four finalists in the coming NCAA Tournament, Villanova and Western Kentucky, would forfeit their finishes because their stars, Howard Porter and Jim McDaniels, had secretly signed ABA contracts. Porter seemed to have an agent for every mood: one who had taken care of him for years, one who signed him with the ABA, a third who got him out of that deal and to the Chicago Bulls.

Even the noble Bruins heard the siren song. Center Steve Patterson, a fifth-year senior, turned down two pro offers to return. Wicks and Rowe would soon be top picks. Patterson says Wooden accused his players of worrying about their pro contracts—"and we probably were."

Oh, yes, the tournament.

Jerry Tarkanian, building a power 20 miles south of Westwood at Long Beach State amid queries from the NCAA, almost toppled the Bruins in the regional finals. UCLA escaped, 57–55.

The Bruins reached the '71 finals in the Astrodome, where they beat Villanova, but not without a career performance by Patterson, who scored 29 points while Wicks and Rowe struggled. And not before Porter and the inspired Wildcats scared Wooden into a stall.

In a touching moment afterward, Wicks bent over from the raised court, shook the hand of a beaming Wooden, and whispered in his ear, "Coach, you're really something." Wicks would have a long NBA career but would never again reach the heights he had under Wooden.

The message seemed clear: No one could stop the Bruins, not even the Bruins.

If Wooden thought he had seen anything yet, he was wrong. From La Jolla, a suburb of San Diego, came Bill Walton and life was never the same.

The 6-11 Walton wasn't Abdul-Jabbar, but he was close. As a sophomore, he was already a walking clinic. Everything he did was picture perfect, like his stance in the post, legs wide apart, arms thrust out, even his fingers spread as far as they'd go.

Walton was fiercely competitive, passionate to a fault, an outspoken political radical, a groupie for the Grateful Dead, and a lover of the outdoors, but he lived for basketball. Of the Bruin stars, he was the most aloof—he had a stutter and disliked dealing with the press—and most romantic. He loved UCLA and revered Wooden, whom he tested almost daily. In Westwood, it was the best of times and the worst of times.

Walton had been a gung-ho recruit. He was one of the dozen players Wooden ever visited at home, but the issue had been settled long before.

"For a high school kid growing up at that time, everybody wanted to go to UCLA," Walton says.

"Denny Crum [then Wooden's assistant] wrote me a letter when I was a junior in high school, saying, 'We hear you're a good basketball player. We want to make sure that if we want to choose you to come to UCLA that you have the right grades and the right academic program.'

"I was so excited. That's all I wanted to do was go to UCLA. I dreamed of playing for Coach Wooden. I dreamed of the fast break, the press and the passing....

"So I wrote quickly back and said, 'Of course.' I told them from the very beginning that I was going to come to UCLA. The first basketball game I'd ever seen on television, ever, at any level, was the '65 championship between UCLA and Michigan. Michigan had all these big bruising guys and UCLA had all these skinny white guys from the suburbs of L.A. Goodrich went for 42 points in the championship game, just with quickness and ball movement. I said, 'That's what I want to do....'

"Wooden was a humble guy. He never talked about himself, what a great job he had done. He always talked about players, but he invented so much of what basketball is today, with the drills and the practice sessions and practice techniques, offensive sets and defensive concepts and philosophies.

"I got to live that with him. What was really great about him, he never let you forget he was the boss. At the time, you're 17 to 21 years old, that's all you want to do is be your own boss.

"He was always there. You know like now, coaches are always off giving speeches and making appearances, doing commercials. He was there every day, in the office every morning. I'd go in and see him, just to talk to him about, 'Hey, what are we doing, why am I playing here, why aren't I doing this, why don't I get more shots?'

"He'd just patiently explain everything. It was great. He had his twelve guys, and that was the focus of his life. He didn't worry about the other teams. He didn't worry about money. He didn't worry about anything, just taking those twelve guys and making them as great as he could."

Gosh, just what the nation was hoping for—another superstar at UCLA.

With three sophomores starting, the Bruins went 30–0 and outscored opponents by 30 points a game. Walton averaged 21 points and shot 64 percent.

The press called them "The Walton Gang," discomfiting Walton, who regarded sports writers as running dogs of the imperialist power structure. He did few interviews, claiming he hated to be singled out. In one, however, he said he'd understand if a black man who resented his success killed him.

The Bruins smoked three opponents in the NCAA tournament by 32, 16, and 19 points, then finished off Florida State, 81–76, in the finals in the Sports Arena. However, the Seminoles cut into a 16-point deficit in the closing minutes with Walton on the bench in foul trouble. The five-point margin was UCLA's smallest of the season. Walton treated the victory as a loss and the press as buzzards.

He made a brief appearance at the post-game press conference, then cut it off, muttering, "I've answered enough questions."

The next season was another thunderclap. The Bruins went 30–0 again and broke the NCAA record for consecutive victories set by USF and Bill Russell. They steamrolled through the tournament, meeting Gene Bartow's upstart Memphis State Tigers in the finals. Bartow tried a zone defense but guard Greg Lee, Walton's best friend, spent the night lobbing passes over the Tigers for the graceful Walton to deposit in the basket. Walton made 21 of 22 shots, another record, and scored 44 points as the Bruins rolled, 87–66.

Afterward, Walton refused to answer any questions at all. "It's just that I'm no longer No. 32 on the basketball court," he said.

"I can be Joe Walton now if I want to. And I'm not talking because I don't want to."

Appearances to the contrary, the going was getting heavy in Westwood. Protesting the mining of Haiphong harbor, Walton was arrested for lying down on Wilshire Boulevard.

"Coach Wooden was very disappointed," says Walton. "He just told me, 'Bill, that's just not the right way to do things. You should write a letter and express your disappointment.'

"So I went in and got some UCLA basketball stationery. You know, it had 'UCLA Basketball, NCAA Champions, '64, '65, '67, John Wooden, *Sports Illustrated* Sportsman of the Year'—the fancy stationery. I typed up this great letter to Nixon, outlining his crimes against humanity, and then I signed it. I said, 'We insist on your resignation. Thanks in advance for your cooperation.' Then I signed it, 'Bill Walton, captain, UCLA varsity basketball.'

"Took it to the locker room, everybody goes, 'Yeah! Let me sign it!'

"Everybody signs it and I take it into Coach Wooden after practice one day and he's standing there, getting dressed after taking a shower.

"I said, 'Coach, I took your advice and wrote a letter and I'd like you to sign it.'

"He says, 'Sure, what have you got, Bill?'

"He starts reading it, and you can just see him just wanting to crumple it up and throw it away. But he didn't. He looked at me with those sad, soft eyes and said, 'Bill, I can't sign this, you know I can't sign this. Please don't send this letter.'"

Walton laughs.

"I sent the letter and sure enough, the guy resigned in a couple months."

There were protests on personal issues, too. Every season at the first practice, Wooden would tell Walton to get his hair cut. The next season, Walton would come to the first practice with longer hair than ever.

"I remember the first practice," says Marques Johnson, a freshman in Walton's senior year. "Bill came in with his hair long, on his bicycle. Coach Wooden checked it out, told him to keep riding, get a haircut.

"Bill left yelling, 'This is fucked!' Came back the next day with his hair cut."

There was an entire cultural revolution, led by Chairman Bill. Walton asked Wooden for permission to smoke marijuana if he could produce a note from his doctor saying it relieved the pain in his knees. Wooden said he didn't care what medical science said, marijuana was still against the law.

Wooden did, however, let Walton and teammates use his office to meditate, perhaps grateful they'd found a pastime they couldn't be arrested for.

"Bill got us all into Transcendental Meditation that year," says Johnson. "We went down and got mantras in Westwood. We'd meditate before games.

"It's funny. Your mantra is supposed to be your own personal secret sound that connects you to the universe. So me and Richard Washington, we were meditating quietly to ourselves. I'm like, 'Richard, you tell me your mantra, I'll tell you mine.'

"He says, 'No man, I can't tell you mine.'

"I say, 'C'mon man, tell me your mantra.'

"He says, 'Tell me yours, first.'

"I say, 'Hi-yeng, Hi-yeng, Hi-yeng.'

"He says, 'That's my mantra!'

"So we're asking the other guys on the team, 'Is your mantra Hi-yeng, Hi-yeng, Hi-yeng?' They say, 'Yeah, that's my mantra too!'

"Then they were vegetarians, Bill was involved and Tommy [Curtis] and Greg [Lee]. I tried to be one, but I liked beef too much so I couldn't hang with them. There was a lot of outside stuff going on.

"They had gone 30–0, 30–0 the last two years. I think mentally everybody just got tired: 'Enough, we're at the breaking point, we can't do it any more, we can't continue this high level of play.' "

They continued it until January 19, 1974, at South Bend, where a Notre Dame guard named Dwight Clay hit a jumper from the corner with :21 left to give Notre Dame a 71–70 victory, ending the UCLA streak at 88 games. It was four days short of three years since the Bruins had last lost.

They lost two more games, their most losses in eight seasons. In their NCAA Tournament opener, they needed three overtimes to beat little Dayton.

They still arrived at the Final Four in Greensboro, North Carolina, as favorites. North Carolina State, the only team that could threaten them, was practically playing at home but looked like it needed the edge; in a game at a neutral site that season, UCLA had blown the Wolfpack out, 84–66.

N.C. State had David Thompson, a 6-4 guard with a 48-inch vertical leap, plus a 7-4 center named Tom Burleson whose size might bother Walton. They met in the semifinals. Johnson, a freshman, says he was so nervous, he was useless. He played only a short stint but learned to appreciate Thompson's jumping ability going after a rebound against him.

"I'm getting ready to go up," says Johnson, "and I looked up, I'm looking at the bottom of his shoes. I'm like, 'Whoa, this is unreal.' "

UCLA led by 11 points in the second half, by 7 in overtime but couldn't hold either. In overtime, Tommy Curtis, who had pointed his index finger at the crowd with the Bruins ahead, committed a key turnover, charging N.C. State's Monty Towe while trying to dribble behind his back. The Bruins lost, 80–77.

"It was almost like this relief," says Johnson. "For the older guys it was like it was finally over, Jamaal [Keith Wilkes, who later changed his name] and Bill and Greg and guys that had had to dig so deep for so many years.

"I remember Bill organizing a boycott of the third-place game, saying UCLA was not going to play in that game. [Trainer] Ducky Drake came by. [Athletic director] J. D. Morgan came by and talked to the team.

"I remember myself and Richard Washington and Bob Webb, guys who didn't get a lot of minutes, we're saying, 'Hey, we'll play! You guys don't have to play, we'll play!' "

Walton made a brief appearance as the Bruins beat Kansas. Another era was over in Westwood.

Before the 1974–1975 season, Wooden told a few confidants—Nell, assistant coach Gary Cunningham—it would be his last.

Wooden only seemed indestructible. He'd had a mild heart attack two years before. He had turned down an opportunity to coach the '76 Olympic team on the advice of his doctor. Nell wanted him to quit. When Wooden had recruited Marques Johnson in 1973, Johnson had asked if he'd stay four years. Wooden said he wasn't making any promises.

Johnson came anyway. Nearing the end of Wooden's run, Marques's story was typical: an L.A. kid (there were still only a few players from outside Southern California) who'd grown up on tales of UCLA's glory and dreamed of being a Bruin as a knight would dream of joining the Round Table.

"I don't know about every kid," says Johnson, "but this kid sure did. Most of my friends that I hung around with did.

"My most vivid memories are the tail end of the Alcindor years but mainly the Wicks–Rowe era. I was in eighth grade, ninth grade, really into basketball, stay up 'til 11 o'clock Friday and Saturday, watch Dick Enberg [then broadcasting Bruin games].

"I never missed a game. Sidney Wicks, I wore his No. 35 at Crenshaw because he wore it at UCLA. Curtis Rowe, I'd try moves he would do. I had my own Curtis Rowe moves, my own Sidney Wicks moves. So, man, I was really, really into it."

By his sophomore year, Johnson, classmate Richard Washington, and senior David Meyers were co-stars. Wooden was back in his no-superstar mode and, his players thought, enjoying it.

"He seemed a lot more relaxed that year," says Johnson, "like, 'This is a group I can control. I don't have any wild cards out here that I can't predict what they're going to do.' I think it was a little easier for him."

The Bruins went 23–3 but took their licks. Late in the season, they lost by 22 points at Washington. "Just annihilated us," said Wooden.

As the NCAA Tournament neared, he complained of trouble sleeping. He began going for his morning walk at 5 A.M.

It was a high-wire act from start to finish. In their first-round game against Michigan, the Bruins were forced into overtime before winning, 103–91. They nipped Montana, 67–64, in the second round.

In the national semifinals, they met Louisville, coached by Wooden's former assistant, Crum.

The game was one of the tournament's classics. Pupil led teacher, 74–73 with :57 left in overtime when teacher's team fouled pupil's best foul shooter, reserve guard Terry Howard. Howard had made all 28 of his attempts that season but missed the twenty-ninth. Richard Washington hit a short jumper and UCLA won, 75–74.

After the game, Wooden told his players he was retiring. "I don't want to," he said. "I have to."

"We were all in the locker room," says Johnson. "Everybody's talking and laughing. Coach Wooden comes in, you know: 'Quiet down, quiet down. I've got something to say.'

"And then saying that the game against Kentucky Monday night was going to be his last game, he was stepping down.

"And I remember sitting there, just kinda stunned. I couldn't really gripe too much because I had asked him when I came, was he going to stay four years like he had told Bill and Jamaal and those guys? And he told me straight up, 'Now, I don't know. I don't want to make that promise again.' "

In the finals, the Bruins beat Kentucky, 92–85. That summer, when Wooden's successor, Gene Bartow, watched film of the tournament games to see what he was inheriting, he marveled at Wooden's final run.

"That championship was Coach Wooden's in every way," said forward David Meyers. "I was the only starter coming back, and we weren't given much chance after losing Bill Walton and Jamaal Wilkes.

"In those days if UCLA was down at all, everyone wanted to step on Coach Wooden. The dynasty was over, that's what everyone was saying. They didn't realize Coach Wooden was the reason UCLA was there all those years. It wasn't the players, it was the coach."

On the other hand, there is so much more to life than winning and losing....

Johnny Wooden loved Nellie Riley.

He'd often say he loved his family first, his religion second, and basketball third and that he was sorry, he knew it was supposed to be religion first and family second.

He loved Nell from the day he saw her at that fair in Martinsville. Loving her, their children, and grandchildren gave his life meaning, and the rest was gravy.

They had been in it together since Martinsville High, where he'd look into the band section where Nell played cornet before the opening tip. She'd make a circle with her thumb and first finger. He'd wave. When he became a coach, he'd turn around before tipoff for their ritual. During games, he clutched his tightly rolled program in one hand and a small cross in the other. In the stands, she clutched an identical cross.

She died in 1985 at the age of 73.

She'd been ill since 1982 when she suffered a heart attack while undergoing a hip-replacement operation and went into a coma for three months. In 1984, they went to their final Final Four, in Seattle. Nell was in a wheelchair. John said it was the last thing she really enjoyed. The following Christmas morning she had to be rushed to the hospital where cancer was diagnosed. She died on the first day of spring and was buried with her small cross in her palm. John's grief was palpable and, it seemed, felt throughout UCLA.

"It was a way of life for him, when Nell was in the hospital," says Cunningham, his former assistant. "His day was, get up, go to the hospital, spend the whole day at the hospital. He did that every day. You do that for a couple years and it becomes a way of life for you.

"He did not want to live.... He went through a period of mourning that was unbelievable. Just sitting at home.

"That's when we started calling him. We would call him and try to cheer him up. I did tell him on the phone one time, I said, 'Coach, you have taught us to overcome adversity and all these principles and right now, you're feeling sorry for yourself. You're not practicing what you're preaching.' "

Somehow he got through it. It made basketball look like child's play, but he made it.

"In our situation you never completely get over that, but it took a year or two to just try to accept things," says Wooden. "My saving was the little great-grandchildren that came along. Now I have nine, and Nellie didn't get to see any of them. The first one was born a few months after....

"She knew she was going to be a great-grandmother but didn't live to see it. They gave me a reason....

"I was down. I'm not ashamed to say that I was down. Not to the point, believe me, that I thought of taking my life or anything of that sort but as I've said, after losing her, I lost the fear of death which, to some extent, I'd always had before.

"I guess that's not unnatural. But that is the only way I ever have to be with her again, and I know that, so I'm not afraid of it any more."

Every Sunday, he visits Nell's grave. At all times he has plenty of company but, as he says, "You can be lonely in a crowd." The sad fact is, while one may get past the passing of one so beloved, one never truly gets over it.

"I'd say in my particular case, that's true," Wooden says. "That might not be true in every case but she's the only girl I ever went with so that is true, yes. I know many people feel that way, and then in a year or so, they remarry. That would never have been a possibility of any sort for me."

He still lives in their homey little two-bedroom condo in Encino. They moved there to be close to their daughter, Nan, and he hasn't changed it since Nell's death.

There's a shag rug on the floor, four Currier and Ives American Homestead prints above the sofa, a bulging bookcase (Tolstoy, Larry McMurtry, Zane Grey, James Whitcomb Riley, Louis L'Amour, Tom Clancy, books on Abraham Lincoln by Gore Vidal, Garry Wills, Carl Sandburg) in the space where they found a wet bar. The Woodens had no use for a wet bar and Nell designated the space for John who'd never had a den.

His basketball mementos are jammed into the small second bedroom. Of the hundreds of awards he's received, only one is displayed in the living room, the Golden Apple, presented by Christian Heritage College in San Diego. It sits on a table next to *Wilmington's Guide to the Bible*.

The phone rings constantly: family, friends, former players, press people. He has an answering machine with a message asking the caller to "please speak slowly." He always returns his calls.

A few days ago, Swen Nater phoned him up.

Nater was Bill Walton's backup, a muscular center who became a No. 1 draft pick despite playing only a handful of minutes at UCLA. Walton remembers him as a young man who lived in the weight room rather than the classroom.

Nater called to say he was sending Wooden a present, a tape recording of the song, "Did You Ever Know You Were My Hero?" Nater sang it himself, replacing the words with verses fashioned out of Wooden's many epigrams.

Wooden puts the tape in his machine and plays it.

"This," he says, leaning back, "is the real joy."

CHAPTER THREE

SAM GILBERT:
HE MADE THEM AN OFFER THEY COULDN'T REFUSE

I'm not part of that athletic department. I'm not under their rules.

—SAM GILBERT, 1978 INTERVIEW, LOS ANGELES *TIMES*

He spun so many tales that I don't think anyone really knows who he was.

—DICK VERTLIEB, FORMER WARRIORS GM

He did what he had to do to protect his family.

Of course, Sam Gilbert had a broad definition of "family," extending it to cover an entire athletic program. As UCLA fan extraordinaire and full-service provider to Bruin players, he had to break some rules in their behalf, but who really cared in the end?

Not the players who flocked to his home for almost twenty years. There is no record of one refusing Gilbert's favors, though some said after the fact they felt funny about the money he paid for their tickets or the drastic discounts he got them on their cars, clothes, apartments, stereos, etc.

Nor were UCLA administrators quick to confront the problem, from Chancellor Charles Young to powerhouse athletic director J. D. Morgan to stern John Wooden.

Nor was the NCAA eager to investigate its Camelot.

Nor did the press pursue the story. Instead, it treated Gilbert as a quasi-official, a spokesman for UCLA players and boosters.

It wasn't because people didn't know something was going on. Gilbert didn't hide. He gloried in his association with his surrogate sons, parading them to banquets like the B'nai B'rith where he might make a grand entrance with Marques Johnson on one arm and Richard Washington on the other.

As if to legitimize his violations of the NCAA code, Gilbert claimed in a 1978 Los Angeles *Times* interview that he had personally informed an NCAA investigator of such activities as paying for abortions for children fathered by players, which he had done for Lucius Allen.

Gilbert wasn't lurking in the shadows. He was a tacitly endorsed fact of Bruin life, a powerful, strong-willed man who played by his own rules and exposed the NCAA code for what it was: an outdated ideal, a guidebook for an innocent world that no longer existed, a sermon the world had nodded off on.

If no one realized that before, here was the living proof and the real significance of Sam Gilbert.

Of course a lot of coaches, lost in the dark Bruin shadow, yearned to let the secret out.

At a clinic once, John Wooden went into one of his homilies, citing the two words he said characterized UCLA basketball, respect and balance. A USC assistant leaned over to the coach next to him and whispered, "I'll tell you what the two words are: Sam Gilbert."

They knew better than to do more than whisper, however. Let's face it, they all had their own Sams, if less flamboyant ones. Who could stop it?

Of course, it was patently unfair of the NCAA to set up a field office wherever Jerry Tarkanian was working and ignore the Bruin gossip. If one didn't believe that, one had only to visit Tark's office years later to hear a catalogue of UCLA violations. Check out Monty's, said Tark, referring to a steakhouse in Westwood see if Bill Walton didn't eat there free.

By real and prevailing standards, however, UCLA ran a "clean" program.

Wooden didn't recruit unqualified students. He would never buy a player. He barely bothered to recruit them and if he sensed an attitude—like the kid who was rude to his mother during one of his few home visits—he pulled the plug.

"Clean," however, didn't mean "pure."

If Bruins like starry-eyed Marques Johnson needed little incentive to enroll, they were still young men of modest means becoming increasingly accustomed to side deals and a society that fawned all over them.

Spending money? Discounts? Free meals?

Bring it on.

When Johnson was a freshman, the older guys took him to Gilbert's house in seaside Pacific Palisades, or as Marques put it later, "They bring you to the godfather."

The older guys told Johnson that Sam could scalp his season tickets for him—the going rate was about $1,000 a season—and he could get him anything for cost: cars, clothes, shoes, tires....

Gilbert and his wife, Rose, an English teacher at Palisades High School, hosted a day-long open house on Sundays. Most of the Bruins hung out there, swimming in the pool, raiding the refrigerator, kicking back or washing their cars. Sam was a stickler for cleanliness. Years later, Johnson—one of the players who broke with Gilbert—would see a spot on his car and think, 'Sam wouldn't have liked that.'

Then there were the talks.

Sam loved to hold court, to exchange ideas with the guys. He had two sons, Michael and Robert, but was on prickly terms with them. Years later, Sam's longtime lawyer and friend, Hubert Sommers, would testify in court that when Michael was young, he sometimes hid under a stairwell when he heard his father coming.

The Bruins basked in the glow of Gilbert's warm side. His home was their retreat, his wide-ranging interests, the anything-goes discussions doors to a new universe.

"All the older guys," says Johnson, "they were out there every Sunday and Sam was barbecuing steaks or we were washing cars or we were sitting around just laughing and talking....

"It was kind of a family thing—a real dysfunctional family thing going. He was the head figure and we were all kind of just there and he would dispense knowledge or advice. Or Wayne Embry [then general manager of the Milwaukee Bucks] would come by occasionally, or Kareem would come by and kick it with us for a day and talk to us. Ralph [Drollinger, former backup center and born-again Christian] would come by and argue about Christianity, he and Sam would get into it. It was a real interesting conversation when you went up there."

Gilbert's father had emigrated from Lithuania, a virulently anti-Semitic country, and Sam sympathized with the plight of American blacks. He gave Willie Naulls money to support his foundation, Soulville, which provided a summer recreation program for kids from Watts. He won the trust of the angry Alcindor, then in the process of becoming a Muslim and fighting with his own father about it.

Sam was more than a sugar daddy, little less than a father for some of them.

"There were two people I listened to," Lucius Allen said. "Coach Wooden as long as we were between the lines. Outside the court, Sam Gilbert."

Had the Bruins known Yiddish, they'd have called Gilbert a *mensch*, a warm, standup guy.

Instead, they called him "Papa G" and Papa G loved it.

Heartwarming or not, it was a massive violation of NCAA rules.

The talks would have been OK and maybe even the free buffet but buying their tickets, the discounts, the fact Gilbert wound up representing the players going pro, these were clear breaches.

Gilbert's flamboyance was unusual but a mountain of anecdotal evidence suggests that nothing else was, that the situation was more the rule than the exception in college basketball and remains so today.

Worse sins, like cash payoffs and cars for players, jobs and homes for parents, are constantly rumored and occasionally documented, even if the NCAA is overmatched, lacking subpoena power, trying to investigate member schools which are increasingly likely to go to court.

On such an ethical frontier, it's a continuing Wild West show.

In the spring of 1987, the lovable goniff, Jerry Tarkanian, sits in his UNLV office, sorting out complimentary tickets for that night's game and introducing a friend to two reporters.

Tarkanian: This is Mike Toney, fellows. He's my main man from the Dunes. Mike, what you need?

Toney: I need six. I need four for Figaro's.

Tarkanian: I'll give you six but they're not going to be all good ones. I'll give you some bad ones, too.

Toney: I don't care where they are. I need two good ones. I got to have two good ones for Jackie.

Tarkanian: Jackie who?

Toney: Jackie Salem, the guy who feeds us.

Tarkanian: Where?

Toney: At Figaro's. The guy who owns Figaro's. The boys are going there every day now for freebies.

Tarkanian: (Sternly) They're not supposed to be going down there for freebies! What are you talking about? (Laughing) You s.o.b.!

Toney: Blow jobs! They're going there for blow jobs!

In 1982, Ron Abernathy, an assistant coach to long-winded, oft-suspected Dale Brown at LSU, drives to nearby Gulfport, Mississippi, to see Kenny Jimerson, the state's player of the year, with $2,000 in a valise—which is then stolen from his car. Perhaps without considering the consequences, Abernathy reports the theft, which becomes public record, obliging him to explain what he was doing with so much cash on a recruiting trip.

Abernathy tells LSU's internal investigation he was out paying bills in Baton Rouge when he got an emergency phone call to go to Gulfport. No action is taken.

At the trial of the thief, Mississippi Circuit Judge James Thomas questions Abernathy's explanation and has a transcript of the trial forwarded to the NCAA.

"Quite obviously, LSU wasn't outraged," Thomas says. "No one from LSU came over for the trial. No one seemed to be particularly concerned. It smelled."

A total of $1,100—all in $50 and $100 bills—is recovered. A certified check for that amount is mailed to Abernathy, who writes back, thanking Mississippi officials.

"He never did complain about the difference," Thomas says.

A fired Clemson coach named Tates Locke wrote a book called *Caught in the Net*, describing his rogue operation in detail.

Perfectly even-handed, Locke blames basketball for his divorce but adds: "Man will bust his ass—say the right things or anything else—to get a woman into bed. But once he's obtained his goal, he will return to real life and work hard. A woman wants much more than that. She wants to put her tentacles around the man."

Apart from demonstrating his own honesty, this scary view of women may be common among the obsessives on the coaching lines but Locke's real contribution comes in the story he tells.

According to Locke:

A wealthy alumnus named B. C. Inabinet gave star center Tree Rollins $14,000 a year for payments for his Chevrolet Monte Carlo, clothes and pocket money.

Locke, himself, gave star guard Skip Wise $1,460 over a three-month period and $300 to another player, Colon Abraham; Locke saw Inabinet offer cash to high school star Phil Ford.

Clemson violated NCAA rules by flying Ford to campus on Inabinet's private plane.

Clemson participated in what amounted to an auction for high school star Moses Malone with Locke personally leading a delegation to Petersburg, Virginia, for an eleven-day stay during which he feared he was being watched by NCAA investigators and calmed his fears with beer and diet pills.

Rollins, Locke's star, acknowledged all particulars and gave his own account of events in the book.

"Once you reach the pros," wrote Rollins, now an assistant coach with the Orlando Magic, "you sort of joke about it amongst yourselves. You say, 'Who got the best deal while they were in school?'

"We'd always ride Phil Ford about it 'cause he joked about Clemson going on three years of probation. We used to tell Phil that the only reason Carolina stayed off probation was Dean Smith had connections with the NCAA board. Phil would laugh and say, 'Yeah, you're right.'

In Locke's five years, Clemson improved annually but the Ford cover-up finished him. Locke sent Ford a fake expense voucher to fill out, which Clemson could show to the NCAA to prove that plane fare has been requested and paid; Ford sent the form and a statement to the NCAA, instead.

Locke was fired just before the NCAA sanctions hit.

Wrote Locke, in what might be termed the Competitor's Lament: "I didn't cheat because the Joneses did or because it made me a big man. I did it because I didn't want to get beat any more. That's all."

His book came and went and only hoop junkies ever hear of it.

In contrast, the 1985 Kentucky scandal was a headline-grabbing sensation. It didn't involve a Johnny-come-lately program from backwater South Carolina but the mighty Wildcats, traditional NCAA powers. It wasn't one disgraced coach's story but the testimony of 31 players.

It was as remarkable for the aftermath, which showed how easy it was for a school to cover up, how hard it was for the NCAA to make anything stick and how little anyone cared. The 31 players recanted their tape-recorded admissions of wrongdoing, Kentucky got off scot-free and the townspeople tried to run the Lexington *Herald-Leader*'s reporters out on a rail.

Kentucky had long been known as one of the most free-wheeling of the major powers but it was an open secret that everyone in town was happy to keep. With power came respectability. UK's chancellor, Otis Singletary, was chairman of an NCAA Division I group exploring ways to tighten enforcement of the rules.

UK had been targeted almost by accident. With the 1985 Final Four scheduled for Lexington, *Herald-Leader* officials heard the Louisville *Courier-Journal* was working on a UK story about Coach Joe Hall's bloc of tickets. Lest it be scooped on a story in its own backyard with the national press in town, the *Herald-Leader* assigned a young business writer, Jeff Marx, and Washington correspondent Mike York to the story.

It didn't take them long to figure out everyone was watching them.

"There were a lot of questions in the newsroom," says Marx, now a free-lance writer in Washington, D.C.

"Why were we even doing this? What did it have to do with Coach Hall's tickets? A lot of the sports writers were starting to take a lot of shit from the people at the University of Kentucky about who were these two guys?

"The first story broke on a Sunday, October 27, 1985. Mike and I left, we were meeting someone. It was after midnight, probably around one in the morning. I had the first copy that I was taking out of the newsroom with me, walking to the parking lot behind the newspaper building. Eddie Sutton [the new coach] was standing in the parking lot at one o'clock in the morning. Literally, standing in the parking lot at one o'clock in the morning. I assumed he was waiting to get the paper when it came off the trucks in the back.

"I went over and we talked, shook hands. He was very cordial. He didn't want to be interviewed but I did wind up giving him that copy and going back in the building to get another copy."

The *Herald-Leader* stories uncovered a well-worn pattern in which assistant coaches pointed new recruits to designated benefactors—developers, physicians, lawyers, mine owners—for stipends.

An unnamed player from the '80s estimated his four-year take at $10,000, but there were occasional windfalls. Jay Shidler, a sharpshooting guard in the late '70s, said he got $8,400 just for selling three years' worth of season tickets to Joe Hall's lawyer, Cecil Dunn.

Scalping tickets was illegal in Kentucky and Dunn was an assistant in the Fayette County attorney's office.

Eleven players said they customarily ate for free at Cliff Hagan's Ribeye, a restaurant co-owned by the former UK star—who was then Kentucky's athletic director. (The NCAA had even looked at Hagan's restaurant seven years before when a player, Dwight Anderson, mentioned it in a newspaper story. Hall wrote a letter saying players weren't allowed to eat for free. The NCAA took no action and, according to players, the ribeyes kept coming.)

The series was a bombshell and it was the *Herald-Leader* that almost blew up.

"There were massive hate phone calls and mail," says Marx. "There were death threats. There was a bomb scare. There was a

'Hate the *Herald-Leader*' rally at a local club. One of the large windows by the printing press was shot out. Everything from a newspaper delivery boy being threatened not to come around with the *Herald-Leader*—things that affected people that had nothing to do with the damn thing.

"In terms of Mike and myself, probably the hardest part was not even the public reaction, it was the personal stuff. Things as personal as my girl friend's family wouldn't even talk to me any more after that. Things like my landlord asking if I would stay somewhere else for a week or so, which I did. Just a lot of different things on a personal level that were even more upsetting than the public stuff....

"I didn't really believe that someone was going to shoot and kill us because of writing a story about basketball but at the same time, when you have more than one death threat, it's something you can't ignore.

"But to be honest, probably the one incident that shook me up the most was a threat that was made to me that I was going to be set up on drug charges by Kentucky State Police. That one day, don't be surprised if I come out of the newsroom and police are taking cocaine out of the tires of my car, was the way it was put to me.

"Now this was said by someone very close to the program and someone who is—put it this way, it was a very believable threat because there's plenty of this documented on the record in Kentucky.... I was very scared about that and I immediately went to my editor and a lawyer, just for nothing else, to have that on the record.

"I mean, I was just a kid. It was my first year out of college. I was 22."

The series won the Pulitzer Prize and obliged the NCAA to investigate. Players began recanting one after another, suggesting a cover-up at work, which the *Herald-Leader* also reported. A player named Scott Courts told Marx of receiving phone calls from assistant coach Leonard Hamilton and Lexington developer Don Webb, whom Courts had identified as his benefactor, asking that he write a statement, denying his comments.

The NCAA ran into a string of denials. The *Herald-Leader* refused to turn over tapes of the interviews, which were by then in a bank vault after the bomb threat. UK dodged the bullet.

Three years later, however, the Wildcats got hit between the eyes when an Emery Air Freight envelope, from UK assistant Dwayne Casey to the father of freshman Chris Mills, burst open in a distribution office in Los Angeles and $1,000 in cash—twenty $50 bills—was found in it, triggering a can't-miss investigation that cost Sutton his job.

(Interestingly, Casey, then a player, had been one of the two the *Herald-Leader* had interviewed who insisted they knew of no violations. Said Casey at that time: "If that makes me look like an oddball, I guess it has to.")

Marx says he and York got a lot of support through their ordeal from other college coaches. The coaches had stories about UK the writers hadn't heard of, although no one wanted to be quoted.

"There is a great, great fear in coaching circles of stepping on anyone's toes," says Marx. "It's been described to us as MAD—mutual assured destruction."

Sam Gilbert was a swashbuckler to hear him tell it, anyway. He claimed to have served in the World War II OSS, the forerunner to the CIA.

He was short and stocky, a bundle of energy, high-spirited, volatile and, he was always warning people, no one to mess with. He commonly hinted of being mobbed up. Asked by reporters about his increasingly controversial association with UCLA athletes, he often threatened to have them killed, thrown out of windows, etc.

Business rivals feared him. In his office in the '80s, he once showed off a shelf full of copies of Mario Puzo's *The Godfather*. He said friends had sent them to him because of the resemblance.

As far as anyone could tell, Gilbert made his money as a contractor. Rose was a Phi Beta Kappa graduate of UCLA but Sam had only attended the school briefly. Sam reportedly helped some 1950s local athletes like prep basketball star Billy McGill but as far as UCLA went, he was only a fan until 1966, when the super freshmen, Abdul-Jabbar and Allen, started grumbling and threatening to transfer to Michigan.

The players had a problem and they weren't shy about it: their lack of pay.

"Here we were in Southern California where money was status and one's personal value was measured as net worth," wrote Abdul-Jabbar in his book. "We were stars and we didn't have shit."

They were referred to Gilbert by a booster friend of Allen's. Sam said he could sell their tickets for them. The problem was solved and a relationship was forged.

"I had very little respect for the NCAA," says Abdul-Jabbar. "That was one thing that Sam really helped me to understand, how we were being exploited.

"The NCAA was partners with the NBA to keep college basketball as an unpaid minor league for the NBA. That's what it's been. Everybody can make money except the players, who are the show. They're exploiting us. I had a very clear understanding of that.

"His whole thing was, 'Don't hurt yourself but you don't have to worry about the moral fiber of all of this because there is no moral fiber there. It's just a facade.'

"Sam was, for me personally, like my uncle or something. He could help people. His idea of helping people was, you helped people and legalities were not that important to him. As a businessman, he knew how people circumvented them and were still considered to be reputable people....

"He took a genuine liking to me and wanted to see me do well. Of course, I would listen to him. I guess his own sons, they rebelled. I was like a pleasant thing in his life because I would listen to him and I benefited from his advice and appreciated it."

They talked about everything: race, religion, politics, even sex. "Although he was at least thirty years older than I was," wrote Abdul-Jabbar in his book, "Sam considered himself a real cocksman."

Abdul-Jabbar became the first Bruin to have his professional contract negotiated by Gilbert. Sam charged him $1.

Gilbert may have overbilled, at that. Abdul-Jabbar wanted to sign with the ABA's New York Nets, which would bring him home. However, he and Gilbert agreed on a bargaining rule: The Nets and the NBA's Milwaukee Bucks could only make one blind offer.

The Bucks' offer was higher and more solid. When ABA officials tried to jump in and raise the Nets' bid, Gilbert and Abdul-Jabbar said they were committed to Milwaukee.

Abdul-Jabbar then spent six seasons in a city he didn't like before demanding the trade that sent him to the Lakers.

However, Abdul-Jabbar still maintains Gilbert did the right thing.

"I came in the league making more than anyone else in the league," he says. "The offer that the New York people put out there, it wasn't the same. It wasn't solid at all."

Abdul-Jabbar and Allen introduced Sidney Wicks and Curtis Rowe to Gilbert. Sidney and Curtis brought the young Bruins of their day. Soon, everyone was hanging at Papa G's.

Wooden, alarmed at all the new fur and leather, warned players about taking stuff. He says he could do no more. His players took that as tacit approval.

"I remember we were on a road trip in Chicago," said Greg Lee, "and five guys all got on the bus together wearing matching coats with fur-lined collars. It was pretty conspicuous. It's not like Coach was an ostrich about Sam but he wouldn't confront the problem."

"He worried me all the time," says Wooden, "but all I could do was talk to my players, warn them of the dangers of things that might be illegal. I had a couple of players that I prefer not to name, that wore leather boots. I didn't feel they had the money to afford them.

"I asked them, 'Did you get those from Sam? Did he give them to you?'

"'No.'

"'Did you pay for them? Did you get a good price?'

"They said, 'Don't you shop to get good prices?' "

"In my opinion, Sam Gilbert had no impact on the program in any way, any more than different alumni at different places—SC, Purdue, Indiana, Iowa, Stanford. Any place you name, you have some of that sort who try to latch on. He tried to latch on. I never heard of Sam Gilbert until we won the first championship.

"There was a lot of misconception about him. You may remember when the NCAA checked very carefully but there was nothing in my years. He worried me but they found no irregularity in my years. They found some after it but I had retired. But not in my time."

Impact is one thing, irregularities were another. Many of Wooden's most prominent players have repeatedly acknowledged receiving improper gifts from Gilbert. However, the NCAA never talked to them.

In 1978, three years after Wooden retired, a former NCAA investigator named Bret Clark testified before the House Committee on Interstate and Foreign Commerce that he had asked to investigate the Gilbert–UCLA connection but had been frustrated by superiors.

"I submitted the memoranda ... and they [NCAA] just sat on it," Clark told the Los Angeles *Times*. "If I could have spent a month in Los Angeles, I could have put them on indefinite suspension.... But as long as Wooden was there, the NCAA never would ever have taken any action."

Clark said Bill Hunt, his boss in the enforcement division, "called me aside and said, 'We're just not going after the institution right now.'"

NCAA officials denied Clark's charge. The fact remains, the NCAA never investigated UCLA until J. D. Morgan died.

There was nothing Papa G wouldn't do for his boys. When Bill Walton was a Blazer, the team owner, Larry Weinberg, once saw Sam bring him a bundle of clean clothes.

Yes, Sam took in laundry, or at least superstars' laundry.

Gilbert wasn't just an easy mark, though. He had demands, starting with numero uno: loyalty. He wouldn't stand for being crossed.

In 1981, NCAA finally placed UCLA on two years' probation, citing the activities of an unnamed booster. A day later in his office, Gilbert, who had consented to be interviewed, asked the Los Angeles *Times*' Alan Greenberg: "Should I press a button on my desk and have two guys come and throw you out the window?"

The *Times* began looking into the story. Gilbert demanded to tell his side, then withdrew. Surprised in the parking lot of his office building by two reporters, Gilbert snarled, "I'm warning you to stop harassing me... If you know my history, you'll stay out of my hair."

The paper ultimately ran a three-part series in which Bruin players described Gilbert's largesse. Gilbert, vowing revenge, tipped TV friends that another *Times* writer, Ted Green, had a second mortgage from Sam Nassi, a friend of Laker owner Jerry Buss.

The item was broadcast. *Times* editors investigated and ordered Green to quit a part-time TV job on a cable network in which Buss was a partner. When Green refused, he was fired.

"Sam didn't play," says Abdul-Jabbar. "I understand that about him. But he had people who tried to muscle him. He didn't play that. Sam dealt with large sums of money.

"Sam's brother, Lou, was an official in the longshoremen's union and Sam knew people. Sam wanted to do honest business deals. He wasn't about breaking people's legs and stuff. He just wanted to do honest business deals and lease these buildings. From what I could see, he was an honest businessman.

"All I knew was, Sam's heart was in the right place as far as we were concerned. He wanted us to go to school and learn how to handle money and be independent of all the sleaze and all of that.

"That's what he wanted for us. That's the only way I can judge him."

Some Bruins stayed close to Gilbert after they graduated. Some, like Abdul-Jabbar, drifted away. Some, like Marques Johnson and Jamaal Wilkes, broke with Gilbert, or he with them.

Wilkes, who'd been rookie of the year for Golden State, retained another agent to renegotiate his contract. Wilkes said Gilbert then wrote a letter to Warriors general manager Dick Vertlieb, denouncing him.

Johnson did nothing more than consult a lawyer, but that was enough to blow up his relationship with Gilbert.

Under Gilbert's auspices, Johnson had tried to sign with the ABA Denver Nuggets after his junior season but the merger agreement with the NBA blew up the deal, with the older league insisting undergraduates were off limits.

Johnson returned to UCLA, where a friend—Walt Hazzard—asked if he was interested in talking to a lawyer named Jerry Roth, a friend of Hazzard's, about the situation.

"I go by Jerry Roth's office," says Johnson. "I call up Sam from Jerry Roth's office and say, 'Sam, I'm in Jerry Roth's office, he wants to talk to me.'

" 'Jerry Roth? What?'—Click! Hangs up the phone.

"Or he might have cussed at me. I knew he was pissed off. I couldn't figure it out.

"Minute later, the phone rings again. Jerry Roth picks up the phone, hands me the phone: 'Uh, Marques, this is Stu Nahan [then sports anchor at the NBC affiliate KNBC]. I hear you've signed with an agent.'

"I told him, 'Stu, I have not signed with an agent.'

"So then after that, me and Sam were like, I was the worst guy in the world. He billed me for everything, every discount he had ever gotten me."

The bill was about $2,000. Johnson paid up.

"Initially I felt kinda like, fuck him," said Johnson. "But then I thought about it and I just wanted to clean the slate, clear the books up, we're even, this is what I owe you, OK, fine. You're outta my life, I'm outta your life....

"When you were young and stupid, he was the master of that. He was a combination of a lot of guys. Some of it was manipulative. I think the guidance and the counseling and all that stuff he'd give you about life was very valid and very useful.

"But he got guys at a vulnerable age and, I don't want to say pimped 'em but he just had a way.... By the time you're finished your four years and it's time for you to hire an agent, you just hand over all your stuff to him without any questions."

Money, however, seemed a minor issue for Gilbert. The NBA general managers considered him a friendly negotiator.

Entree, that was something else.

"There were situations, too, like the B'nai B'rith," says Johnson, "where me and Richard [Washington], he'd call us up at the apartment—this happened on at least 10 occasions—'You guys want a steak dinner? OK, I'll pick you up in 10 minutes.'

"We'd have our jeans on and a T-shirt. Pick us up, go to a big affair, everybody in a suit, 5,000 people or 500 people, he'd walk in, two big Bruins on his arm.

"He'd be, 'Marques, this is so-and-so, this is so-and-so.' I'm shaking hands. We'd sit down, eat good. Sam might get up and say something, introduce us. We'd wave, you know.

"We're so stupid, we're just like, 'Hey, good steak.' "

Entrenched in the Wooden era, Gilbert would prove impossible to dislodge afterward.

Coaches came and coaches went, the NCAA ordered UCLA to sever his connection to the program time and again, but Sam remained a player at the school.

He would be Gene Bartow's arch-critic, Gary Cunningham's ally, Larry Brown's bitter enemy and Larry Farmer's most ardent sponsor. He would still be active at the time of his death in 1987 during Walt Hazzard's tenure.

In the spring of 1984, three years after the NCAA ordered UCLA to bar Gilbert, he walked up to the press section in Pauley Pavilion, told the Los Angeles *Herald Examiner*'s Pam King he didn't like her coverage and slammed his hand down on the table in front of her.

The coach was then Larry Farmer, a player so close to Gilbert they were like father and son. After that season, UCLA administrators decided Farmer need to be shored up with fiery assistants and chose Walt Hazzard and Jack Hirsch. When Farmer met with them, it was in Gilbert's office.

In 1987, with Hazzard coaching, another NCAA investigation again cited the famous "unnamed booster," producing two Gilbert checks for a total of $2,357, paying for the rent and security deposit of Carl Pitts, a UCLA recruit. This time, UCLA turned him in, when the new athletic director Peter Dalis self-reported his program.

The NCAA took away two scholarships and again directed UCLA to sever the Gilbert connection.

Two months later, Gilbert died at 74, of cancer and heart disease.

Three days later, federal marshals, unaware of his passing, came to his home to arrest him on charges of laundering money for a

Florida drug-smuggling ring. The story seemed to confirm Sam's claims to having been an underworld figure although questions remain what it meant.

The drug ring was headed by Ben Kramer, the son of a man Gilbert knew in the construction business. Kramer, now serving a life term on a drug-trafficking charge in Illinois, was alleged by federal authorities to have made $50 million in the early '80s smuggling marijuana into Florida.

The government charged that Gilbert had been brought in to launder the cash, setting up companies in Liechtenstein and the Virgin Islands, then had used $12 million of the take to build a casino in Bell Gardens, California, in which his three children and a woman described as his mistress became part owners.

The casino, called the Bicycle Club, was a gold mine. Michael Gilbert's lawyer, Michael Pasano, said his client made almost $2 million a year.

A courier named Charles Podesta testified he made several flights to Los Angeles, delivering up to $7 million to Sam, who made the pickup himself, usually in the garage of his office building in Encino.

"He would drive his car around next to mine," Podesta said. "He had a gray Mercedes 450 SEL. Then I would transfer the boxes.... Because of his age I couldn't expect him to lift the boxes. They were pretty heavy."

Gilbert never had a chance to answer charges and his lawyer, Hubert Sommers, denies them. Michael Gilbert and several other alleged members of the ring were convicted on similar charges. Michael remains in jail.

Pasano, Michael's lawyer, says the trial established Sam's involvement but argues it was a late-life fling.

"It's still an enigma why a Sam Gilbert late in his life, having accomplished everything he did, did what he did," says Pasano.

"The trial established unfortunately and unequivocally that Sam had gotten in bed with Ben and Jack Kramer. It did not establish why he did it.

"I think it's very clear and uncontested that Sam liked people to believe that [he was a mobster]. I think you can somehow view his relationship with the Kramers as part of that. Sam enjoyed being viewed as that. But there has never been a scintilla of evidence that it [the mob tie] was real."

In the annual UCLA basketball yearbook is a page devoted to thanking the 104 donors to an athletics campaign. Donors gave at least $100,000 and received "special recognition as part of a unique display in the UCLA Athletics Hall of Fame."

Sixteen contributed in the name of the basketball team, including Pooh Richardson, Willie Naulls and Coach Jim Harrick and his wife, Sally. The last one on the list reads, "In memory of Nell Wooden."

Fifth from the top, in alphabetical order, is "Rose Gilbert (in memory of Sam Gilbert)."

So he is with them, still.

CHAPTER FOUR

THE BARTOW YEARS:
CLEAN GENE DOESN'T
LET THE DOOR HIT HIM
IN THE REAR END

I figure this nostalgia for Coach Wooden will pass in about a year. As long as we keep winning.

—NEW UCLA COACH GENE BARTOW, FALL 1975

I wasn't worried about getting fired. Now, assassinated, that's a different thing.

—GENE BARTOW, AFTER LEAVING UCLA

It was obvious what the Bruins needed to succeed John Wooden: another Wooden.

That was Gene Bartow who was as Midwestern as Wooden, as straight an arrow, as devoted to his family, as trustworthy, loyal, helpful, friendly, courteous, kind, obedient, cheerful, thrifty, brave, clean, and reverent.

Bartow was known as "Clean Gene," because he ran a good program. His origins were as humble and small-town as Wooden's and he had come up slowly, like Wooden. He was nice, like Wooden.

When Bartow and Wooden posed together for the cover of the UCLA media guide, people said they could have been father and son. If Bruin fans wanted someone who would work hard, treat his players well, graduate them and in general run a program the right way, Gene Bartow was their man. Of course, if they'd need another 10 titles in 12 years, he was in trouble.

Predictably, they fell on him like a turkey at Thanksgiving.

Players laughed at his country ways and rolled their eyes at his non-Wooden methods. Fans skewered him in letters to the editor. Boosters plotted his overthrow, starting with the one and only Sam. After Bartow's last game—a second-round loss to Idaho State in the NCAA Tournament—students rioted.

Bartow's decision to leave was part economics and the greater part self-preservation. It turned out to be the smartest thing he ever did.

Of course, the dumbest was coming in the first place.

It's almost 20 years since Bartow left Westwood to coach at a school that wouldn't field a basketball team for a year, with the catcalls ringing in his ears.

They've been good years, too. He's been at the University of Alabama at Birmingham ever since. Three years after beginning play, he had his new program in the NCAA's Sweet 16. In their fourth year, they made the Elite Eight.

They have a modern, new on-campus arena, sleek and low-slung. There's an adjoining suite of offices, with the big one on the first floor reserved for the athletic director. That's him, too.

Marques Johnson, who thought Bartow tiptoed around the Wooden holdovers, came down to spend a season as a UAB assistant and saw a different Bartow than the one he remembered.

Said Johnson: "He told one guy, 'I'm running this program and the president of the college is a good friend of mine so I'm going to be here awhile so you better get used to it.'

"I realized what kind of guy he is, what kind of class gentleman. I just felt bad for all the little things I did.... It wasn't like there was any kind of friction or dislike. It was just hard for us, I think, to accept that difference, being 18, 19, 20 years old at the time."

The UAB basketball program is like an extended family. Bartow pages through the yearbook to show off the page of pictures in which he's posing with his wife, children and grandchildren. His oldest son, Murry, is his top assistant.

Of course, Bartow is still not the type to ignore a dark cloud on the horizon, or one that's off-white, but how much better can it get than this?

That was UCLA's gift to him: It showed him what was important.

The trouble began the way it always did in those days, with a phone call from J. D. Morgan.

In J. D.'s mind, this was like an invitation to move to Paradise and conduct the Heavenly Choir. The Bruins would only be able to indulge themselves in this fantasy a little while longer; in the next six years they would have to hire three more coaches.

For Morgan, who had inherited Wooden, this would be his first basketball hire. But if anyone was up to the task, he was. A powerhouse in his own right, Morgan ran an empire that *Life* magazine once called the "Athens of Athletics" with a strong arm and an iron will.

Wooden's dynasty was but one jewel in J. D.'s crown. In Morgan's 17 years as athletic director, the Bruins would win 20 other NCAA titles: four in track, six in tennis, seven in volleyball, three in water polo. He'd built his own dynasty, coaching the tennis team to seven NCAA titles and building it into a colossus that lured stars like Arthur Ashe, Charlie Pasarell and, after Morgan moved upstairs, Jimmy Connors.

Morgan was tall, distinguished and outgoing. He captained the tennis team at UCLA, fought in the Golden Gloves, commanded a PT boat in World War II.

"He was like somebody from central casting," says Kareem Abdul-Jabbar. "Big guy, big voice, big presence. Should have been on television, like a game show host."

Morgan was appointed to his post in the summer of 1963, the day before the coronation of Pope Paul VI. Local columnists liked to say that J. D. sometimes forgot which he was, pontiff or athletic director. Jim Healy, a local radio provocateur, called him "J.D. Boredom."

With an in-town arch-rival at USC, detractors were abundant and Morgan was also called arrogant and pompous. Pac-8 basketball coaches once voted to ban him from the UCLA bench where his harangues had the officials wondering if they'd ever work in this town again.

Taking over a department $136,000 in debt, Morgan launched a building program that replaced the "B.O. Barn" with Pauley Pavilion, with a track stadium named after Ducky Drake next to it. He eased aside Drake, the longtime coach, keeping him as athletic trainer, bringing in Jim Bush who won four NCAA titles.

Morgan could be tough—he fired Billy Barnes, the football coach he inherited, after 2–8 and 4–6 seasons—but he was better known for standing by his people. He was a Wooden stalwart, which was easy. He would back others like football coach Terry Donahue and Bartow when it was not.

Morgan was a power in NCAA circles and within the UCLA community, practically autonomous. Chancellors Franklin Murphy, the man credited with bringing UCLA out from the Berkeley shadow, and Charles Young, who succeeded him in 1968, let J. D. run his own show, or in the words of a *Daily Bruin* sports editor, "J. D. Morgan wouldn't give Chuck Young the time of day." Morgan and Morgan alone would handle the passing of the torch.

Wooden hoped one of his assistants, Gary Cunningham or Denny Crum, would get the job but in Wooden style, tended to his own knitting.

Morgan might have gone for Cunningham but he took himself out of the running, going to work in the Alumni Association. J. D. didn't want Crum, a decision that would be much speculated about for only the next fifteen years or so.

Morgan had another candidate he thought would do just fine.

Gene Bartow was corny as Kansas in August and came by it honestly.

Like Wooden, a Hoosier, and Morgan, a native Oklahoman, and a significant percentage of the emigrants who were flocking to Southern California, Bartow was a Midwesterner, born in small-town Browning, Missouri. His wife, Ruth, was from nearby Galt.

He had come up slowly and respectably: six years coaching in Missouri high schools, three at Central Missouri State, six at Valparaiso, four at Memphis State, where'd he won national attention by reaching the NCAA finals.

He was now in his first season at the University of Illinois in Champaign-Urbana, his reward for turning around Memphis State but no bargain on winter days when the prairie wind nipped at his nose—and a lot less appealing after Morgan telephoned.

"J. D. called me and asked me if I would have an interest in listening to him," says Bartow.

"I had been at Illinois less than a year. It was fascinating, of course. I found myself thinking, 'That is something that, I wouldn't sleep good, ever again maybe, if I didn't take a hard look at it and probably accept it.'

"It was out of the blue but it was in early February. John had told J. D. that he was going to get out of coaching before the night down there in the NCAA Tournament....

"Yeah, I was surprised. Although, a year or two earlier, I believe George Raveling [then Washington State Coach]—George knows everything—George had mentioned to me that J. D. had thought I did an excellent job with coaching and was a good person and fit the mold."

A cautious man might have thought, "Follow Wooden at UCLA? How?"

Bartow thought of the beautiful UCLA campus, the returning All-Americans Marques Johnson and Richard Washington. He remembered the velvety Southern California weather from his days as an assistant at UC Santa Barbara. He felt bad about up and leaving Illinois but how could he live the rest of his life amid the cornfields, knowing that once they had wanted him on the Coast?

Said Bartow: "It was like a small-town mayor that was suddenly asked to be governor. Here I was, a small-town guy being asked to coach at the best basketball university in America.

"What more could you ask for?"

Be careful what you ask, you just might get the answer.

The Bartows—Gene and Ruth and the three kids—moved into a house in Northridge. Thirteen orange trees in the backyard. Big pool. They had arrived just before the real estate boom and got it for $68,000. It was fortunate because Bartow wasn't coming for the money. He made $30,000 at Illinois and took the UCLA job for $33,000, which, as Morgan noted, was what Wooden had made.

At Illinois, however, Bartow had been guaranteed radio and TV shows, worth another $20,000. At UCLA, it was pretty much straight salary. This was Hollywood; they didn't need basketball coaches cluttering up the airwaves.

The bespectacled Bartow, wearing a blue blazer, tie and double-knit patterned slacks, appeared with Wooden in a photo on the inside cover of the 1975–76 basketball guide.

Bartow was accepting a basketball which the bespectacled Wooden, also in blazer and tie but without the double-knits, was presenting to him.

"Yes, this picture symbolizes the passing of the (basket)ball," said the caption, "the ending of one basketball era at UCLA and the beginning of another....

"These gentlemen also appear to be saying, quite simply and sincerely, 'Good luck, John,' and 'Good luck, Gene.' "

One of them was going to need it.

Isn't it nice when your new neighbors call to welcome you? One day Bartow got a phone call from a Sam Gilbert, inviting him to breakfast.

Bartow didn't know who Gilbert was but when he asked, was told that he was somebody he should meet. They got together at the Holiday Inn on Wilshire Boulevard. Bartow won't discuss it. A UCLA official says Gilbert bluntly informed the new coach of everything he was doing for his players. "Almost down to the dollar amount per player," says the official.

"Gene told me, 'I knew who he was after breakfast. Boy, was he loud!' "

Roy Hamilton and David Greenwood, stars at nearby Verbum Dei High School, had already decided to go somewhere together. Wooden had recruited them but they hadn't signed when he announced he'd leave.

Suddenly, all bets were off. Bartow went to see them. They thought he was different but nice.

"You could tell he was very sensitive," says Hamilton. "Just the way he approached me, you could tell he was very warm and gentle and he cared about me, my family, how I was going to do in school. It was very sincere, at least I felt. Maybe it was the southern style of his. He just cared and he cared deeply about what was going to happen at the program....

"It was still UCLA and the sad part was that Coach Wooden wasn't going to be there because I at least wanted to have one year experience with him. That was very disappointing to me, but the magnitude of the program was just so powerful. It still had the mystique of the strongest university at the time in college basketball.

"I had some mixed feelings about him. I talked to my high school coach, George McQuarn. He had been a student at UCLA. He said, 'I'll tell you, Roy, UCLA is going to be UCLA. That part is never going to change. There's just too much tradition built....'

"It's really funny, looking back at it now. Obviously we can reflect and say, 'Hey, anybody who takes that job is really going to be in trouble, at least for a couple of years.' But they had so many players back from the national championship team, you figure, 'At least, we're going to be in the Final Four....'

"You know, it's funny, coming in myself as an 18-year-old kid, not thinking that, 'Hey, whoever replaces Coach Wooden is really going to be in a hot seat.'

"Hey, he took the job, you figure he can do it."

Bartow didn't have a southern accent but a Midwestern twang, although the distinction was lost on his Southern Californian players, to whom he might as well have been Jed Clampett.

That wasn't the last time Bartow would be misunderstood. Despite similarities in origin, dress and lifestyle, Bartow was not Wooden, no matter how much everyone seemed to want him to be Wooden. He had a different personality, coaching philosophy, temperament.

However, he had Wooden's players.

Even Wooden, who would quickly tire of talk of the pressure his success had placed on his successors, would say that in Bartow's case, it was real.

"It's been tremendously overdone," said Wooden. "The only time when perhaps it really mattered was with Bartow, who came immediately after me....

"At the same time, any coach would have loved to step into that situation. I could see three or four years for sure that UCLA was going to be very outstanding when I left. I made sure the cupboard wasn't bare when I retired."

Wooden's old players, veterans of the '75 championship run, eyed Bartow with a keen interest.

Says Marques Johnson: "Coach Bartow, he just seemed like a nice guy. He had a southern kind of twang and that was something we had fun with, behind his back. I'm not going to lie. Everybody had his *Jay-uhn Bore-tow* impersonation. Everybody could do it."

Bartow eyed them with as much interest.

"Well," he says, twenty years later, "it was a championship team but Pete Trgovich graduated. David Meyers graduated. There were three, I believe, of the first seven.

"It was a team that Washington had beaten by 30 points [22 actually] in January. It was a team that, if anybody studied their last five, six, seven, eight games including the NCAA, every one of them went right to the last second and they won every one of them.

"You go back to Louisville and the game before that and the game before that. Michigan, for example. Michigan had them beaten in the first round, all the way, and they miss a little six-foot jumper off the glass that would have won the game there at the end and it goes into overtime.

"What I'm saying, out of all the miracles that John created—and I think that he's the best that ever lived in any sport—of all he created, the biggest miracle of all may have come in his last season 'cause his talent level wasn't national championship caliber.

"Now I had inherited good players. Marques Johnson and Richard Washington, both of them were big-time players. And we had a lot of other big, big-time players. But David Greenwood, Roy Hamilton and Brad Holland were all freshmen.

"Ralph Drollinger was a good big man. Andre McCarter was a good guard. Jimmy Spillane was a good guard but I mean, when you think of national championship-type players...."

Whatever they were, they were opening the season on national TV in the Checkerdome in St. Louis, where the Bruins had beaten Bartow, against Indiana and Bobby Knight.

To say that Knight was eager for the game is like saying Ahab went out to do a little fishing. An aspiring dynast himself, Knight revered the great coaches, with an interesting exception—Wooden. Knight was especially close to former Cal Coach Pete Newell, a Wooden rival of many years. Knight frequently praised Newell as the best of them all.

In the Checkerdome three years before, Wooden's Bruins had beaten Knight's Hoosiers in a taut NCAA semifinal that turned on a call when IU's Steve Downing picked up a key foul in a collision with Walton. Knight never forgot it. Knight had nothing personal against Bartow but that blue and gold UCLA uniform was something else.

"I knew going into that game it was going to be a real difficult game," Bartow says. "Indiana was 26–1, I believe, the year before and had everybody back. They were ranked No. 1 in the country.

"Now if I had it to do all over again, we wouldn't play that game. J. D. asked me right after I took the job should we do it or not? Because I think he could feel if we happened to go back there and get beat, it might be tough. It was not a good game for us to open a coach's career on."

No, it was not, not with this particular coach's problems. Bartow waded through the skepticism, just trying to get to the opening tip of his first game.

Says Johnson: "He handed out these detailed scouting reports on Indiana and some of the comments were, like, 'Kent Benson, he's so mean, he'd fight a junkyard dog.' And 'Wayne Radford, he's so tough, he'd fight a buzz saw.'

"So we're reading this stuff and it's like, 'What is this, UCLA or the Beverly Hillbillies?' "

Wooden, of course, had never used scouting reports, with or without pithy commentaries. His oft-stated belief was the Bruins should play their game and let the opponents worry about them.

Nor did it inspire any confidence in the new regime when Indiana laid a fearsome 84–64 pounding on the Bruins. If one regular-season game couldn't doom a coach, not even at glory-drunk UCLA, this one went as far as one game could.

"That kinda set the tone," says Marques Johnson, "kind of like us feeling that here's a guy who's in over his head.

"Like, here's a guy who's in L.A. and who's got this ... I don't want to say country-bumpkin thing going but I mean, that's kinda how we perceived it at that time. And I think it kind of eroded some of the respect we might have had for him as a coach right off the bat."

For his part, Bartow went home, discovered the media storm breaking above his head and squealed like a stuck pig.

Whoever hoped to follow Wooden would have to have a tough hide or enough charisma to jolly the newsboys along. Bartow had neither.

He had grown up and worked in small towns, which was more the rule in the NCAA. A big city like Los Angeles, with its two glamour schools, was the exception. In small towns, a local university was a major industry and a source of great pride and was treated gently. In Los Angeles, where the schools competed with each other and pro teams for entertainment dollars and space in the press, the distinction between collegians and professionals blurred.

And Bartow was not one who enjoyed being pricked under any circumstances.

"You know," he says, "I was very naive, there's no doubt.

"I had been very fortunate as a high school coach and we won big and won the state championship in Missouri. I got the head job at Central Missouri State. We'd won fairly big and I'd moved on to Valparaiso and we'd won fairly big and went on to Memphis and their program had been in shambles, and we played for the national championship three years later.

"I'd been on a ride, goin' up, and I'd never had any real scrutiny or any media. Everything had been, 'Oh, Gene's a good guy, good coach.' Everything had been positive written about me in the media.

"Anyway, I get to Los Angeles. The beat writers there were fine, but the columnists, two or three of them, were very critical when we lost games. I'm not sure they saw any practices or games. But I didn't adjust very well to that....

"I was not all that surprised that Indiana got us pretty good. The thing that surprised me was the media reaction after they got us good.

"And I still to this day—if you dug out those papers the day after Indiana beat us and looked at the articles and the headlines, and I'm not sure I ever said this to anybody, if you looked at them and then you took John Robinson who followed John McKay the following year at USC and I believe it was his first game, he got clobbered, they didn't make that big a deal out of it. But UCLA basketball, with a new coach following Wooden, they made a big deal out of it."

It was true.

73

No, not that the press hopped on UCLA. USC football was huge in Los Angeles and Robinson's first season, in which he went 10–1 after an opening-game loss to Missouri and finished No. 2 in the nation, was closely scrutinized.

It was true that where USC was concerned, UCLA was institutionally paranoid, a dangerous environment for someone already predisposed in that direction, like Bartow.

USC was the private school with the Waspy, wealthy student body (in Westwood, USC stood for "University of Spoiled Children") that had educated Southern California's power elite for so long.

The Trojans clung to their memory of UCLA as a commuter school full of dweebs and grinds who lacked college spirit. As they said at USC, "A Bruin for four years, a Trojan for life."

It was Dean Cromwell, a USC track coach in the '30s and '40s, who damned UCLA forever with a compliment: "gutty little Bruins." For years, that was how Los Angeles thought of UCLA: disadvantaged.

"The schools had a pretty major political disagreement," says the Los Angeles *Times*' Jim Murray. "There were different philosophies between the schools.

"Over the years UCLA would get beaten 72–0 in football. USC had great track teams, great football teams. USC always took care of the athletic side of things.

"UCLA came up with the great black players, Jackie Robinson and Kenny Washington, but even that edge was taken away. USC became very aggressive as soon as it realized blacks could run the 40 in 4.3."

The hiring of Red Sanders in the '50s presaged UCLA's ascent in football. The rise of Wooden and college basketball in the '60s shattered Trojan domination. By the '80s, coverage of the two schools was carefully balanced; actually, it tilted toward Westwood, since the Bruins had become more competitive in football than the Trojans were in basketball.

Not that the Bruins found that easy to accept.

They clung to their gutty-Bruin identity and complained at the slightest provocation, including the ones that were self-inflicted.

Each Saturday, the *Times* ran letters to the editor, a bow toward participatory democracy which often saw readers criticizing the paper's editors and writers. No one abhorred the letters like UCLA administrators, whose fans were particularly volatile. UCLA fans blasted their coaches when their teams did badly or *Times* writers for criticizing their Bruins when they did well. In any case, a UCLA fan was hard to please.

Wooden, who had little to fear, had taken a tolerant posture, suggesting the letter-writers weren't really UCLA people.

Bartow, who got zinged weekly throughout his first season, favored a more traditional Heartland approach: censorship.

"Those Saturday morning letters cut me to the core," he says. "Just cut me to the core.

"Who was the sports editor, Bill Shirley? I said, 'Bill, I'd like to sit down over lunch and talk to you. We go 28–4, we're third in the nation, we won our conference by two full games, we signed four high school All-Americans, I mean, why should I have to put up with that?'

"We're into April, we're recruiting for the next season—28–4, third in the nation, signed four high school All-Americans! I may be exaggerating a little there, there may be only two of them who were high school All-Americans, but they were all on everybody's top 50. Why did I have to put up with this? Do you hear where I'm coming from? Can you see a guy getting a little paranoid?"

If one couldn't, one had only to stay tuned.

Rebounding from the Indiana loss, the Bruins won 11 in a row. Sure, like a little 11-game winning streak was going to mean anything at a school where the record was 75. People complained that the victories weren't crisp or efficient or something and, in fact, the Bruins had a different look. Instead of Wooden's high-post offense, Bartow pounded the ball in to Marques Johnson and Richard Washington in the low post.

The Bruins called it Bartow's "star system." Players like Hamilton thought it made the other 10 guys tentative, afraid to shoot because they didn't have the coaches' confidence.

To show what a fix Bartow was in, even Johnson and Washington, who got to take all the shots, didn't like it.

"That was the thing Coach Bartow had with me," says Johnson. "He wanted me to shoot 20 to 25 times a game, me and Richard. But that concept was just totally alien, dominate the ball and shoot it every time. And so that kinda didn't sit well with me initially. So there were some things—it was just different.

"Looking back on it now, I'd love to shoot the ball. I should have taken him up on it. That probably would have led to greater success but it was just changing from one system to another system that quickly for me, at that age."

Bartow suffered.

There was no hiding his suffering. He was operatic, a Pavarotti of torment. The more he tried to suck it up, the more it showed.

If one man's misery could have balanced all of Wooden's success, Bartow's two seasons in Westwood would have sufficed but, of course, that would require several more decades and coaches.

Bartow was in it alone, too.

On his popular radio show, Jim Healy would play a tape of Bartow, his voice rising, answering a question suggesting the Bruins were weak on fundamentals, over and over.

"Sounded almost like a pig squealing," says Marques Johnson. "It was just hilarious. We'd listen to it, the players.

"Coach Bartow was thin-skinned. The places he had been before, Memphis and Champaign, Illinois, you're the biggest game in town and the media are kind of coach-friendly to you. Now all of a sudden, you've got Jim Healy talking about you on his show. And Coach Bartow was the kind of guy who wore his emotions on his sleeve. I mean, he just looked like a worry wart. He called the media 'the kooks.'

"He'd say, 'There's a kook element out there, gentlemen. There's a kook element in the media and they're out to get me, I'm telling you, they're out to get me. But they're not going to get me.' "

Wooden had been a master at keeping pressure off his players. Bartow didn't know how.

"During the course of that year, he lost a lot of weight," says Roy Hamilton. "I felt bad for him. We all knew as players what was going on. A lot of alumni were on him, just fans in general on him....

"It was funny with us because of the way he talked. He had the southern accent. He'd call us in a huddle and he'd start talking to us. And he'd start telling us about all the stuff that was happening to him.

"We were looking at him like, 'God, Coach, that's really sad.' It was almost funny but it was sad.

"He was saying, 'Well, that stuff doesn't matter, it doesn't bother me.' But we knew it bothered him because if it didn't bother him, he wouldn't talk about it.

"It was really bad. I mean, he would tell us what was happening and that was nice because he let us be a part of that whole thing. And that made us want to try harder to play for him, to make his system work. It was just different for those other guys that had been there, to make that system work."

Remarkably, given everything that was going on, the Bruins went 24–3 and won the Pac-8.

Not that that cut any ice for Bartow. UCLA fans booed as the Bruins lost at home to Oregon—the first game they'd lost in Pauley in six seasons and the third since the building opened ten years before. That was how it worked in Westwood: Losses were monumental and an NCAA title the only victory that counted.

UCLA marched back into the Final Four in Philadelphia's Spectrum, where Indiana awaited them again.

The Hoosiers were 30–0, making them 61–1 over two seasons. A fond projection of their coach, the Hoosiers were tough and imposing. The once-lordly Bruins swallowed hard.

"The players on Indiana," said Roy Hamilton, who had missed the first game, "I said, 'My God, these are the biggest players I've ever seen in my life!'

"I mean, they had Quinn Buckner and Bobby Wilkerson in the backcourt, 6-7 and 6-5. And then Kent Benson at center, Tom Abernethy and Scottie May."

It wasn't a humiliation like the first meeting but it was still one-sided and dominated by Knight's rages. Indiana pounded the Bruins into submission and won, 75–61.

"All I remember was Gavin Smith [a UCLA reserve center] and Bobby Knight," says Marques Johnson. "We were making a run and Gavin was playing well. So Bobby Knight called a time out. So Gavin's walking by Bobby Knight, going 'Yeah! Yeah!'

"So Bobby says, 'Fuck you, Smith!'

"So Gavin goes, 'Fuck you, Knight!'

"So they go back and forth—Fuck you, Smith! Fuck you, Knight! It was a pretty wild scene."

"It was a game that I was very upset about because I thought we'd beat them back there," Bartow says. "And we started out really well.

"Benson got in foul trouble and Knight went crazy out on the floor at the officials and just took the game over. He just took it over and there was nothing I could do about it. Benson probably wound up playing 35 minutes, even though he'd been in foul trouble. As I remember it, he got three fouls in the first 10 or 12 minutes.

"At half, he [Knight] raked them. Jim Bain, a Big 10 official, was the lead official. The night before the third-place game, I told Jim, I said, 'What happened was disgraceful, Knight in the Indiana game.'

"And he agreed. And he insinuated that a couple people on the tournament committee had even gotten on him at half-time about calling the game fairly loose. The game was really rough in the second game, which went to Indiana's advantage.

"Maybe it shouldn't have. Maybe we didn't adjust very well, but it was the kind of game Knight likes. Now, Knight's a friend of mine. We've never really talked about this game because he plays 'em and I play 'em and you don't win every one of them. At that point, it was difficult for me to take because I really felt we were playing well as we went down the homestretch and that we could win the national championship if we beat them.

"Now, would that have changed my life at UCLA if we'd won that national championship? In my mind, no. I don't think it would have changed a thing and I didn't then.

"But I thought, even after everything, 'Well, I'm going to stay three, four years on this job. I'm going to stay and make a decision what should I do, go into athletic administration, whatever.' "

If Bartow felt obliged to stick it out, his stars did not.

Richard Washington announced he'd give up his senior year to enter the NBA draft early, the first Bruin ever to do so. Johnson, Washington's best friend, says Richard had no particular problem with Bartow. Maybe it was just the same gentle disdain most of the veterans had. Another player, Ralph Drollinger, remembered that Washington "used to make smirks a lot" at Bartow.

Bartow says he wasn't surprised that Washington was leaving.

"Not really," he says. "after his agent got involved. For your book or anybody, I don't want to get involved with his agent, but you know who his agent was. Nothing really surprised me."

Washington's agent was Sam Gilbert, who was also acting for Marques Johnson. Marques intended to leave, too.

"I knew Richard Washington was leaving," says Johnson. "He wanted to go hardship and play in the NBA. He was ready to be out of there. He was just ready to leave. He pretty much stopped going to class after the last quarter started.

"We both were leaving, as a matter of fact. The Nuggets were talking to both of us. We flew down to Denver, along with Sam Gilbert. I fell in love with [Coach] Larry Brown. They made a contract offer and the terms were agreed upon. Then the NBA people got wind of it and told Denver it would affect the merger if they signed some underclassmen improperly, without going through the draft so they had to pull out at the last minute.

"I was gone. I was out of there. Coach Bartow didn't have anything to do with it. I just felt like I was ready to play on that level."

Bartow had already figured out he was in the wrong place at the wrong time but, at least, things couldn't get any worse, could they?

As a matter of fact, they could.

His second season was a replay of the first. What would have been a good season anywhere else was sub-par in Westwood. The Bruins went 23–4 and won the Pac-8 but lost at home to Notre Dame, always a bad day since Digger Phelps was such a hot dog and knew 100 ways to rub it in the papers. They lost at home to Dick

Harter and Oregon's Kamikaze Kids in what was supposed to be the revenge game for the preceding season.

Bartow was like a man out of water in the desert, with all the buzzards wondering what time dinner was. It was his first season all over, the misery, the weight loss, the siege mentality.

"Even my senior year," says Marques Johnson, "we'd sit down at the breakfast table and I'd read the L.A. *Times* and Coach Bartow would say, 'Marques, what's it say about our game last night?'

"I'd say, 'It's right here, Coach, you want to read the paper?'

" 'Oh, no, no, I swore I'd never touch another L.A. paper as long as I live. Could you read it to me?'

" 'OK. The Bruins ran their offense effectively'—reading the paper to him."

"It was definitely getting to him."

Before the first round of the NCAA tournament in Pocatello, Idaho, a friend who hadn't seen Bartow since he went west said, "He looked like he had aged thirty years in two."

At practice before the Bruins' opener against Louisville, Bartow sat in the stands with the Cardinals' Denny Crum, a friend of his. According to a Cardinal assistant, Bartow told Crum, "You want this job, you can have it because I'm out of here! There's a letter in the paper every day, saying 'We want Denny Crum.'

"Denny said, 'Is it that bad?'

"Gene said, 'I can't stand it anymore.' "

UCLA had finished that season the nation's No. 2–ranked team. In the NCAA opener, it beat Louisville, 87–79.

The next opponent was Idaho State, standard tourney fare for Bruins en route to the Final Four. Bruin fans were already peeking into the next bracket at their upcoming meeting with Jerry Tarkanian's UNLV Running Rebels with Reggie Theus, the Smiths, Robert, Tony and Sudden Sam, and their 107-point average.

Instead, the Bruins fell to Idaho State with a thud, 76–75.

Bartow says he could almost see it coming.

"Maybe it's because that week leading up to Idaho State, Marques had missed practice," he says. "He may not even remember this but I remember it. His agent, who was the same man, took him out of practice. I'm not sure he practiced all week. He had a wisdom tooth that was killing him. I didn't even know until game day for sure, as I remember it, if he was going to play.

"I was disappointed. We shot horrible from the perimeter. Idaho State had the big guy [Steve Hayes], seven-footer who ended up playing in the NBA for 10–12 years, and I knew they were a pretty good basketball team. They packed it in a zone and if you didn't shoot a little from the outside, you had problems."

In Westwood, there was chaos. Students in the dorms rioted after the game, pitching mattresses out the windows. The Bruins' flight home was funereal. There were boosters on the plane and they weren't sympathetic.

Bartow started forlornly out the window. A player joked that he was afraid the coach might ask for a parachute. Chris Lippert, a reserve forward, joked, "He might jump without it."

"It was vicious," says Roy Hamilton. "You knew there were going to be changes. You just heard things the alumni were saying. [In Pocatello, Sam Gilbert had confided to NBC's Billy Packer that the alums were buying out Bartow's contract.] They were very unhappy. And I think it was starting to get worked out right after that game. To lose to Idaho State—you got to be kidding.

"I looked at Coach, you almost felt like someone had died, someone in his family. I mean, he had lost so much weight again that year. He was so worn down. I felt bad for him.

"And you knew the end was coming. It was like OK, enough was enough, at least for him."

Enough was not enough, however, for J. D. Morgan. J. D. was not faint-hearted, nor under pressure from university officials. Morgan was sticking with Bartow and that was that. It looked like Bartow would be back, until the night he went on The Steam Room.

The steam room was a radio talk show hosted by Bud Furillo, also known as Steamer. Several weeks after the season-ending loss, stung by calls from angry fans, Bartow snapped "Hogwash!" and stormed out. Shortly thereafter, he accepted the job at Alabama Birmingham, a new school that wouldn't field a team for another 18 months.

"We were good friends," says Furillo. "He was one of the nicest guys who ever lived. He came in studio and it's pretty hard to get coaches to come in studio.

"A 19-year-old kid called in and told Gene he didn't know fundamentals. He just didn't know basketball fundamentals and went on and on. And Gene threw off the headphones, walked out of the studio and, as I liked to say, all the way to Alabama."

Bartow insists he didn't leave because of the radio show, even if it was embarrassing. He says he left because UAB came up with a fat offer—three times what he was making at UCLA.

Of course, he'd have gone for less.

"I think," Bartow says, "when I went to J. D. Morgan in that June of 1977 and told him I was considering coming down here and starting this program, I think he thought, 'This guy is stressed out completely. He's lost it, to think about going somewhere that doesn't even have an athletic program, from UCLA.'

"But J. D. didn't know that financially, it was three times better than what I was earning at UCLA. And it was a chance to get any stressful thing off my back completely. And there's no doubt, I had stress at UCLA."

It's summertime in Birmingham and the living is easy.

The Bartows have a place in Palm Springs. After every season, they go to the Springs, where Gene plays golf with coaching friends like Norm Stewart and Eddie Sutton.

Then there's the annual midsummer Bartow family reunion. This year it was in Branson, Missouri, where there's a country music show. Relaxed and at ease, Bartow is back in his office, getting ready for recruiting season.

He jokes about his team: The good news is they're all coming back and the bad news is they're all coming back. It'll be OK, though. He's seen fire and he's seen rain. This is just college basketball.

"I'm not sure," he says, "if you scrutinized every column written while I was there [UCLA] and every article written while I was there, if it's really that bad. I think I reacted very poorly 'cause I'd never, ever had it happen to me before.

"As I look back and followed Gary Cunningham and Larry Brown, and Larry Farmer and Walt Hazzard and all of them right on down—it's Los Angeles. It's any big city. It's Philadelphia. It's New York City. We've got it here, even though it's not so big. In any large city, you're going to be more scrutinized. You're going to be under the microscope. And I didn't really understand that at that time.

"I visited with Larry Brown about it a few times and Gary Cunningham a time or two but when Farmer took it, we visited from time to time and I better understood it after I got away from it a couple of years.

"It's a different type job. Alabama football's a different type job. Ask Bill Curry. Notre Dame football's a different type job. Kentucky basketball. There are not very many of them but there are three or four that are different type jobs.

"UCLA basketball's one of them. Probably at the top."

Of course, people are who they are. In 1993, a letter Bartow wrote to NCAA enforcement chief David Berst, complaining about in-state rival Alabama, leaked into the press.

In it, Bartow thanked Berst for "possibly saving my life" by not investigating UCLA while he was there, adding he believed Gilbert was "Mafia-related and was capable of hurting people." Embarrassed, Bartow said he'd only been joking about Gilbert.

But as stories go, Bartow's has a happy ending. Self-knowledge is a precious thing, especially if one survives to enjoy it.

"He was different," says Roy Hamilton. "He had his philosophy. Once you understood his philosophy, you said, 'OK, I've got to adjust my game because this is the way it is.' The problem was, he had so many of the Wooden guys there.

"I see him a lot. We joke a lot. He says, 'Roy, you know that place is just too crazy. You guys are too crazy.'

"He looks so happy. A weight was lifted off his shoulders. You can tell he's happier. He's more at ease with himself. That was just—oh my God, what a roller coaster."

CHAPTER FIVE

DENNY, COME HOME: THE BRUINS DISCOVER THE AGE OF LIMITS

Where could I afford 55 acres in Southern California? Probably not even in the Mojave Desert.

—DENNY CRUM, ON TURNING DOWN THE UCLA JOB IN 1977

We were all sad when Coach Crum went to Louisville. We wish he would come back. They're still singing the blues in Westwood.

—BILL WALTON, BEFORE CRUM'S INDUCTION TO THE HALL OF FAME IN 1994

It was obvious what they needed now: Denny Crum.

It's interesting to wonder what would have happened if they had ever gotten him, which they didn't despite more than fifteen years of speculation, wishes and occasional published reports he was on his way.

He seemed perfect: a player and assistant under Wooden, a success in his own right who'd made Louisville one of the nation's elite teams. He was young—38 when Wooden retired—and had star power. He was good enough to do the job, slick enough to handle the press and the alumni.

Roy Hamilton says the UCLA players wanted Crum. Sam Gilbert wanted him. Wooden was in his corner. Even J. D. Morgan, who had reservations, seemed to come around.

Somehow they missed connections. In the beginning, when Crum wanted to be the UCLA coach, he despaired of ever getting the chance and left.

In 1977, when they wanted him they offered him peanuts. When he turned them down, it was the first glimmer that they had already lost their place at the center of the basketball universe.

It would take years for a hard truth to register on UCLA administrators: They were state of the art only in expectations. Other powers were building larger arenas, playing to a higher percentage of capacity, soaking the alumni more for premium seats, generating more revenue, budgeting more for recruiting and lavishing higher salaries and all manner of perks upon their coaches.

J.D. Morgan still thought he was doing people a favor, offering them that $33,000 that Wooden had worked for, along with an opportunity to ride the barrel over the waterfall.

Wooden had given the Bruins a dynasty for peanuts. A child of the Depression, he accepted their modest salary without complaint. Nell used to bristle at the bargain Morgan was getting and John

85

could surely have forced the issue but never did. Were it not for his summer camps and speaking engagements, his retirement would have been precarious.

UCLA coaches, in general, led unpretentious lives. They couldn't afford the pricey neighborhoods near the school. Bel Air, right across Sunset Boulevard, the campus's northern border, was out of the question but so were Westwood, Brentwood, and Santa Monica, where $1 million homes were common. Most lived over the Sepulveda Pass in the San Fernando Valley where it was hotter in summer, colder in winter and they had to get up early to beat the rush-hour traffic.

UCLA perks were similarly modest. Wooden himself hadn't been allowed to hold his summer camp in Pauley. Instead, he held it in Thousand Oaks, 30 miles away.

He kept his camp after his retirement and dominated the field. Bartow had made $20,000 a year on a camp at Illinois (on university facilities, standard procedure elsewhere) but when he arrived at UCLA in 1975, found he was far down the totem pole.

Bartow says his two-week camp in 1976 drew a disappointing 110 kids. He understood the local star system. He sent his own son, Murry, to Wooden's camp.

Meanwhile, Denny Crum was living like a prince in Louisville, on a 55-acre ranch outside town. He heard the siren's song but he was no fool.

The funny thing was, Crum lived for the UCLA job.

He had made his share of sacrifices, which was the Bruin Way. When he graduated in 1959, he went back to Pierce Junior College as a coach and P.E. teacher and came over to Westwood at night to help Wooden's assistant, Jerry Norman, coach the freshmen for free.

(Norman was Wooden's first full-time assistant. Before him, Bill Putnam, the assistant athletic director, doubled as assistant basketball coach, although he wasn't able to help with recruiting. In the mid-'50s, Norman became the first to relieve Wooden of that duty. That was how low-power the UCLA program was.)

Norman's pay was typical Bruin subsistence level. In 1968, he left to become a stockbroker and Crum got his job.

That entailed still another sacrifice.

"I took a $3,000 cut in pay to go from Pierce to UCLA as an assistant," says Crum. "Course at that time, the cost of living wasn't what it is today. I think I was hired at $11,500 or something like that."

Crum stayed three seasons during which the Bruins won three titles. The strong-willed young assistant may have been as much a challenge as some of the players—Wooden banished him to the end of the bench after an argument in the '71 title game against Villanova—but there was no doubt of Crum's devotion or Wooden's loyalty.

After the '71 title game, Crum got offers from Virginia Tech and Louisville. Anxious to prove himself, and to move up to $20,000 a year, he took the Louisville job, intending to stay just long enough to prove himself to Morgan and succeed Wooden. The Louisville people assumed it as a given: When UCLA called, Denny would go.

Crum didn't lack confidence. NBC's Al McGuire would name him "Cool Hand Luke." Thirty-three years later, at his Hall of Fame induction, a mellow Crum would admit, "In my younger, cockier days, I suppose I would have said I expected to be here one day."

Wooden, rooting for one of his assistants to succeed him, says he thought that Crum would be the one if he did well at Louisville, which Wooden expected him to do.

"I tell you how I felt," says Crum. "I felt that J. D. Morgan would not hire an assistant coach to coach UCLA. That was my feeling.

"Course, I wanted to be a head coach. I wanted to prove I could be a head coach and be successful at that level. And in my opinion, because of his vision of UCLA, that UCLA was way up here, he thought—and these are my thoughts, I can't read his mind—but knowing him like I did, I felt like he would not hire an assistant coach to take that job when Coach Wooden retired."

Nor did Crum waste any time proving he could be a successful head coach.

The Cardinals had a long tradition of winning seasons under Peck Hickman but only one Final Four appearance. In Crum's first season, he took them there for a semifinal meeting with ... the Bruins. Before the game, Bill Walton, whom he had recruited, teased him about what the Bruins would do to his new team and they did: UCLA 96, Louisville 77.

They seemed bound by fate. Four years later, Crum was back in the Final Four at San Diego for a classic matchup with the Bruins in Wooden's last hurrah.

"That was only twenty years ago," says Crum. "I remember it like it was yesterday....

"Junior Bridgeman was a forward on Pete Trgovich's high school team. I had recruited Trgovich to go to UCLA and had not recruited Bridgeman and when I took the Louisville job at the end of that year, I didn't think it was ethical to try to get Pete to come to Louisville just because I was going there. But I did go in and start recruiting Junior.

"We had a guy named Wesley Cox on that team who had not practiced in over a month because of a hamstring pull that he had to have numbed to even be able to play in the games. And yet in the game, he had like 13 rebounds playing against Marques.

"We were ahead and Trgovich had fouled out. Coach Wooden put a freshman guard, [Jim] Spillane, in there and I'm sure he told him not to foul Terry Howard.

"And the kid got a little overzealous, the official called a foul on him and Terry missed the first free throw.

"Now that wasn't why we lost the game. We also made three turnovers against their press in the last couple minutes there. But we missed a shot and they came down and Richard Washington hit a jump shot and tied it up. Then we lost, 75–74, in overtime."

After that game Wooden announced he'd retire. From that moment, speculation about his successor dominated the weekend and Crum's was the first name on everyone's tongue.

"We were there with all our fans from Louisville," says Crum. "And the rumors were flying hot and heavy that I was going to go back to UCLA. And all the Louisville people were concerned and upset, they thought I was going to be leaving.

"At that time, I didn't want to leave because we hadn't accomplished what I wanted to. I wanted to win a national championship there. Now we had been in two Final Fours, got beaten both times by UCLA but we could have just as easily won the last one....

"I didn't want those people thinking I was gonna leave. I called a press conference and announced that I had no intention of going to UCLA, I was staying in Louisville until I accomplished there what I wanted to accomplish.

"At that point, nobody had even offered me the job. I didn't want them thinking I was even considering it."

Louisville insiders, however, say there was another reason Crum took himself out of the running: He knew he wasn't getting the job.

"He held a press conference to announce he was not a candidate," says one, "he hadn't accomplished what he wanted to do at Louisville. The truth is, he had been told that Bartow had already been given the job. The reason was J. D. Morgan hated him. They really clashed. He really had a dislike for Denny.

"I think Wooden came to his hotel room [in San Diego]. Denny was all set to go to Tijuana for lunch with a bunch of people. Afterward Denny told some people, 'Bartow's got the job.' They said he was almost in tears because he felt he was going to get that job."

Morgan, who died in 1980, never discussed his reasons for bypassing Crum. There are several theories: that he was upset at Crum for having left; that Crum was too brash, too flamboyant, not enough like Wooden.

Whatever Morgan's objections, he seemed to have gotten over them two years later. When Bartow left, J. D. first offered the job to Crum.

Crum flew to Los Angeles for the interview and decided to take the job. Then, according to the story he's always told, he flew back to Louisville and thought better of it.

"When I left after talking to him [Morgan], I really had the feeling I was gonna say yes," says Crum. "Until I got back to Louisville and got off the airplane and got back to my office.

"The phone rang and somebody asked me to go play golf. I was thinking about going fishing and getting stuff off my mind for a bit.

"I said, 'Well, L.A., where could I do that?'

"I mean, it was just a total different way of life and the opportunities out there were just not the same....

"Financially, when you consider the cost of living, the pay out there was way below par. I always felt that Coach Wooden was grossly underpaid, too. He was probably paid about one-third of what some of the top coaches were making at the time....

"So I called them and told them no, I'd changed my mind, I wasn't interested."

Insiders have another version of this story, too. Crum knew all about the different lifestyles but interviewed eagerly, intending to accept if the job were offered. However, he was shocked when Morgan offered him that old $33,000. Crum's salary had risen far above that. Crum told friends that J. D. had lowballed him, knowing he wouldn't accept, just to get the alumni off his back. No one is sure how Morgan really felt about Crum, but Denny thought J. D. hated him.

UCLA would call one more time. After Walt Hazzard was fired in 1988, Pete Dalis, the new athletic director, asked if Crum was interested. Dalis wanted a star and UCLA was finally willing to pay market price.

By then, thoughts of UCLA no longer made Crum's heart go pitter-pat. This time he was genuinely disinterested.

In the years after he turned the Bruins down, Crum went on to prove just what a great coach they'd let slip away.

His Doctors of Dunk, led by Darrell Griffith, won a national title in 1980—beating the Bruins in a close game at Indianapolis.

The Cardinals won again at Dallas in 1986, led by freshman Pervis (Never Nervous) Ellison.

In all, Crum has taken Louisville to six Final Fours. Among active coaches, only Dean Smith and Mike Krzyzewski have been to more; Bobby Knight has been to one fewer.

The program cooled off after that—Louisville hasn't been to a regional final since 1986—and there was an embarrassing feature by "60 Minutes" on its graduation rate but Crum has already secured his place in the profession. In 1994, he became the third active college coach, with Smith and Knight, to be inducted into the Hall of Fame.

Wooden escorted his former assistant to the stage. In Crum's speech, he thanked Wooden, "the Man o' War of coaches and the Secretariat of people."

"The Hall of Fame was special," said Crum later, "but it was even more special since Coach Wooden got to come....

"He wasn't feeling well when he made that trip. To travel that far at his age, that's really unbelievable to me. I'll never forget that night as long as I live."

Someone else was going to have to pick up the torch.

In Los Angeles, where half the population arrived after World War II and passions ran shallow, the Bruins could feel their fan base eroding.

"We seat 18,800 and something," Crum says of Louisville, "and we average 19,000-something....

"I think it's because there's so many things to do and so many other interests [in Los Angeles]. You've got the mountains and you've got the beach and you've got the Lakers and the Clippers. You've got SC and Pepperdine. There's so many different things. There's the hockey, there's the Dodgers.

"I mean, there's so many different things to do that people divide their affiliations so many different ways so that not any one thing is as important. When you're in Louisville, we have Triple A baseball and Louisville basketball. We have the Derby a week or two during the spring. And that's it.

"It's a big difference. Our fans' attentions are toward us all the time, year-round. You walk into a restaurant in the middle of the summer and you'll hear people talking about basketball and recruiting."

In Westwood, people sat at outdoor cafes in the middle of the summer and wondered where they were going to find another wizard who'd work for $33K.

CHAPTER SIX

THE CUNNINGHAM YEARS: BOTH OF THEM

*He could have stayed as long as he wanted to be there.
I mean, out of all the guys who were there, he could
still be there now if he wanted to....*

*The alumni liked him, the players liked him. He was
good for the program. He was the ideal guy.*

—ROY HAMILTON

It was obvious now what they needed: a Bruin.

Gene Bartow's biggest problem had been being an outsider, ignorant of Bruin tradition and city ways, a stranger to Bruin players, a figure of scorn to Bruin fans.

So they hired Gary Cunningham.

With Denny Crum out of the running, Cunningham was a logical choice. He lacked Crum's charisma and, unlike Crum, had no track record as a head coach but otherwise he was qualified as qualified could be. Like Crum, he had played for and coached under John Wooden, was popular with the players and the boosters.

Unlike Crum, Cunningham was willing to work for $33,000. He knew that was how it was at UCLA and besides, he wasn't looking to break the bank. When the Bruins turned their plaintive eyes to Cunningham and told him how important it was that he take the job, he didn't know how to say no.

He might have proved a good choice, too.

The legendary pressures sat easily on the broad shoulders of the 6-7 Cunningham. He had that Wooden self-assurance. It was something you had or you didn't but without it, a UCLA coach was a steak among piranha. If Cunningham's finishes—No. 2 rankings in both his seasons, no appearances in the Final Four—were disappointing, he said he could live with it. Unlike Bartow, he betrayed no torment and had no foibles to latch on to. Even the thick-skinned Wooden had delighted in chiding critics. Cunningham never seemed to take offense at anything.

Not that the critics were much of a problem.

"I think that people accepted Gary," says Jim Harrick, then his assistant. "There was never a negative word written or spoken about Gary Cunningham in the two years I was here. He was the coolest, calmest individual. Stayed on the seat of his pants to coach. Would punch me once in a while to say, 'Yell at the officials.'"

Cunningham might have been the one to calm the spoiled Bruin fans, to introduce them to the real world. He only had one problem.

He didn't want to be a basketball coach.

It would be easy to put Cunningham down as one more refugee fleeing Wooden's shadow.

After all, he stayed two years, quit unexpectedly and shortly thereafter left UCLA forever to take a job at tiny West Oregon State College. Someone who's been hounded out of town might want to get as far away as possible. Who else makes such a move of his own free will?

How about someone who wasn't yet caught in the rat race and didn't want to be? Who had a life, a young family he wanted to enjoy and a spirit of adventure that went beyond camping on some high school kid's doorstep?

Someone like Gary Cunningham, even if no one wanted to believe it.

"When I went back to coaching, I just didn't want to do it," he says, sitting in his office at UC Santa Barbara two decades later. "I don't know how to say it any other way. I just didn't want to do it the rest of my life. And I wanted to get on with my life, as far as getting into administration. I really had a hard time during that era—I haven't had these questions asked of me for years—convincing people that you could walk away from one of the top five programs in the nation and there wasn't something wrong with you.

"I just made a decision and I went to Oregon. I went to a small school, which no one can understand. You've got to walk to the beat of a different drummer sometimes."

At first glance, he'd seemed like the others. He was an L.A. kid who starred at Inglewood High School, got a scholarship to UCLA and finished as one of the top twenty-five scorers in Bruin history. In 1962, he co-captained UCLA's first Final Four team.

After graduating, he played on an AAU team in the Philippines and taught school there. He and his new wife, Barbara, whom he'd met when they were both at UCLA, toured India and the Orient on their way home. Gary enrolled in a master's program at UCLA and took a job as a P.E. teacher when his life was changed by a chance meeting with Wooden.

"The way I got into college coaching," says Cunningham, "he was in the student union having lunch and I saw him there and said, 'Can I sit down with you, Coach?'"

"He said, 'Well, I've lost my freshman basketball coach, would you like to be the coach?'"

"I had no intention of going into coaching. I was going to get my doctorate and go on to the academic world."

In the ensuing ten years, Cunningham worked his way up to the varsity staff, then, after Crum left, the No. 1 assistant's role. Although Cunningham worked hard at his job, he wasn't obsessed by it. He and Barbara had two daughters. They went fly fishing and camping together. They were devoutly religious, although Gary didn't advertise it.

And then, before the 1974–75 season, Wooden confided to Cunningham it would be his last. Cunningham decided it would be his last, too.

J. D. Morgan would later say the job would have been Cunningham's, but Gary immediately took himself out of the running. As Morgan was turning to Bartow, Cunningham was going into administration as he'd always planned, as executive director of the UCLA Alumni Association. He spent two years there, happy ones for him, less so for UCLA fans who wailed and gnashed their teeth at Bartow. When Bartow's time expired, Crum said no and North Carolina's Dean Smith said he wasn't interested in interviewing. Morgan came back to Cunningham with a plea to reconsider.

So Cunningham reconsidered.

"It was emotions, I think," he says. "They appealed to me, we need you, serve the university, etcetera. I think it was an emotional decision. So I gave my job up that I really loved and went back and coached."

His return was hailed throughout Bruindom. Former teammate Jim Milhorn, now a UCLA official, said he didn't want to criticize

Gene Bartow, "but with Gary it will be back to the basics that weren't there before. Sure he'll lose some games, but only to teams that are more physical and more talented. He won't lose games he shouldn't lose."

Sam Gilbert, described in the Los Angeles *Times* as "an Encino contractor and long-time adviser to UCLA athletes," said Cunningham was "in the Wooden mold," adding that David Greenwood and Roy Hamilton had told him, "they learned as much from Gary in two hours at a clinic as they've learned all year under other coaching."

Bartow, of course, had done the "other coaching." Gilbert didn't even want to mention his name.

The players were, indeed, fond of Cunningham.

"I thought it was great," says Hamilton. "Gary recruited me. I thought it was great to have him back as a part of the program again. I used to visit with him my first two years there. He had an office there on campus just like Coach Wooden did, so I thought it was a tremendous opportunity for him.

"The players really liked him. They thought it was great. At least it's someone who obviously has known their system for a long time and was part of the program."

The august Wooden endorsed Cunningham.

"Gary is a very excellent basketball man," said Wooden. "He has good rapport with the players and is a stronger person than some people might believe. You can be a strong person without ranting and raving and fighting with everybody. Gary has the solid strength to command respect, although he's not a showman or flashy."

All in all, everyone was overjoyed, with the possible exception of Cunningham, himself.

A reporter close to him described him as having "no ego, no need for the limelight, no chip on his shoulder, no scores to settle, no backroom debts to pay"—in other words, all the normal coach's motivations.

"Gary is capable, intelligent, moral," asserted his new assistant, Jim Harrick. "I worry about what will happen to him in this world."

For the moment, Cunningham sounded happy enough.

"I think sometimes a person has to get away from what he's doing to know what he really enjoys," he said upon assuming the post. "When this opportunity came, I felt it was something I wanted very much. I am really elated."

This was effusive for a man who once joked that he ran at 33⅓ in a profession in which everyone was at 78. Cunningham was patient, long-suffering, and soft-spoken, too, none of which added up to charismatic.

And yet there was something about him. Larry Farmer, who had been an assistant under Bartow and was staying on, remembered a time when Wooden had been ill and Cunningham had taken over for a week. The players got set to do the old substitute teacher routine, until Cunningham blew his whistle. After that, Farmer said, everyone just fell in line as if Wooden was there.

With Cunningham, now the head coach, everything fell in line once again. If Bartow had been haunted by Wooden, Cunningham was like Wooden's son.

In Cunningham's office, he hung a picture of Wooden, who had signed it "To one of my boys."

Cunningham's first team went 24–2 in the regular season, losing only two close games to Notre Dame, finishing No. 2 in the nation. The fans and the boosters were happy. Cunningham had gone back to Wooden's offense, and the games had that familiar JW look, with none of that infernal standing around while they punched it into the low post as they had under Bartow.

Of course, Cunningham was likely to go into a dissertation at his weekly press breakfast on the joys of some administrative task like scheduling while the writers smiled politely and glanced at their watches. But everyone liked him and everything ran smoothly.

"It was fun," says Hamilton. "I think when you start in a new place and a different kind of environment, everyone's starting from scratch. I think that made it different and fun for everyone because we were all starting over again....

"They ran the high post. Everything, as the old guys told me, was just like Coach Wooden. The practices were the same. The offense was the same."

And yet, it wasn't the same. It never would be again.

Al McGuire, making a splash as a mad savant on NBC's broadcast team with Dick Enberg and Billy Packer, announced out of the blue during a game at Pauley that the Bruins wouldn't win another title in the century. By the '90s, it would look like the prediction of the century, but in the '70s the UCLA name was still magic.

"It was a good solemn statement," says McGuire. "You only had 23 years to go. I remember Dick looking at me with those big, soft puppy eyes. And Billy looking at me with his pit-bull type eyes. It was in the Pavilion. These two guys are looking at me, like, 'Here's another Neanderthal statement from this guy.'

"I made the statement, that I would bet that UCLA would not win another championship in this century because the odds were in my favor, by far. By far."

UCLA was talented but hardly overpowering. McGuire called Greenwood, their best player, "a velvet player, not a cement mixer like Kentucky and Notre Dame's big kids."

As if to prove it, the Bruins' fine season ended abruptly in a 74–70 second-round NCAA upset at the hands of Eddie Sutton's Arkansas Razorbacks, led by the "triplets," Sidney Moncrief, Ron Brewer, and Marvin Delph.

"I guess, looking back on it, I didn't think Arkansas was as good as they were," says Cunningham. "They were well coached.

"Defensively, we did not do a great job on their guards. They really hurt us. They were quicker. They got open and they hit the shots."

"We were flat in that game," says Hamilton. "It was disappointing. We were good enough to beat them but not that night. It was disappointing but everyone was happy because we were playing the way that UCLA normally played. It was like, we didn't quit, we didn't get blown out, we were in the game and we came back, the way UCLA teams always come back. And we had the whole team coming back, except [Ray] Townsend."

In the summer a coach's thoughts are supposed to turn to thoughts of recruiting, but Cunningham's didn't.

At UCLA, the torrent was slowing to a trickle. Since the bumper crop of Greenwood, Hamilton, and Brad Holland—recruited by Wooden, signed by Bartow—they had lost every big-name prep like Herb Williams and Clark Kellogg who visited.

"It amazed me when I would meet players that came to town," says Hamilton. "I couldn't understand why they didn't come to UCLA. Herb Williams came on a recruiting trip. Maybe it was like it was with me because I knew I couldn't leave home. I wanted to stay here in Los Angeles and when I had an opportunity to play at UCLA, it was like a no-brainer for me. Maybe that was the key thing, kids didn't want to leave their environment.

"I know it became very difficult. Television changed it tremendously. When I was coming out of high school, the selling point for UCLA was, you knew yourself, they didn't have to tell you, you were going to have four, five games on national television. No other school could have come to me and said, 'Hey, we're going to be on national television four or five times.' Because they weren't."

A Bruin official says recruiting bedeviled Cunningham, taking up his time, and convincing him he was in the wrong business. In fact, Cunningham brought in only three players: Michael Sanders, a dark horse who became a star, and two insignificant players, Tyren Naulls and Rennie Kelly.

Of course, Cunningham had recruited well enough under Wooden. It was Cunningham who had sat in the high school gyms watching the young players develop and delivered the prospects to Wooden's office where the wizard would close the deal.

"I think my record speaks for itself, as far as recruiting," Cunningham says. "I think some of the things that have been directed at me—maybe I didn't recruit well or whatever—I think the record speaks for itself. I recruited a lot of great players.

"We didn't need a lot of players because I had them all coming back. We had a lot of people lined up the next year because we needed four or five, and there were some very good players that we had an in with and Larry [Brown] ended up getting some of those players....

"It was getting more intense. I would be wrong to tell you it wasn't getting more intense. It's your lifeblood and people develop new techniques and whatever you want to call it. But I always felt like we could recruit at UCLA. We had a great thing to recruit to. We had Pauley Pavilion, we had tradition, we had a great academic school. I mean, we had a lot to sell. But I just got tired of selling. The bottom line is, I used to think, 'God, I'm just doing the same thing over and over again.'

"Same speeches, same procedures. And I wanted to do things that were maybe a little more creative in my life. But you have to recruit. Recruiting's hard work. It's scouting the prospects, it's getting to know the coach, it's talking to the prospect on the phone, getting them to commit to a visit, all of those things. Yes, it was getting more intense, but in a lot of ways, I was just bored with it."

New techniques, indeed.

If fawning could be termed a "technique," then recruiting was undergoing revolutionary changes as the game got bigger, the players more valuable and the competition more frenzied.

Once, whole segments of the country had scarcely mattered. Southern schools wouldn't recruit blacks. The Eastern independents got little TV exposure. But with time, integration, rising profits, the rise of the Big East, and the advent of ESPN, the playing field leveled and the competition went beyond intense into vicious. The recruitment of high school star Moses Malone in 1974 was a new high/low point in the art of procurement, with several assistant coaches introducing more new "techniques" like taking up residence in hotels near his Petersburg, Virginia, home for months at a time.

Showing he had grasped the process perfectly, Malone chose Maryland's package (soon after enrolling, he posed for *Sports Illustrated*, sitting on the hood of his new Chrysler, acquired in what was termed a "lease-purchase" deal), then signed with the Utah Stars of the ABA before classes started. If this was an auction, what was he doing taking anything but the best bid?

The more the coaches fawned, the more players and parents demanded.

Recruiting was a free-for-all with one winner and everyone cutting up the front-runner. If a coach wasn't a living presence in a prospect's life, rivals claimed he didn't care. Yesterday's lack of proportion became today's standard of behavior.

A new monster appeared on the scene: the starstruck parent. Years later, Harrick would say at banquet appearances, "The players think they're Michael Jordan—and the parents think they're better."

Since the parents were often dirt-poor, it should have been no surprise they were keenly interested in the economic potential their golden children might represent. Some wanted payoffs. Some wanted to chart their sons' courses to the NBA, choosing schools on the basis of guarantees of starting jobs and the promise to play their "pro positions."

"Now so many people believe unrealistically that their son has a chance at the NBA," says Utah Coach Rick Majerus, once an assistant and recruiter for Al McGuire at Marquette. " 'What does he need to do, what can you do to get him to that next level?'

"I mean, I can't grow him bigger, I can't grow him taller. Everybody wants to play a position other than what they really are. The fives [centers] want to be fours [power forwards], the fours want to be threes [small forwards], the threes want to be twos [big guards], the twos want to be ones [point guards].

"Only the ones are happy with what they are. There's never been a one that wanted to be a two. They want to control the ball. They know where it's at.

"The things that are always asked—When will I play, how soon will I play, will I play as a freshman, a sophomore, do you slot me? There's more people promised to play as freshmen than were at the Harvey Haddix 13-inning no-hitter. That's question one, and question two is, what position will I play?

"And the most important questions of all, the ones that everyone without exception should prioritize as being the most important concern in the whole process, the academic issues, those are buried under television exposure, climate, topography of the campus, press coverage. It's sad."

There was a change in tone, too.

No longer were coaches representatives of proud institutions, offering a valued educational experience. Now they were supplicants, and their assistants, dug in on the front lines, were worse, toadies and hit men.

A memorable piece by *Sports Illustrated*'s Bill Brubaker in 1984 compared the correspondence sent by various coaches to high school stars Chris Washburn of Laurinburg, N.C., Institute, Danny Manning of Greensboro, N.C., Page High, and John Williams of Los Angeles Crenshaw.

Washburn received letters from North Carolina's Dean Smith and Louisville's Denny Crum before he ever played in high school. Crum's letter congratulated Chris on his "past achievements."

Said Washburn to Brubaker: "I didn't know what to make of it. My ninth-grade season hadn't even begun. So when Coach Crum wrote about my 'past achievements,' I suppose he meant my eighth-grade season at Grand View Junior High."

Washburn and Manning got smarmy letters from Duke's Mike Krzyzewski.

Wrote Krzyzewski to Washburn: "You looked in great shape and the young lady with you did not hurt your appearance."

And to Manning: "Danny, I spoke to a couple members of the Page girls' team. They had nothing but fantastic things to say about you. I stood next to them at the game and they cheered like crazy for you."

Williams got letters from UNLV assistant Mark Warkentien, reminding him that attendance at UCLA was down and no one cared about him like the Rebels.

"Do UCLA, Louisville, Houston and LSU feel the same way that we do? Why don't they come to your games like we do? THINK ABOUT IT."

Williams got the same form letter three times from Syracuse's Jim Boeheim.

Washburn received 278 pieces of mail from North Carolina State, most from assistant Tom Abatemarco.

Abatemarco started writing Washburn as an assistant at Virginia Tech, describing Coach Charlie Moir as "a great person and coach." After going to work at N.C. State, Abatemarco shifted gears smoothly, assuring Washburn that Jim Valvano was also "a great person and coach."

Abatemarco wrote Washburn's mother, Savannah, proclaiming: "Chris means the world to me.... Chris is very important to us as a player and person."

Valvano wrote Washburn, "I've never met someone who enjoys life and lives it to the fullest as much as you do."

After attending three high schools, Washburn chose North Carolina State because, "Those letters showed me how much N.C. State really cared about me. State just wanted me the most."

Questions were raised about the recruitment of all three players. Soon after going to Raleigh, Washburn was seen driving a Subaru. He claimed his girl friend bought it, but that his name had been put on the purchase agreement so he could drive it.

Manning went to Kansas after Coach Larry Brown hired his father, Ed, a former NBA player who was then driving a truck, as an assistant coach.

Williams went to LSU after a free-wheeling recruiting fight that was so messy, the winning coach, Dale Brown, announced he wanted to put $150,000 in a valise and offer it to Williams as an object lesson in the indignity of selling oneself to the highest bidder.

Washburn, then a college freshman, told Brubaker he was keeping all his correspondence.

"Someday when I have a family, I'm going to show this mail to my children," he said. "And when these kids see all the letters that I received from all these schools, I think they're going to be proud of me."

Washburn stayed at State for two years before leaving to become the third pick in the 1986 NBA draft. His pro career lasted two seasons before collapsing under the weight of his substance abuse problems. Today, he's a footnote in basketball history, one of those players whose name is synonymous with "wasted potential" and those letters are probably scant comfort.

Gary Cunningham wasn't worried about recruiting. One season into his coaching career, he knew it wasn't for him.

Sitting around after the Arkansas loss, thinking of the season, he began to realize he didn't want to do it. Before he started his second season, he went in to break the news to J. D. Morgan.

"I knew after the first year I wanted to be in administration," Cunningham says. "I told J. D. going into the second year, 'You have a year to find a coach.'

"I said, 'I will coach the team, I'll do the best I can for you, I will recruit for you. I will not in any way short-change you. But I'm not going to be the basketball coach after this year.' "

Only Gary, Barbara, and Morgan knew the secret under which the Bruins played the 1978–79 season. Cunningham, anxious to secure his assistants' futures, started talking them up behind the scenes. The Pepperdine athletic director was interested in Harrick. Cunningham told Harrick it was something he should pursue—but Harrick didn't want to.

"Jim didn't want to leave me," says Cunningham, smiling, "and I couldn't tell him I was leaving. So I kind of pushed him. I really pushed him to the Pepperdine job."

Amazingly enough, the secret held and the season was successful and uneventful. The team came together nicely with Brad Holland replacing Ray Townsend at guard. Within two years, four of them (Greenwood, Hamilton, Holland, and Kiki Vandeweghe) would be No. 1 draft choices. At mid-season, a Eugene, Oregon columnist predicted that Cunningham wouldn't return, intriguing insiders—Cunningham had family in the area—but everybody let it pass.

The Bruins went 23–4, won the Pac-10 again, then won their first two games in the NCAA Tournament, blasting Bill Cartwright's big USF team in the second round and advancing to the Western finals for a rematch with DePaul.

DePaul's Ray Meyer, an ancient and beloved figure who'd coached George Mikan, was a sentimental favorite, but his team, built around freshman star Mark Aguirre and guards Clyde Bradshaw and Skip Dillard, was thin. Meyer had to play his starters almost all the minutes. In an early-season meeting, the Bruins had bombed them, 108–85.

This time, when it counted, it was DePaul 95, UCLA 91.

"We had set all the NCAA field goal percentage shooting records that year," Cunningham says. "We'd beaten DePaul earlier in the year by 23 points. And we go out and shoot 13 or 17 percent in the first half. They stalled the ball and we come all the way back and we had a remote chance to win the ball game.

"And I really felt we had as good a team—I think we could have gone and played with Magic [Johnson] and Larry Bird and those people in the Final Four that year. My decision was all settled, but I was terribly disappointed and even today I am.

"I think back on it and I really felt we had a Final Four team. I really felt we had the chemistry and the players to win a national championship.

"We just had a bad shooting game. I mean, a really bad shooting game. The ball didn't go in. I made a calculation on a DePaul kid. I didn't think he could shoot—[Jim] Mitchem, their center. He drilled several shots from 17 feet. I told David Greenwood to play him soft. Get back in the middle, play him soft, he can't shoot. He just started putting them in. We kept missing.

"It's a long time ago, but that is probably my biggest disappointment."

"The thing about it," says Hamilton, "we had played so well against San Francisco the game before. That's the game we should have lost, that everyone thought we were going to lose because we were so small and they had like almost all seven-footers across the front line.

"Well, we knew we shouldn't have lost. Coach Cunningham was proud of us because we didn't quit. He was really good at the end, in the locker room. He commended everyone on their effort and said he was really proud of us because we didn't quit, we fought all the way to the end.

"I think the public handled it pretty good. I think the media handled it pretty good. We lost but we lost the way a UCLA team played."

Five days later Cunningham announced his resignation. The secret had held to the end. Jaws dropped all over campus.

"I think I found out from Coach Farmer," says Hamilton. "I was surprised. That was really a shock. I never imagined him doing that. I just thought he really was happy. The team was successful. The program had turned around. The respect was there. We were nationally ranked so I was just amazed."

At a farewell press conference, with Chancellor Charles Young sitting at his left elbow, Cunningham said the game had changed. Now there were summer leagues and all-star games a coach should see and what ever happened to the off-season?

"As I did the job," Cunningham said, "I was away from home an awful lot. There were times during the season when we worked 25 or 28 straight days. I'm not saying I don't want to work hard, because I've worked hard all my life and that doesn't scare me.

"I just like to have a day off every once in a while."

Young had told Cunningham there would always be an administrative job waiting if he didn't want to coach. There was—his old post, director of the Alumni Association. Cunningham never complained but friends say he had his eye on another job higher up and was disappointed.

In his final surprise, Cunningham resigned his new job two months after going back to it, to become athletic director at someplace called West Oregon State College. As far as his former peers in basketball were concerned, he was Columbus, sailing off the edge of a flat world.

"There was some discussion of another job," says Cunningham, "but the promise was never made. And I had a little bit of disappointment, to be honest with you.

"To leave UCLA—I was only on that job two months and left it—that was kind of an abrupt leaving, too. All of those things have been mended since, but at the time, it was kind of abrupt just to take a job and two months later, to leave it.

"You have to make choices in life. I wanted to live in the Pacific Northwest, always wanted to."

The Cunninghams only stayed in the Pacific Northwest two years, though. He decided he wanted to get back to Division I and accepted an offer from the University of Wyoming in Laramie, another outpost far from the bright lights of L.A. Another five years and he moved to Fresno State in the sun-baked San Joaquin Valley.

In 1983 when the UCLA athletic director's job came open, Cunningham applied but it went to Peter Dalis. Since Cunningham was popular and eminently qualified, it is hard to believe that his departure didn't count against him.

Cunningham stayed at Fresno for nine seasons. He moved to UC Santa Barbara in 1995, reportedly exasperated at the hiring of Jerry Tarkanian by the school president after a messy job search in which the victory-starved townspeople all but marched on the campus.

As it was, a member of Fresno's athletic board received a threatening phone call, advising him to vote for Tarkanian. After the hiring, Tark made a late run at verbally-committed prep stars like New York's Stephon Marbury, reportedly offering to hire one of Marbury's brothers as an assistant coach. Marbury went to Georgia Tech as planned and no one else broke a commitment to switch to Fresno but Tarkanian didn't apologize for the furor.

"If anyone thinks I came here to lose and go out to eat some good Armenian food," Tark said, "they're wrong."

For the record, Cunningham says his plans to leave predated Tarkanian's arrival, that his "batteries needed recharging." For whatever reason, Cunningham came to Santa Barbara, a lower-power program but a beautiful school set stunningly on a bluff overlooking the Pacific.

Cunningham says he doesn't regret his decisions although he does note in passing he might have left coaching "prematurely."

"I guess," he says, sitting in his new UCSB office, "I was young enough and naive enough that I never felt pressure that the coaches that have come after me have felt. I always felt I was family, part of the whole thing.

"I had never known anything but winning and I always felt we were going to win. The pressures that I felt were self-imposed, but as far as eating me up, no, it wasn't eating me up. I felt the fans were with me, we were all on the same page....

"I felt that I could have stayed as long as I wanted because I was one of them. That's not arrogance. I think I could have.

"I had great training. I had the opportunity to work with Coach, to play for him, to understand. I think I was a good teacher. I was a very good teacher of fundamentals and I thought I was a good strategist in the game. I think probably my former players would tell you that."

In administration as well as coaching, one wins some and loses others, but Cunningham did get to watch his daughters grow up. There's a theory that coaching is a test of one's sanity—and if one leaves it, he passes.

Cunningham aced the course.

CHAPTER SEVEN

THE BROWN YEARS:
THE PIED PIPER HANGS
A U-TURN

Larry was the kind of coach, he was the kind of guy where you're always going to feel there's hope. We've been in games, down 15 with two and a half minutes left and he'd call time out and say, 'Hey, we're fine! We're getting ready to press, steal it twice, score two times.' He'd call time out with a minute to go in games you had no chance to win and tell you how proud he was of you. He always encouraged you, he always created an atmosphere of hope.

Some coaches panic, lost it, cursed you out, snapped, talked to you in a condescending way. He didn't do any of that.

He never lost his composure. And the things he was saying to us, they all happened.

—MICHAEL HOLTON, CLASS OF '84

It was obvious what they needed now: a star.

Luckily J. D. Morgan had had his eye on one for a while. And J. D.'s prospect was available.

And so Larry Brown came to Westwood.

What followed was two years of the highest highs and the lowest lows the Bruins had ever known. They seemed to crash to earth weeks into Brown's tenure, then saw him lead them on one of the most remarkable post-season runs they would ever experience. The students adored him as they had never adored a UCLA coach, John Wooden included. Wooden had been a kindly grandfather. Brown was so young, so outgoing, so hip, so obviously one of them in spirit, a kid in adult's clothing.

Then after taking them back up the hilltop overlooking the promised land, Brown abandoned them. It was the damndest two years UCLA had ever seen.

Of course, for Brown, it was pretty much like any other two years in his career.

In the years that have passed since that fateful day in the fall of 1979 when he first sat down in Wooden's old office, many things have happened to Brown.

He has had five more jobs, delivering five more teams to heights they hadn't previously reached and leaving four of them. In 1979, however, that was all ahead of him. He was 39 and a boy wonder, whose Denver Nuggets were widely admired for their entertaining uptempo style and collegiate enthusiasm.

He had taken the Nuggets smoothly from the American Basketball Association into the NBA before falling out with management over the acquisition of George McGinnis. McGinnis was a traditionally nonchalant NBA superstar, and when he objected to

Brown's gung-ho style after their first practice, Brown offered to trade him on the spot. Calmer heads—whose head wasn't?—soothed Brown, but only for the moment. Midway through the season, Brown worked out another resolution to the conflict: He quit.

It seemed unremarkable. Brown had been in Denver for five seasons. Only his friends knew how flighty he could be and he hadn't even shown them the whole act yet.

They had a clue, though. His first coaching job—at Davidson—didn't appear in his record. It couldn't. He quit before the first game.

"It's true," says Indiana Pacers president Donnie Walsh, once Brown's assistant in Denver, laughing.

"First of all, he was taking over a team that, the year before, had been a great team. They were all coming back plus they were adding a guy coming off their freshman team averaging 30 points a game. Larry was like a shoo-in to get into the Eastern regionals.

"He called me up, he asked me about the team, I told him, 'Hey, you've got a great team. You can't miss.'

"And he called me about two weeks later and told me, 'I'm quitting.' He said, 'They didn't change the carpet in my office.'

"I said, 'Larry, you're out of your fucking mind! You'll never get another college job again!' Obviously, I was wrong."

Obviously, this was not your standard boy wonder.

Brown was born in Brooklyn and raised on Long Island but his father, a traveling furniture salesman, died when he was six. It was so traumatic for the family, his mother didn't tell her kids for weeks.

They moved constantly as she strained to make ends meet. She remarried when Larry was 18 and although his stepfather was nice enough, he stopped coming around. The family bristled with dysfunction. Larry and his brother, Herb, who would coach the Detroit Pistons, weren't close as kids. As adults, they went years without speaking.

Brown, searching for father figures, revered his basketball coaches. If business intervened and one appeared to abandon him, as did the magnetic Frank McGuire who recruited him for North Carolina before going to the NBA, Larry was heartbroken.

Brown was a fine player and he had that Isiah Thomas imp quality. He was so nice, it could break your heart. He was the type of guy who would see a kid reporter walk in for the first time, scuffing his shoes because he was too shy to talk to anybody. Brown would walk up, offer his hand and say, "Hi, I'm Larry Brown."

At 5-10, he wasn't going to become the next Oscar Robertson, but he played in three ABA all-star games. As a coach, however, he was a gaint. In his first four seasons, he was ABA coach of the year three times.

Nevertheless, he worried.

Coaches all worried and obsessed, but Brown could out-coach, out-worry and out-obsess any of them. He lived in constant fear of being fired and needed constant reassurance. When the unsinkable Doug Moe left Brown's Nugget staff to take over the Spurs, he found himself on the phone with Larry nightly, consoling him as before. One night it struck Moe that his team was 4–6 and Brown's was 9–1.

Whenever Brown landed a new job, he would say the same thing, as if surprised: "Someone out there thinks I can coach."

That was what he said that day in Denver in the spring of 1979, when J. D. Morgan called and asked if he'd be interested in the UCLA job.

After that, the Bruins were off on the ride of their lives.

Actually, J. D. had called Brown once before, in 1977 after Bartow left.

"Mr. Morgan said to me," says Brown, "out of the clear blue he said, 'I'm going to offer the job to somebody that I feel a real, strong responsibility to and he's done a lot for our program'—and he mentioned Gary [Cunningham].

"He said, 'But I don't think he's going to take it.' And he said, 'If he doesn't take it, I've been following you and I'd like you to come here.'

"And I had never met the man or anything. I was in a state of shock. You know, I never perceived of myself as a pro coach and still don't. So at the time I said, 'I'm just honored you would even consider me.'

"Then he called me back and said Gary, in fact, had taken it. He said, 'But Larry, a lot of funny things will happen.'

"I said, 'Mr. Morgan, opportunities like that never happen again but you just gave me the greatest honor in the world.'

"And he said, 'Well, I'll be in touch.' "

J. D. was right, funny things happened. In two years, Cunningham left and the Bruins needed another coach. Brown needed a job, though his phone was ringing off the hook. The Celtics' John Y. Brown called, and the Bulls' Rod Thorn, but after his Denver experience, Brown wasn't wild about another pro job. He had always yearned to be a college coach, anyway, like his mentors, Frank McGuire and Dean Smith.

Brown flew to Memphis State with his wife, Barbara, for an interview and fell in love with the place. He was all set to accept the job when Barbara marched him out of a cocktail party and urged him to see what other offers came in. The Browns flew back to Denver and that was when Morgan called again.

Thus ended the selection process, on both sides.

"Mr. Morgan invited me to Scottsdale," says Brown. "He had just had open-heart surgery and was recovering. I sat down with him and his wife and I thought it was an interview. He said, 'I've picked you to be the coach.'

"Of all the things that have ever happened to me in basketball, that was the greatest thing that's ever happened."

It was everything Brown had ever dreamed of: a college job, a beautiful campus, a storied program and the compliment of being chosen to follow in the footsteps of John Wooden. So what if he had to take a cut from the $200,000 in straight pay he'd gotten in Denver to $40,000 plus perks?

"I never even asked them my salary," Brown says. "Forty was fine. He [Morgan] told me I was going to have a little TV show, a radio show. We didn't even talk about money.

"He said, 'Larry, to be honest with you, coaching UCLA—money shouldn't matter.' I didn't even think about it. I didn't get into coaching for money."

Brown was a romantic and he was in love. Nothing that happened would ever change his feeling for UCLA, but these were the dizzying first days when Cupid's arrow pierced his heart.

"I can remember the first day I met him," says Steve Hartman, now a talk radio host in San Diego. "I was sports editor of the school paper. When I walked into his office, he was putting up all these *Sports Illustrated* covers of Wooden and the players. Somebody had taken them down.

"He was telling me, 'I can't believe they did this, took these down. I feel like I have the greatest job in the world. I'm pinching myself. I'm the head coach at UCLA. I'm the happiest guy in the world.' "

Brown was never happier than that summer, puttering around his new office, thumbing through the old yearbooks, wandering around the campus.

"I'm coming from Carolina," Brown says, "and I look at our book and I'm proud of the unbelievable success Carolina basketball has had. They've got ACC champs, a special thing there, and Eastern regional champs, a special thing there. Well, at UCLA I keep turning the pages and it's all national championship pictures.

"First thing I did when I went to UCLA was look for the championship trophies. It only looked like they won three because they were stacked, one behind the other, in the bowling alley. And I was pinching myself, I was just so tickled."

Reality had to start seeping in sometime.

"Barbara and I started driving up and down looking for places to live," Brown says. "We wanted to live close by campus so the kids [his players] could come around. I knew you had to spend a lot of time traveling and I didn't want to spend a lot of time on the highway. I wanted to be close to school so at least I could spend some time with my family.

"We were driving, I remember, up one of the canyons by UCLA and some lady was wheeling some garbage out and she had a sign, 'For Sale' and it looked like kind of a nice house. Barbara jumped out of the car and asked, 'We're not trying to be rude but how much are you asking?'

"It was a little ranch house. She said something like $975,000. This is 1979. And we cracked up.

"We started looking around. We found a small house off Bundy [in Brentwood]. They wanted three hundred-and-something thousand dollars. It was a tiny house but it had a fence where we could put our dogs. Three bedrooms. Well, when I figured it out, I couldn't buy it, so some UCLA alums bought the house and helped with the rent. My paycheck didn't cover the rent. The deal was, I would pay back and buy the house when I could afford it."

Then there was the team he was taking over.

It wasn't very good by any standards and the Bruins hadn't seen anything like it in decades. Graduation had taken David Greenwood, Roy Hamilton, and Brad Holland, all No. 1 draft picks. Only one returning player, Kiki Vandeweghe, had ever averaged more than six points a game.

"When Mr. Morgan hired me," Brown says, "he gave me a couple interesting comments. He said, 'Larry, you're going to have a tough time your first year. It's going to be impossible your second year. Next year, you lose four seniors'—Kiki, James Wilkes, Gig Sims, and Darrell Allums.

"And then he said to me, which was the greatest: 'I will do everything for you to help you succeed. I'm going to ask you a couple things: get Sam Gilbert out of the program and make sure you win.'"

Oh yes, Sam.

Brown says Morgan didn't say why he wanted Gilbert's entree ended, but he didn't have to. Brown had heard about Sam's involvement, which was notorious throughout the biz, and could read between the lines of J. D.'s request: Cut him off before he lands us on probation.

Shortly after arriving, Brown was invited to a booster's function at a Chinese restaurant in Century City. He remembers arriving to find his players sipping cocktails with Gilbert. Offended—"I would have never ever thought about drinking in front of my coach"— Brown left. The next day, he asked the players not to do it again.

Brown says he never put Gilbert off limits, never confronted him personally—Sam was, after all, a significant donor and a boon to the program as well as the players—hoping to keep him aboard but at arms' length.

However, there was no doubt who the surrogate father of any Brown team was going to be: Brown.

"He always had a genuine concern with what was going on with you," says Michael Holton, one of Brown's first recruits. "His thing was, if you had a problem, you'd better bring it to his office. He didn't ever want to hear about it anywhere else.

"So if you had a problem with your girl, I mean, he knew. If you were struggling with a class, he knew. He wasn't a kind of coach that delegated. So many coaches delegate. This guy handles the academics, that guy does the recruiting, this guy does that, that, and that—and I golf.

"He was so accessible that way. He told you, 'You know, I expect you to peek your head in here.' When he saw you and he said, 'Hey, how you doing kiddo?'—which is how he talks. What he meant was, Come into my office, sit down and visit with me for a few minutes.

"Sometimes you walk through the coach's office and you see Coach, you say hi, he says hi, you go on about your business. I got to the point where I didn't go there with anybody. When I'd go through there, I knew I needed to have 10 or 15 minutes blocked out. Because if I bumped into Coach, we were going to visit. But that's warmth and caring and concern. What it created was a relationship where you would always give him 100 percent. I mean, willingly. And be upbeat about it."

Not one to be tuned out, Gilbert fumed about the gall of this interloper. "I could cut his balls off and he wouldn't know it until he pulled his pants down," he confided to a reporter.

All Gilbert could do was talk, though. He would remain a force behind the scenes at UCLA because of his old alliances, but his Godfather days were over.

Yes, there was something about the new coach that grated on the traditionalists.

Star power notwithstanding, Brown was clearly Not A Bruin. Despite his lavish kowtows toward UCLA and Wooden, he had North Carolina Tarheels written all over him, and in Westwood all that Carolina-Dean Smith-If God Isn't a Tar Heel Why Did He Make the Sky Carolina Blue?-stuff didn't mean diddly.

They Shoot Coaches, Don't They?

UCLA as Wooden found it in 1948: Bruins face the hated USC Trojans before a rare sellout of 2,400.

John, in his Navy uniform, and Nell with their first two children.

Walt Hazzard (42), Wooden, and the '64 champs who started the whole thing.

Kareem Abdul-Jabbar, hooking over the no-longer-known-as-Big E, Houston's Elvin Hayes in the '68 Final Four payback period.

Bill Walton at UCLA, before discovering capitalism, TV, and hairspray.

Bruins on parade: Sam Gilbert at home with his wall of autographed pictures.

J.D. Morgan, future A.D. and dynast in his own right, with one of his seven NCAA tennis champions. Star pupil Arthur Ashe is on the far right.

The '69 champs, one of the best college teams ever. Wooden (bottom row center) has Denny Crum on his right, Gary Cunningham on his left.

Gene Bartow and Wooden in their "father and son" shot in the 1975–76 UCLA media guide. As the original caption put it, "These gentlemen also appear to be saying, quite simply, 'Good luck, John,' and 'Good luck, Gene.'" One of them would need it more than the other.

Marques dunking: In Westwood, there was only one.

Roy Hamilton,
in period Afro,
drives in 1976.

Young Larry
Brown at the
start of the 1978–
79 season, the
greatest of his
life.

Larry Farmer in action. Note the Wooden-style rolled-up program; the nuances were easy to copy but nothing else was.

Gerald Madkins, going hard to the hoop, as usual.

Ed O'Bannon, enjoying the moment with his trusty videocam during the '95 tournament run.

Seattle dresses up for the '95 Final Four: Corporate bazaars downtown, the Bud Light "ladies" walking around for a photo op. Good thing they haven't let this thing get over commercialized.

Jim Harrick and his staff in the Arkansas game, watching their dreams come true.

When the Bruins went to Japan in Brown's second season, they were given new uniforms by the Descente company with a lighter blue. *Carolina blue!* moaned Bruin fans. Brown's assistant, Larry Farmer, got letters urging him to stand up for the tradition.

But the students loved Brown and rightfully so, because he loved them.

He was one of those grownups who would chase his adolescence through his adulthood. His college days had been a joy and the Carolina program had offered a sense of warmth and family he had missed growing up. No matter what he did as a pro coach, before and after UCLA, he'd always say he was really a college coach and intended to go back one day.

Brown loved "the kids," players and students alike. He loved talking to them, winning their confidence, getting them to confide in him. He was just a grownup kid himself.

In Brown's mind, a college program was not run for the benefit of the fat cats. They had their role and he was willing to profit from it and to acknowledge them, but he was leery of them, too. They were adults.

Brown told the players, most of whom lived in apartments off campus, he wanted them back in the dorms, among the students. He wanted Pauley reconfigured, with student seats in the empty space behind the baselines to heat up the old sterile atmosphere. When students camped out overnight to buy tickets for games, Brown and the players showed up, passed out doughnuts and led cheers.

"We would sign the Icky La Boom Ba cheer with them," says Holton, laughing. "I don't know if you're familiar with that: 'Icky La Boom Ba, Icky La Picky Wicky, Opa Tee Ah.' That was the thing. We would sing that and cheer. We would go out to the football games and say that cheer."

The students, who could recognize one of their own when they saw it, reciprocated in kind.

One night, Brown accepted an invitation from Lambda Chi Alpha fraternity to speak. The Lambda Chis had heard that Brown had been in a Jewish house at Carolina, but he told them he hadn't, that he might have joined a Gentile house, but couldn't because Jews were barred.

"Our rush chairman literally kicked me under the table," says Steve Samms, then a Lambda Chi, now a Los Angeles attorney. "He said, 'Hey Steve, can we bid this guy?'

"I said, 'I'm pretty sure we can.'

"Without any further ado, he stood up and said, 'Well, Coach, on behalf of the brothers of Lambda Chi Alpha, we would like to extend you a bid to become our first new associate member in 1979.'

"He stood up and said, 'Wow, that is one of the neatest things anyone has ever done.' "

Brown put his pledge pin on while the Lambda Chis' hearts swelled. Of course, they suspected he was just being nice—until one day Samms spotted him shopping in Westwood, wearing his pledge pin.

Samms told Brown that he didn't really have to wear it, that although they were all proud of their house, etc., they didn't make their pledges wear their pins everywhere.

"He said, 'Well, Steve, I'm always proud to wear that pin,' " says Samms. "He wore it every day."

Samms ran home to tell the brothers that one. Who cared what some old fart in Pacific Palisades like Sam Gilbert thought? On campus, Larry Brown was a god.

Had Mr. Morgan told him to make sure he won? Did Mr. Morgan know what he was asking?

The cupboard wasn't bare but it was close to it. Gary Cunningham had gotten a bunch of verbal commitments from local stars—the best were Leon Wood and Darren Daye—but with a new coach coming in, all bets were off. Brown set out to sign whom he could.

Wood, one of the top point guard prospects in the country, dropped out. Brown says someone had told Wood's mother that the new coach was a racist. Daye said he'd come. Cliff Pruitt said he'd come. ("Cliff said, 'In spite of you, I'm coming to UCLA. I don't care who the coach is,'" says Brown, laughing. "He was my first signing, so I was in love with him.")

With Wood gone, Brown made a late run at Holton, a guard whom the Bruins hadn't been recruiting, and signed him.

Dean Smith recommended a guard from Chicago named Raymond McCoy. Brown flew in to see him, but McCoy didn't show up. Brown called him the next day to see what had happened.

"He said, 'Well, I'm going to go to San Francisco. I signed with San Francisco last night,' " Brown says.

"I said, 'Why wouldn't you call me, give me the courtesy?'

"He said, 'Well, I didn't think it was any big deal.' I said, 'Well, Raymond, I'm going to go find the quickest little guy I can find in America. And we're going to press you when you get off the airplane and you can count on that. I'm going to schedule your ass.'

"So we ended up getting Rod Foster. Everybody thought he was going to LSU. Dale Brown said something nasty about him in a *Sports Illustrated* article—'Obviously Rod got a lot of money to go to UCLA.' "

So Brown had a team, more or less.

His first inclination was to go with the veterans. Under the circumstances, he had a good freshman class—Daye, Foster, Holton, and Pruitt—but they were hardly the nation's top prospects. Brown, a noted sentimentalist (as a pro, he customarily started his lowliest benchwarmers in their home towns), felt for the older Bruins who had never known the glory that was supposed to be UCLA. In Brown's revered Carolina system, Dean Smith regarded a player's senior year as his reward for all the hard work he had done.

So seniors Vandeweghe, Wilkes, and Allums started, along with junior Tony Anderson and sophomore Tyren Naulls. And the bottom dropped out of the program.

Of course, it didn't take much. After a 3–0 start against small fry (Idaho State, Hofstra, and Santa Clara), the Bruins lost, at Notre Dame and at home to DePaul. *Sports Illustrated* wrote its "The Bruins Are in Ruins" piece, declaring, "Now UCLA is just a team, Pauley Pavilion is just a building and the song girls are just cheerleaders. Gone are the awe, the mystique, the glamor. UCLA, R.I.P."

A three-game losing streak—UCLA's longest since the '50s—dropped the Bruins to 8–6 and Brown decided, screw sentiment.

"We were 8–6," says Holton, "and everything seemed to be falling apart. We were being talked about as the worst team in UCLA basketball history, etcetera. I just remember taking a lead from Coach Brown—that it wasn't the end of the world. It wasn't a catastrophic time. It really was a special situation. For us to have a chance to believe in ourselves and pull together and to rebound from those circumstances and that situation and that predicament was special.

"I remember him doing something as a coach in transforming that situation. He basically called us in and said that he had tried to do things the way they'd been done there.

"He said, 'Guys, I tried it. I went with you, and at this point I gotta go my way. I gotta do what I feel is right to do. You guys who were in the program when I got here, I'm sorry but I don't owe you anything. I gave you a shot; it's not working. I gotta go with what I think's going to work here. I hope you'll be able to handle that.'

"I remember him having that conversation. It was not nice.

"They didn't say anything because he challenged them in that meeting. They didn't say anything. And he told them that he felt they hadn't performed. Now this is not all of the seniors because this didn't really affect Kiki, but the other ones; he thought they were soft. He told Gig Sims and Darrell Allums that he didn't think they were showing manhood.

"That was the first time I saw a coach tell a player something like that. And he just said it! He challenged 'em! I thought it was super-intelligent, what he did. Because he created an environment after that meeting where you're either stepping up or you're stepping down. You're not going to stay the same.

"He put Rod in the lineup and a couple games later, he put me in the lineup and we began a transformation of our team."

Brown didn't expect a miracle. He thought they weren't going anywhere and might as well play their youngsters. Michael Sanders, a 6-5 sophomore, became the center with Foster and Holton at guard. Daye and Pruitt completed the seven-man rotation. Things improved, if not dramatically. They lost by 16 at Washington State, by 12 at Arizona State.

They were 15–8 going into their last home game, fourth in the Pac-10, but still alive for the NCAA Tournament by grace of the new rules that had expanded the field from 32 teams to 48 in two seasons. For their final home game, against Washington, Brown started five seniors as a going-away gift—four 6-8 forwards plus walk-on Chris Lippert as a makeshift point guard. Brown says the seniors played well, but the regulars struggled when they got in. The Bruins lost on a last-second shot, 72–70, but the way Brown remembers it, everybody thought it was neat.

Well, almost everybody. The headline in the Daily Bruin said: "UCLA Says So Long to Seniors and NCAA Bid."

The Bruins finished 17–9 and squeaked in. There was some sneering that they were the last selection but they were seeded No. 8 in the West, meaning they'd have gotten in even if it had been a 32-team field.

Not that anyone expected them to stay around long.

In the first round in Arizona's McKale Center, they dispatched Old Dominion, although Brown had to tell his players where and what Old Dominion was. "That was hysterical," he says, laughing. "I was telling these guys, we're playing Old Dominion, the Monarchs. And they're saying, 'What's an Old Dominion?'

"You know, UCLA kids...."

Their second-round matchup was DePaul, the nation's No. 1 rated team, and that was supposed to be it for them. But something was happening; the Bruins had become a tough defensive team. In Wilkes, Brown had a fine low-post defender to put on the Blue Demon star, Mark Aguirre. Instead of the predicted blowout, the game turned tense and taut and UCLA won, 77–71. Aguirre, whose career would be studded with such disappointments, ran out of the arena, sat down, and cried.

Of course, everyone knew what an upset this had been and how far the Bruins were in above their head, no one more than Brown.

"After we beat DePaul, they have the typical press conference," says Brown. "So my assistants, Farmer and Kevin [O'Connor], went to see the second game, Arizona State against Ohio State.

"Arizona State was great, they had Byron [Scott], Fat [Lever], Alton [Lister]. They had beaten us that year twice. Ohio State had Clark Kellogg, Kelvin Ransey, and Herb Williams. I remember, I walked in after the press conference and looked at the score and Ohio State was up 20—at Tempe."

He laughs.

"I grabbed Larry and Kevin, I said, 'Look, quit scouting this game, let's celebrate this win. These guys are going to kick our ass the next game!' "

One thing his guys had going for them, there was no pressure on them. Nobody expected anything, Everyone else might be up to their eyes in expectations, but for once the Bruins were on a lark.

"He did such a great job of coaching," says Holton. "We took it one game at a time. We didn't have any pressure. And then, he was funny.

"I remember him before we played Ohio State. The people at Ohio State were just huge! Herb Williams, Clark Kellogg, they were just huge! We're getting ready to run out to warm up and he says, 'Hey, I don't want anybody to take their sweats off before the game starts. Because I don't want them to see how small we are.' "

UCLA won that game, 72–68, as the 6-8 Wilkes held the 6-11 Williams to 10 points.

"They had a big lead early and dunked it about nine times in the first 15 possessions," says Brown. "Each guy dunked the ball. And then we just hung on.

"I remember we had a one-point lead, and they were making a run at us and I was trying to get a time-out. When we wanted time-out, everybody on the bench stood up. And Darren Daye didn't hear me, drove in and made a three-point play. I said, 'Yeah, Darren!'

"I also remember, I told them about 'the power [an old North Carolina superstition].' I had 'em [players on the bench] all holding their left nut. Michael Holton tapped me on the shoulder and said, 'I'm dying here!'

"Then we beat Clemson in the regional finals. I was getting numb. After that, I thought we'd beat everybody. Our freshmen were, like, nuts. Darren was like Stinky in 'Our Gang,' made everybody angry at him in his own way. And Rod, he didn't understand. Rod didn't know if there was 50,000 people watching or he was playing in the playground."

They were in the Final Four.

It had only been three years since the last UCLA appearance, even if this had nothing to do with the old days. Brown looked around Indianapolis Market Square Arena at the public workout the day before the semifinals and shivered with excitement.

"We walked into that shoot-around," Brown says, "and I saw Coach Smith and Coach Meyer and Coach [Pete] Newell—all these guys watching us work out. Coach Meyers, Coach McGuire [Al McGuire, by then an NBC commentator], and Coach Smith came by and said something.

"And I was thinking to myself, 'You shouldn't take these things for granted. They might never happen again.' When you realize all the great coaches and great programs that sometimes don't even get there or at this particular moment are watching you play, it was pretty incredible."

Their semifinal matchup was another Big Ten powerhouse, Purdue, located in nearby West Lafayette, which made it practically the home team, led by 7-0 Joe Barry Carroll, considered the top big man in college. The Bruins were again underdogs.

Once again, they won, 67–62, as Wilkes held Carroll to 17.

"Kiki dunked on Joe Barry with one hand, off the dribble and that just turned the game around," says Holton. "You know how Kiki picked the ball up in one hand off the bounce? He drove baseline and did that to Joe Barry twice! It just let us all know, OK, we're going to be all right. We're going to slay the giant."

They were in the finals against Louisville. Of course, the Cardinals were favored. Like Purdue, they were just down the road and they had a superstar, player of the year Darrell Griffith.

The Cardinals were Denny Crum's version of the first UCLA champion, a small, athletic team that pressured opponents out of their game plans. Unlike any Wooden team, the Cards were free-spirited and mouthy. They called themselves the Doctors of Dunk and blithely informed everyone all season, "the 'Ville's going to the 'Nap."

With four minutes left, the 'Ville was going into the tank.

The Bruins had a 56–52 lead, and Vandeweghe was on a fast break, having just stolen the ball. A layup would make it a six-point lead and the title would be the Bruins' to lose.

The only Cardinal back was 6-1 point guard Jerry Eaves, but all he could do was try to strip the ball as Kiki went up, foul him or watch.

Eaves cut in front. Vandeweghe went up, hesitated in the air as best he could, trying to glide past the defender... and missed the lay-up.

"He hates when you bring this up," says Holton. "We're up four, Kiki breaks away. I'm like, he dunks this thing and we're in great shape, we can manage the clock. There's no shot clock at that time. We could take a minute off the clock next possession. But Jerry Eaves cuts in front of Kiki and he double-clutches it and misses the lay-up.

"They get it and now instead of it being a six-point game, they score, it's two. They score again, it's tied. The wind just went out of our sails."

The Bruins didn't score again. The Cardinals scored the last nine points of the game and won, 59–54. For UCLA this was a fairy tale after all, and the clock had just struck twelve.

"I remember Larry coming to me and asking me to speak at the little post-game thing they had set up with all our alumni," says Holton. "I'm sitting there, *heart-broke*.

"I remember it vividly. Everybody was saying, 'Oh, great job, we got there, we turned around, great year.'

"I remember saying when I got up to the podium: 'This is the greatest thing about this, that our families were all able to be here and we're together at this moment. But let's not kid ourselves, we came here to get something done that we didn't get done.' "

Everyone else marveled at what the Bruins had accomplished. Washington State's George Raveling called it the finest job of coaching anyone had ever done at UCLA.

"I hate to compare teams but obviously, it was my first college coaching job," Brown says. "I always wanted to be a college coach and I'm thinking about that all the time. I can't think of any better experience anybody could have in coaching than I had, coaching at UCLA. That was pretty remarkable."

Of course, it was still UCLA.

"I used to joke about all the things I did at UCLA when I got the job," Brown says, grinning. "I was the first coach who didn't win a Pac-10 championship. I was the first coach to lose to SC in a number of years. I was the first coach to lose two games in a row at Pauley—things like that. And I always teased about that.

"And then, I remember when I was walking off the court that game. Somebody came up to me and said, 'Congratulations, you've got another one. You're the first coach in the history of this school to take us to the final game and not win.' "

Happy days were there again.

They had Michael Sanders and the now-famous Four Freshmen coming back. They had two local blue-chippers coming in: Kenny Fields, a power forward who would wear Marques Johnson's 54 and, hopefully, inherit his mantle, and Ralph Jackson, rated the top point guard in the nation. Almost unnoticed was a hulking junior college transfer, 7-4 Mark Eaton.

Of course, Brown's experienced big men, Vandeweghe and Wilkes, were gone. More important, J. D. Morgan was on his deathbed.

J. D. had been ill for years, and he succumbed early that season at 61, having seen UCLA teams win 30 national championships in his 17 years as athletic director. Brown missed him keenly. Morgan had always backed his coaches to the max and Brown needed that kind of assurance. When the kindly vice-chancellor Elwin Swenson began making the trips instead of Morgan, Brown looked at him skeptically; his bond had been with J. D. Who was this guy and what did he want?

The season became a disaster.

Fields was not the second coming of Marques, but a gifted young man with a soft body and stage-door parents. Brown was never one to tiptoe around what he considered half-efforts. Fields sulked and his parents exploded.

"The problem wasn't Kenny," says Holton, "it was his parents. I don't think Larry ever had a problem with Kenny until he had a problem with his parents. His parents are going, 'He's not going to make it to the pros as a center, da, da, da, da-da.'

"I remember his mother went in the coaches' locker room after a game and cussed Larry out. I remember because the next day Larry called a meeting and he told our team, 'I want you guys to know something, I'm coaching this team. I'm not coaching families and nobody's family is coaching this team. I'm coaching this team and if that's a problem, maybe you need to look elsewhere.' He made a real blatant statement about that. He took a stand.

"And shortly after that, Kenny quit the team and had his famous walk on the beach. That's what we all called it.

"It was hilarious. When he came back, a reporter asked him what did you do? He said, 'Aw, I went and walked on the beach and I thought about some things.' We kid him to this day.

"But Larry did something in that situation. He said that he would never coach Kenny again. He gave himself no out. He said, 'If he comes back, I won't coach him, I'll never coach the kid again.'

"When Kenny came back, I felt that Larry was gone. I just felt it in my heart. The kind of straightforward guy Larry was, had he been responsible for Kenny coming back or working that out, he would have said that. But I believe it was more of an administration thing.

"That's not Larry Brown. So I felt that was the end. Because it just wasn't the same after that."

With Fields gone, Brown played Eaton and the Bruins snapped to life. Then Fields' father, Don, said that Kenny hadn't quit, he had just been thinking things over, wanted to return and would apologize.

Holton was right. Brown took Fields back because he'd already decided to leave, himself.

"The thing that was obvious to me," says Brown, "was I wasn't going to be back and Larry [Farmer] was going to be the coach and that was his favorite kid. He had started recruiting Kenny when he was a little kid. And I made the accommodation to him [Farmer]."

By then Brown had a list of reasons for leaving as long as Mark Eaton's arm. He missed Morgan. He had noticed the facilities were second-rate. He was having marital problems and thought the financial strain (Barbara was working as a travel agent to help make ends meet) might be causing them.

After the Bruins' run the previous spring, he was hotter than ever. Brown's agent, Joe Glass, another of his surrogate fathers, was getting big-bucks feelers from the Nets. Why did Larry Brown need to live hand-to-mouth?

Rumors of a Nets deal wafted over the final weeks of the unhappy season which ended, suddenly and appropriately, in an upset at the hands of Danny Ainge's BYU Cougars in their NCAA Tournament opener.

"I think I heard it, but I felt so close to him I didn't believe it," says Holton. "I didn't know him in terms of leaving jobs and all that. I think he filed a disclaimer with us, don't listen to all that stuff, I'm here, I'm your coach. And I believed him.

"But the second we lost to BYU in the first round, I could see he was gone. I never will forget it. We played in Providence, Rhode Island, and it was a situation where the hotel was across the parking lot from the arena, so we walked. And after the game, I can remember walking back to the hotel after we lost and Larry started to talk about what I needed to work on.

"And I felt that he was having his final talk to me."

UCLA officials hunkered down to wait for Brown to break the news to them, a final indignity. Finally, it came: He was taking the Nets job.

It wasn't an easy decision and Brown was even more torn than usual. The night after he made the announcement, he ran into the Los Angeles *Times'* Mike Littwin, an old friend, in Westwood. Brown said he'd just made the biggest mistake of his life.

"I made a hasty decision to leave," says Brown, "and it was almost no turning back....

"They were all things that, when you look back at it, meant absolutely nothing. But at the time they looked like they were so big and things you couldn't overcome, and I made a hasty, dumb decision. I didn't get into coaching to make money, but I felt really inadequate because we were driving a car that one alum had allowed me to have. Some alums helped me with a second mortgage on a house. I felt almost like dehumanized, like everybody was giving me things.

"So that was a problem, but when I look back on it, I could have had everything. I mean, there wasn't one thing that I wanted that they wouldn't have done for me. I just didn't know how to ask."

You could get dizzy following this career.

Brown didn't feel that he could change his mind after announcing he'd leave in 1981.

In 1987, he would accept an offer to return to UCLA, but this time he did change his mind and walk away.

Since leaving UCLA, he has coached five teams: The Nets made their first two NBA playoff appearances under Brown; Kansas won its only post-Phog Allen NCAA title; the Spurs had their two best seasons to that point; the Clippers made their only playoff appearances in Los Angeles; the Pacers won their first NBA playoff series.

"Each time I've left," Brown says, "I've really thought I had a legitimate reason, one that if somebody would sit down and think about, they could maybe say—with them analyzing me personally—they could maybe say he was justified.

"But the bottom line is, I've always wanted in the back of my mind to always stay in one place. Somewhere where you can have the guys come back and be part of it. That's what I'm all about.

"Unfortunately, I got a little off the track."

One infers changes in such ingrained patterns of behavior at one's peril but for whatever it means, Brown is now working for an old friend, Donnie Walsh, in Indianapolis. Brown has married for a third time and, at 53, fathered a son they call L. J. Larry, noting he saw little of his three daughters' childhoods because he was busy coaching, intends to be part of it this time. He has also hired his estranged brother, Herb, as an assistant coach.

Brown still talks wistfully of Westwood, of the things he did, the mistakes he made. He still yearns for college basketball.

The young Bruins, players and students, who knew him then and have grown up since, pine for him still, but UCLA officials shiver when they hear his name.

At least they'll never forget him.

CHAPTER EIGHT

THE FARMER YEARS: MORE WOODEN THAN WOODEN

I am family. I have been the constant at UCLA. With all the stuff that's gone on the last decade, there's one face that people have seen around here and it's mine.

—LARRY FARMER, NEWLY-NAMED UCLA COACH IN 1981

A host of heavenly angels couldn't coach that team. Success there is 30 wins. They don't realize such great success is unobtainable.

People don't realize the funeral's over, the hearse is back in the garage. They've seen the passing of an era.

—GEORGE RAVELING, WASHINGTON STATE COACH

It was obvious what they needed now: another Bruin.

It was OK if he wasn't brilliant. After two years of genius, they were worn out. He didn't have to be the name on everyone's lips. After two years of Larry Brown, they just wanted someone who wanted to be at UCLA.

So they chose Larry Farmer.

Farmer was a Bruin through and through. He had spent almost half his life in Westwood. He'd been a member of Bruin teams that went 89–1 and won three titles. He had played for John Wooden and assisted every coach since. He had married a UCLA song girl.

He was popular as popular could be. Everyone liked Farms, administrators, coaches, players, press people, boosters, and none more than the most influential booster, Sam Gilbert.

Farmer was such a happy choice, the fact he was UCLA's first black coach was barely remarked upon. If the sheer weight of numbers proved blacks were at a huge disadvantage, the right black man could rocket through the ranks, and Farmer had. He was 30 when he got the UCLA job, the youngest man ever to coach UCLA basketball. He had turned down Cal State Fullerton the year before, and the Bruins didn't want to lose him.

That was how it had always been for Farmer. He respected his elders, followed their advice, worked hard and everything always worked out, just as they had told him it would....

Until he became the UCLA coach. After that, nothing worked the way they had told him it would.

The NCAA finally caught up with Gilbert and the sins of the godfather were visited upon the head of the godson.

Farmer tried to emulate Wooden, his idol. His players snickered at him. He wasn't Wooden. He wasn't even Larry Brown. He was a rookie head coach in a crossfire.

The job challenged Farmer's belief system first, his personal life second. He left before it got to his sanity, although it was close.

He had always been the All-American boy.

Farmer was from Denver, one of three sons of doting parents. His father was an electrician and a "very, very strict" disciplinarian who, Farmer said, "didn't put up with any crap from me." His mother was a caterer. He was close to them; he called his mom almost every week.

At Denver's Manual Arts High, Larry was an all-state basketball player, president of the National Honor Society chapter and a lieutenant colonel in Army ROTC, the second-ranked officer in the state. He wore his military uniform proudly and at every conceivable occasion. His high school basketball coach remembered him as being "like a 45-year-old when he was 17."

Colorado wasn't known for its prep basketball and Farmer's best offer was from Drake. For the heck of it, he sent a game film to UCLA and it paid off. The Bruins lost a forward they thought they were getting and invited Farmer to visit. He remembers sitting in Wooden's office, Wooden offering him jelly beans, Wooden talking. Farmer doesn't remember what Wooden said. He was awestruck.

When they offered him the scholarship, he was theirs. They could have floated him back to Denver on a cloud.

Not that they'd need a lot from him. When he joined the varsity in 1970, the forwards were Sidney Wicks and Curtis Rowe. Coming in a year later would be Keith Wilkes and a year after that, David Meyers.

However, Wooden always balanced out his teams with unselfish hard-working players and that was Farmer: MVP of the freshman team, outstanding first-year varsity player as a sophomore, most improved as a junior, captain as a senior. In three varsity seasons, he played in one losing game (82–89 at Notre Dame, his sophomore year).

Drafted by the Cleveland Cavaliers, he got a $10,000 signing bonus but was cut in training camp and came face to face with a sobering truth—"I wasn't good enough." He returned to Westwood and became assistant jayvee coach.

He spent a year playing in West Germany. The money was good, $2,000 a month, but Wooden was leaving, Gene Bartow was coming in, and there was a spot open on Bartow's staff.

Farmer was a model assistant, hard-working and unswervingly loyal, even if he was "Bruin family" and two of his head coaches, Gene Bartow and Brown, were outsiders whose departures from UCLA tradition angered Bruin fans. Brown, a connoisseur of loyalty, said he never had a moment's worry about Farmer.

Black assistants were often pigeon-holed as recruiters but, although Farmer pitched in, he was never the chief recruiter. Under all three coaches, he was the staff's academic adviser.

Now it was his staff.

"I don't know of any coach who went into a specific situation with as good a basic apprenticeship as Larry has had for the UCLA job," said Wooden, endorsing the selection. "It wouldn't have been the same for him to take over the Purdue job or Notre Dame or Kentucky. But for UCLA, no one possibly could be better prepared."

Farmer was 30, the golden boy, always in the right place at the right time, or so it seemed.

Actually, what it was was ground zero.

The Brown years seemed to offer Bruin fans a sense of continuity with the glory years, suggesting they were on their way back. In fact, the glory years had ended, the program had run down to nothing and had been revived for a glorious month in the miracle of the '80 post-season.

UCLA fans thought of it less as miracle, more as prelude.

There was another hot freshman class led by Stuart Gray, a 7-0, 250-pound, red-headed (sound familiar?) center who had been hyped beyond recognition after outplaying young Patrick Ewing at the National Youth Festival. Gray was supposed to be the next in the line of great UCLA centers. Since his predecessors included Hall of Famers Kareem Abdul-Jabbar and Bill Walton, Stuart had his work cut out for him.

Allowing himself to be sucked in and piling the pressure ever higher, Farmer noted Gray was "more physical than either one of those guys were.... a more massive human being."

Gray was supposed to be the missing center. Kenny Fields and Michael Sanders would go to their natural forward positions. The guard corps was three-deep with Michael Holton, Rod Foster, and Jackson. They had won 20 games the year before without a big man, amid turmoil, with their coach negotiating to leave.

Farmer set upon the transition with a vengeance, going back to his interpretation of the Wooden years: high-post offense, precision drills, dress code, no-nonsense atmosphere, a stern but warm coach.

Even the actual Wooden hadn't been as stern as Farmer. Some prison wardens weren't.

"If practice is scheduled for 2:30 and a player shows up at 2:31, he doesn't practice," Farmer explained soon after he arrived. "Coach [Wooden], he might let you practice. I take it one step farther. Each player has my phone number and the numbers of my assistants. Someone is always available.

"When we travel, we wear coats and ties. They love it. I don't mind sweat suits when we're around the hotel, waiting to go to a practice. But it's different on an airplane or in an airport. They have an obligation. They are part of the mystique of UCLA. I want them to be different from what people might believe sports groups to be....

"This is the gospel truth, they [players] love to hate it. A few years ago, the length of hair was a lot longer and we tolerated it. But Richard Washington and Marques Johnson came to us and said they preferred shorter hair. I just make one promise. I tell them I won't ask them to cut off anything that won't grow back. There's more to life than bouncing a basketball."

There was more to basketball than short hair, too, like the consent of the governed. One must command it or earn it. The players had known Farmer as a nice-guy assistant, a confidant, a sounding board for their doubts.

This didn't seem like the same man.

The contrast, between Brown and Farmer, between old Farms and new Farms, shocked them. In the old days, they'd hung around Brown's office, watching TV and eating the candy on his desk. Soon after taking over, Farmer discovered Tony Anderson in traditional posture—feet up, cheeks bulging, remote in hand—and told him to stop wasting time around there. And in the future, if he wanted candy, ask first.

"I miss Coach's jokes," said Anderson, alluding to Brown, before Farmer's first game. "I miss having fun with him."

"I liked Larry Farmer," says Holton. "My first recruiting trip to UCLA, he drove out and picked me up. I talked to him a lot. I felt close to him. I didn't have a problem with this. I just missed Larry [Brown] and it was because the relationship involved more than basketball.

"Larry Farmer just changed. You know what I mean? He just changed. I guess you have to.... He was fun [as an assistant]. He was loose. He was approachable. He had all this UCLA history under his belt, how things were and how they were supposed to be, who was who. And then when he became head coach, it was just different. He wasn't approachable. When he became head coach, it was like he had self-imposed pressure immediately. And I could never figure that out.

"I think he resented the way Larry [Brown] ran his program, so his thing right away was to let us know he was going to get back to the glory days, the good old days, how UCLA basketball was sup-posed to be. No dunking in practice, no dribbling through your legs in practice. He'd go back to all this Wooden stuff—and that was a shock for us. It was stunning. It was restricting. It was confining. It wasn't comfortable.

"Larry Farmer threw Ralph Jackson out of practice for dribbling through his legs. Threw him out! 'Told you, we don't do that here!'

"You know everybody's like, 'This guy's lost it. This is crazy.' You know? It was that type atmosphere."

Given time for a young coach to relax and establish his own identity, it might have worked out, but at UCLA there was never time.

There was another problem: an NCAA investigation.

After ten years of gossip, the NCAA had finally begun looking at the years from 1977 to 1981, the tenures of Gary Cunningham and

Brown. The verdict came down a few weeks into Farmer's first season, truncating it neatly. UCLA got a year's probation from the NCAA tournament, had to forfeit its 1980 second-place trophy and was ordered to "dissociate one representative of its athletic interests" from its basketball program.

That was, of course, Sam Gilbert.

For Farmer, it was a cruel irony. No Bruin, coach or player, had ever been as close to the Godfather. It began his freshman year when Gilbert heard that Farmer, who couldn't get home to Denver, ate Thanksgiving dinner by himself at a Hamburger Hamlet.

"He said it was tragic," said Farmer, "and it would never happen again to somebody from out of state. Then I knew he cared about me, the person, not the basketball player."

If there had been something... different... about Sam, he still seemed perfectly respectable to a young straight arrow like Farmer. All the older players went to his house. Papa G. loved to hold court, to be admired. Farmer was always drawn to authority; he could remember "sitting and talking to him... being spellbound by the things he did in his life."

When Farmer was cut by the Cavaliers, he was invited to try out by the Denver Nuggets. Farmer's father, Larry Sr., told his son to pursue it if he wished.

Gilbert advised him to forget it and Farmer did. Not only that, Gilbert brought him back to Westwood.

"He told me not to go to Denver," says Farmer. "He told me the NBA was not a life for me and told me to stay by the phone, he'd call me back. That was a Friday."

The next day, Gilbert called back to say Farmer could become UCLA's new graduate assistant. The job paid peanuts, so Gilbert invited Larry to move in with his family, which he did.

A year later when Farmer, unable to get playing off his mind, went to West Germany, it was Gilbert who called him with the news that Wooden was retiring... and if Farmer could fly right back, there was a slot for him on Gene Bartow's staff.

Gilbert wore one of Farmer's championship rings. Now Farmer had to enforce Gilbert's exile, ordering his players to stay away from the old Bruin refuge in Pacific Palisades.

Said Farmer: "As much as that hurt him, that's how much it hurt me."

His players didn't care much. Brown had already cut the cord (not that the Bruins had become squeaky clean; other younger boosters had stepped into the vacuum). Farmer noted sadly that Sam's stories didn't interest his players as they had interested him, that Sam was "getting lonely."

Behind the scenes Gilbert would remain Farmer's confidant and adviser, but as a rookie coach Farmer had to foot the bill for their relationship. The price was his first season.

Stuart Gray wasn't happening.

Big players develop slowly and he had a long way to go. On a team that didn't need a lot from him, he did less and struggled awkwardly. To say the least, there was no resemblance to Kareem or Bill.

"Hmm," says Michael Holton, "Stuie....

"He was going to be the center we never had. [Laughing] He turned out to be the center we never had.

"He was just OK. He was good in flashes, wretched.... At times, he did some things like, man! And at other times he was frustrated. It was just that he wasn't a kid who can handle that type of pressure and hype. He showed up believing it. That was what we didn't like.

"Nobody had a problem with him. It's just, Stuart is just a guy who—I think he put pressure on himself because he was frustrated a lot of the time. Kind of like a raging side of him, trying to live up to what he thought he was supposed to live up to."

If they didn't have a problem with him, they weren't anxious to throw "Stuie" the ball, either. There were noses out of joint all around. With Gray joining a lineup that had five returning starters, someone had to leave and it was prickly Darren Daye.

Holton, erstwhile team leader, was now leading from the bench. Farmer had decided to go with the ballyhooed Ralph Jackson, even though Ralph's freshman season had been unimpressive. Jackson never lived up to his billing but Holton never got his job back.

The Bruins went 20–7 and sat out the NCAA Tournament, satisfying their probation. In Farmer's second season, with only Sanders gone, they started 13–1 and grabbed the No. 1 spot in the polls for the first time in four years. They finished 23–5, ranked No. 7. They won the Pac-10 and entered the NCAA Tournament as the West's No. 2 seed.

In their opener in Boise, the only tournament game they'd ever play under Farmer, 10th-seeded Utah gunned them down, 67–61.

That was it for Farmer's honeymoon. There was an alumni storm breaking over Westwood by the time the Bruins' plane returned home. The letter writers awoke with a vengeance.

To the editor:

Undisciplined Chokers Lose Again.

> Lew Riley,
>
> Fullerton

There were reports of players acting up, being disrespectful to their coach in a pre-game meeting which Daye had interrupted with a belch, prompting a Farmer explosion.

Daye claimed later his belch had been taken out of context.

"What happened was, I belched," Daye said. "We'd just eaten our pre-game meal. I covered my mouth. I said, 'Excuse me.' What are you supposed to do, run outside the room and hold your mouth?

"Coach was really upset about it, you know. I didn't know what to do about it. It was before a big game so I didn't say anything. I just wanted to let it pass.... It was a situation where everyone had a little tension in them. Coach got a little excited."

Said Rod Foster: "Darren was just playful and sometimes he played at the wrong times."

Michael Holton says the problem wasn't the belch but the season that preceded it.

"There was so much talent [eight of them would play in the NBA], we could win even if we didn't play well together," Holton says. "A lot of games I went home thinking we hadn't played well, we hadn't played together. But things get smoothed over when you're winning.

"It was a unique blend of characters. We got along better off the court than we did on it. Guys liked each other better as people than we did as players. We didn't have problems off the court but we had problems on the court that Coach Farmer didn't resolve.

"I talked to him about it. He said he didn't see those differences."

For two years, Farmer had been as safe from criticism as Gary Cunningham but now he was beginning to resemble Gene Bartow. Nor was Farmer cut out for heavy sledding; the dutiful son had never had people unhappy with him and it scared him.

That summer, the administration extended Farmer's contract for one year. Farmer asked that no announcement be made. He told a confidant he didn't want anyone to think UCLA was stuck with him; if the Bruins didn't want him back, he'd leave gladly.

Before the next season, he asked another reporter doing a story on the Utah upset, "Will my mother be able to read this?"

"I was an assistant here to three coaches," Farmer said before the season. "I saw what they went through.

"But it's like when you see someone put his hand on a hot stove and get burned. You really don't know how it feels until you do it yourself."

Somehow everything was different.

A coach, as Farmer could tell you, was no longer a man who automatically commanded respect. Instead, he was examined, second-guessed, even held up to ridicule.

The watershed Michigan State–Indiana State meeting in the 1979 finals, still the highest-rated basketball game at any level, had turned the college game into a major league spectator sport with attendant pressure.

Everything, however, paled in comparison with the great transfiguring institution of the twentieth century: television.

Television and its particular chemistry, the relationship of action, camera and the small screen, would decide what would prosper or wither. Football was perfect for the TV screen and became preeminent. Baseball, the National Pastime with its old-time atmosphere, epic feel and far-flung action, was not easily captured by a panning camera and found itself in a losing battle for young viewers.

Basketball, once small potatoes, a sneered-at "YMCA sport," was actually perfect. The court was small and easy to cover with a few cameras. The players were acrobatic, even balletic.

And there was a new technology: cable.

Until the '80s, there had been only a handful of nationally televised games so a power, like UCLA, that could guarantee several appearances had an immense recruiting advantage. Now there was something starting up called ESPN, the Entertainment and Sports Programming Network, whatever in hell that meant.

The first reaction, even among fans, to the news that there would now be a network devoted entirely to sports, was lukewarm. What were they going to show, rodeos and tractor pulls?

What they showed, instead, was college basketball.

It was live, exciting, inexpensive to put on the air. Right fees and production costs were bargains. There was an audience for it. If the audience was small—for all its impact, cable's numbers were a fraction of what the networks pulled—it was influential. The kids, the future recruits, the lifeblood of any program, watched religiously.

Almost overnight, it seemed, cable TV redrew the map, tilted the country. The Big East games came on in prime time on the East Coast and early evening out West but a West Coast game would start at 10:30 P.M. on the East Coast.

West Coast kids grew up watching the Big East and the ACC. In 1985 the Big East, which was not yet 10 years old, had three of the Final Four teams. In 1987, the two best high school guards in Los Angeles, Stevie Thompson and Earl Duncan, went off to play in the ice and snow at Syracuse.

And a new sound was heard in the land....

SLAM, BAM, JAM! DIPSY-DOO DUNKEROO!

It was another phenomenon, Dick Vitale, ESPN's first and most controversial star, a former coach with a passion for the game and a voice that could scare the family pets. Suddenly basketball fans were intoduced to an entire new glossary—PT, pub, light, paint, J, rock—not to mention the mute button on their remotes.

Vitale was the game personified. Before fame came out of nowhere and tapped this self-described "bald one-eyed Italian from back in Jersey" on the shoulder, he had given his adult life to it, not to mention his first marriage and parts of his stomach.

His had been a Basketball Life: the humble start teaching grade school at $4,500 a year, coaching the state championships at East Rutherford High, the hundreds of applications and rejections until he caught on as an assistant at Rutgers, the trips into the poorest ghettos to recruit players like Phil Sellers ("Phil used to tell me, 'Coach you can't come to my house, not a white guy by himself,'"), the big break at last at the University of Detroit, the dream opening with the Pistons, the firing one season and 12 games later.

"How'd I start?" says Vitale of his broadcasting career. "I got fired by the Pistons—November 8, 1979—and I was as low as I'd ever been in my life. I'd always had the philosophy, a boy, a ball, a dream. I'd climbed the ladder of success from junior high coaching all the way to the pros, without shooting a jump shot.

"I was no player. Believe me, I was a non-player. I played like one year at Seton Hall [at the Paterson branch, actually] as a walk-on. I couldn't run, I couldn't jump and I couldn't shoot. But, oh man, could I talk about the game!

"Then I got to the pros and I found out it wasn't the rose garden. I was fired with a 4–8 record in my second year. That was when Scotty Connal called me from ESPN. I didn't know. But my wife told me, 'Hey, what are you going to do, sit around the house and mope?'"

Yo, Dickie Vee, how's this for a surprise? You're going to be a star!

Vitale was that network exec's dream, an Everyman the viewers could identify with, a basketball version of John Madden. Vitale was personally likable, lively, fun, opinionated and, if you could endure his shrieking and egregious hot-dogging, he could teach you something about the game.

Of course, the execs liked to think announcers mattered—it gave them important decisions to deliberate upon, careers to make and break—although the evidence suggested viewers couldn't care less. The execs liked if their announcers made the columns of the key TV critics (the most closely watched was the amiable Rudy Martzke in *USA Today*) and one thing about Vitale, he was impossible to ignore.

And besides, the networks, over-the-air or cable, were making so much money, they had to do something with it.

"It's almost been scientifically proven that not one extra person will tune in because they say, 'Oh look, they've got Pat Summerall and Madden instead of Don Criqui and Beasley Reece," says Norman Chad, the great gadfly TV critic, late of the Washington *Post, The National* and *Sports Illustrated.*

"You're watching the game because you want to watch the game. I can see where Fox wanted to get more credibility their first year [televising the NFL] so they gave Madden $7 million. Even then, you could get Pauly Shore to work with Madden but they said we need to get Summerall, they gave Summerall close to $2 million. It's stunning to me.

"Even with Vitale—you can make the argument that along with Billy Packer, he's the greatest ambassador in the history of college basketball. His presence at a game for ESPN does not add 1/100th of a ratings point. I would argue that anyone with a brain cell, during the course of a game, it actually decreases viewership by 1/100th of a ratings points if you can't find the mute button."

Anointed by the system Vitale's opinions counted, and he had so many of them.

This conference was great; this one stunk. The Pac-10 was a particular target in the '80s, on merit. This coach was The General (Bobby Knight) or Michaelangelo (Dean Smith). Arkansas' Nolan Richardson asked why he couldn't have a nickname, too? This coach was hot; this one was a comer. Of course, if someone didn't get canned—Vitale hated to see coaches fired, it hit too close to home— there would be nowhere for his comers to move up to.

Suddenly, there was scrutiny not to mention wisecracks.

An influential key audience was tuning into another ESPN show, SportsCenter, for the scores of the day's games. Where once a UCLA fan got his spin from the friendly anchors in Los Angeles, ESPN had a national perspective which soon grew irreverent. By the '90s, the Sports-Center anchors were comics like Dan Patrick, Keith Olbermann, and Craig Kilborn who specialized in acerbic commentary while narrating highlight reels and passed up no straight lines.

If a coach didn't have a thick skin, he was in trouble. If he didn't like being lampooned, he'd better win or retire.

Every day that went by led them from the dignified past when they worked in college athletics, to the prosperous future whose name was show business.

Farmer, a tortured Bruin rather than a dancing bear, was already halfway to the door.

His final season was a disaster. Holton, Foster and Daye had left. Gray and Jackson were busts. There were no recruits of note; the only promising freshman was a 6-6 scarecrow named Reggie Miller, whom they'd taken after the three players they wanted, Reggie Williams, Antoine Joubert, and Tom Sheehy, turned them down.

There was another fast start against the cupcakes (10–1), raising them to No. 6 in the polls, followed by a sorrier than usual finish (7–10), dropping them out of the top 20.

Farmer all but assumed the fetal position. His marriage had broken up. He wasn't working at recruiting. He confided in a few trusted friends and otherwise holed up.

"He withdrew," says a member of the traveling party. "It was sad. You never saw him on the road. He'd have Vic, the team manager, go out and get food for him."

Pauley was like a tomb. After upsetting the Bruins there, New Mexico Coach Gary Colson said that it was like playing at a neutral site. Before Valentine's Day, Farmer opened his weekly breakfast media session, asking, "Everyone here have a heart?"

Farmer's players bristled at the speculation that now dogged his every step. In a rare display of solidarity, they invited the Los Angeles *Times*' Tracy Dodds into the dressing room to attack his critics.

"I don't understand why some of our alums, some of the people who are supposed to be our fans, are so busy trying to run off our coach," said Stuart Gray. "Why can't they leave him alone and let him coach the team?"

The ever-sensitive Kenny Fields said the revolving coaches were killing recruiting and the apathetic fans were deserting them.

"We were at a meeting of the Bruins Hoopsters last night," said Fields, "and a lady there told me she was all cheered out. That's what she said. She's done so much cheering for the Bruins over the years that she's all cheered out.

"So then I say something about the fans—not talking about the student section at all—and I hear they want to boo me. Now what kind of support is that?"

Another time, Fields said, "The problem we're having is John Wooden. He won too much. Now our fans can't accept anything less."

The Bruins missed the NCAA Tournament and were invited to their first NIT. Farmer came out publicly in favor of accepting. The new athletic director, Peter Dalis, turned it down.

There would be worse records and worse Bruin teams but there would never be as much whining and bleating. There was only the matter of putting Farmer out of his misery but nobody seemed to know how.

So they invited him back?

It was amazing but true. Morgan's old assistant, Bob Fischer, had been eased out and the new AD, Dalis, had been making strained statements about waiting to evaluate Farmer until the season was over. Privately, he'd been critical of Farmer.

However, when the magic day came, the most Dalis could get from Chancellor Charles Young was permission to fire Farmer's assistants, Craig Impelman and Kevin O'Connor. Dalis intended to replace them with firebrands Walt Hazzard and Jack Hirsch, the ex-Bruins who were now coaching at little Chapman College, in the hope they could shore up the reluctant head coach.

Now, who could get Larry in line?

How about Sam Gilbert?

Gilbert was still ostensibly backing Farmer but grousing about it, too. Late in the season an alarmed Impelman had even called Bartow, who was still friendly with Farmer, and asked Gene to plead Larry's case to Gilbert.

Of course Gilbert hated Bartow, and Bartow hadn't planned on talking to Sam again in this lifetime but he made the call. In another surprise, Gilbert took it. When Bartow made his plea, Gilbert launched into a list of things Larry had done wrong. Larry was stubborn, Larry wouldn't listen, etcetera.

For his part, Farmer was wondering where he ended and Gilbert began.

Farmer was close to Impelman, wasn't sure he wanted to stay if it meant firing him, and wasn't sure he wanted to stay in any case. Asked if he shouldn't be tougher about it, Farmer replied: "Maybe I should have a job and no friends?"

Hirsch acknowledged having heard that Farmer was "petrified of or intimidated by us." Gilbert hosted a meeting at his Encino office where Farmer could talk to his new assistants. Everyone said soothing things.

Farmer decided to accept the university's offer, a two-year extension. There was a press conference to announce it. Farmer said he'd been "burned out" but claimed he was now "hardened" after going through his "baptism of fire."

Four days later, he changed his mind and resigned. Dalis hired Hazzard within the hour and the Farmer era was mercifully over.

If he wasn't a Bruin, what was he?

Farmer spent a season doing color commentary on Denver Nugget broadcasts and married a UCLA grad student he had begun dating in his last season as coach.

Still, he had the coaching bug. He found his name still meant something and there were schools interested in him. He accepted an offer from Weber State in Ogden, Utah, a little hotbed of a town of 80,000 where 8,000 attended games.

Farmer's first season was a success. His Wildcats started 10–0 and finished 18–11. In his next two, however, it all blew up in his face again. Weber went 7–22 and 9–21.

"They told me they wanted to be nationally ranked, to be on television, the usual," Farmer said later. "So we devised a tough schedule and we began to lose."

Says a Weber official: "Larry only knows one way, the John Wooden way. That high-post offense is one thing with Bill Walton in the middle, but with Harry Willis in the middle it isn't the same thing."

Some things were universal, Even in Ogden, there was disappointment and pressure. Attendance dwindled to half of what it had been. Farmer says he was stung when he was fired but the Weber people say it was inevitable.

Farmer thought that would be it for his coaching career until he got a call from Sheik Fahad Al Ahmed, the head of the Kuwaiti Olympic committee. That was Kuwait, as in the Arabian Peninsula. The one in the Middle East.

In 1976, when Farmer was on Bartow's staff, he had befriended a young Kuwaiti player who had been sent to the United States to learn basketball. The Kuwaiti went home and recommended the nice American to Sheik Al Ahmed.

The first time the Sheik offered him a job, Farmer was still at Weber, which seemed infinitely safer. Utah might not have been teeming with blacks but it had more than Kuwait. When Farmer was fired, the Sheik called again with a better offer. Farmer, thinking he should look at such a nice piece of change, joked that he answered, "I'll come over for a week or two and if I didn't get shot, I'll stay."

He has coached summers there ever since, returning to the States in winter to do color commentary on college basketball games for the Raycom syndicate.

One thing about the Kuwaitis, they knew how to put together a benefit package. Like local citizens, Farmer pays no taxes. Education and medical care are free. The goverment pays for his apartment in a modern high-rise. The fans in the Sultan Center get in free; the ones at courtside relax in plush leather armchairs under a huge portrait of the Emir.

Of course, there are the indignities, like the censoring of mail that every foreigner must endure. Once Farmer sat in the post office, watching the censor go through one of his magazines, cutting out the ads for Calvin Klein jeans with a razor. Nightlife didn't exist and he had to wangle an invitation to the U.S. Embassy for the occasional cold beer.

But at least they let him coach the game he loved. He could teach someone the fundamentals Wooden had taught him, and his players would be as grateful as he was.

"I don't have any worries," Farmer told the Los Angeles *Times*' Peter Greenberg. "I don't worry about the budget because it's limitless. I have no alumni breathing down my neck, no ticket sales to drum up, no NCAA officials...

"Every once in awhile, I'll be getting ready for a game. I'll be sitting on the bench and I'll look around at the crowd, at the players and it will suddenly dawn on me that this isn't Pauley Pavilion and I'll wonder what I'm doing here. I was never very good about predicting my life. My career has always been a step ahead of me. So here I am in Kuwait.

"I'm sure there must be some reason for me to be here and I'm not complaining. Please tell everyone back in Westwood that right now, Larry Farmer's doing just fine."

CHAPTER NINE

THE HAZZARD YEARS:
FOOL FOR LOVE

He's black, that's one strike against him. He's a Muslim, that's strike two. It's pretty incredible that Coach Hazzard got this job.

—ASSISTANT COACH JACK HIRSCH, FALL 1984

I had heard the legend of Coach Hazzard, played the point on the first championship team, and there he was.

First thing he said when he got the job was, "I'm going to change this thing around."

—NIGEL MIGUEL, CLASS OF '85

It was obvious now what the Bruins needed: someone hard-nosed with a burning passion for the game and a UCLA background.

Also, someone they could get in a hurry.

That was Walt Hazzard. He was tough, indeed, with a glower that could stop a truck, and he'd proven his love for the game over and over.

UCLA background? He bled blue and gold. He had turned down full scholarship offers to prep at Santa Monica College before leading the Bruins to their first title. During the football season, he was a cheerleader. He didn't just sit in the stands and cheer, he was an actual cheerleader, with the sweater, the megaphone, the whole bit. He met his wife, the former Miss Patsy Shepard, the first black UCLA pom-pom girl, on Bruin Walk, the avenue between campus and the dorms.

She could remember it years later. She was a freshman. He was a junior. He was wearing a letter sweater, shorts, and thongs, talking to Arthur Ashe.

He told Ashe, "That's the girl I'm going to marry."

"I think he was just showing off," she said later. "I said, 'Not if you don't wear socks.' "

But they got married and had several kids, one of whom became a Bruin, too. If pedigree, devotion, and industry would have been enough, Hazzard would have been one of the all-time greats, but it would take more. Among coaches, Hazzard would be an innocent at a convention of used-car salesman, blunt, candid, quick to erupt, proud to a fault.

When he arrived, the program was at its low ebb. Though he strove mightily for four years, he was never able to nudge the boulder much up the hill.

His teams split between his players and the Farmer holdovers. There was a meeting that almost turned into a brawl when Farmer

148

players said they didn't want to play a game. Three players, including a talented 7-footer, transferred out. The program was hit with NCAA sanctions for more violations by Sam Gilbert.

The boulder rolled back down and squashed Hazzard. He was fired, making him the only UCLA basketball coach to suffer that additional indignity.

All in all, he'd have been better off if he hadn't loved UCLA quite so much.

Hazzard's hiring, the day Farmer resigned, was a stunner.

It dominated conversation at Seattle, site of that spring's Final Four. It was one thing to bring an inexperienced assistant off one's bench, another to give one of the game's glamour jobs to a man who'd never coached at a Division I school.

For Hazzard, it was as if someone had lowered a ladder from heaven. Long in search of himself, he had journeyed far, learned a lot about himself and come full circle to basketball. Now he was back at UCLA, not as an assistant, which was as much as he'd hoped for until the moment Farmer walked, but as the man.

"My son from Stanford was home and he kept repeating, 'Compton to Pauley, Compton to Pauley,' " said Hazzard. "The more he said it, the more unbelievable it sounded. I had never heard anything like it."

He'd spent his whole life listening, too.

He had always been a hard driver. When he transferred to Philadelphia's mighty Overbrook High where Wilt Chamberlain had gone, he brought the yearbook from his school in Maryland where he'd played on a state champion team as a freshman. "I just wanted to be able to prove who I was," he said.

He was a fierce competitor. He played 10 NBA seasons and was once an all-star, averaging 24 points for the expansion SuperSonics. More often, he was in the wrong place at the wrong time. He played only that one season in Seattle, which traded him to Atlanta for Lenny Wilkens. In Hazzard's UCLA office, he would hang a picture of himself, cleaning out his locker at 4 A.M. He said he never wanted to forget the hurt. He quarterbacked the Hawks to a first-place fin-ish, saw them draft Pete Maravich and trade him to Buffalo, another expansion team.

"Eventually, we got a chance to go to Buffalo for a lot of money," said Patsy. "Believe me, it takes a lot of money to get you to go to Buffalo."

It wasn't politics or deference that kept him around. When he saw the owner of one of his five teams fondle his wife, Hazzard says he told the man he'd kill him.

The Hazzards became Sunni Muslims and took new names. Walt was Mahdi Abdul-Rahman. Patsy was Jaleesa. "That was it for my career," he says.

He would later reassume his original name for professional pur-poses although he remains a Muslim. The son of a minister, he took his conversion seriously. He went on a pilgrimage to Mecca. He vis-ited Libya at the invitation of Muammar Khaddafi. He wondered later about some of the people who advised him.

"I was used, no doubt about it," Hazzard said. "I was naive. To tell you the truth, I didn't have a clue."

He moved back to Los Angeles after his playing career, coached in youth leagues and looked for a way to get back in the game. He was willing to start humbly and did, at Compton College, a junior college near Watts with a low-budget program.

Jack Hirsch, his rich-kid buddy since their playing days at UCLA, came along as assistant. Hirsch, the self-described "screw-off" and "odd Jewboy on the team," had been retired at 28.

"When Walt asked me to come to Compton," said Hirsch, "I said, 'Are you crazy? I don't want to be the White Shadow.' "

"He wasn't doing anything," said Hazzard, "just sitting at home and watching the stock market. He needed something to do."

They went 24–3 and 29–6 and were even mentioned as candi-dates for Larry Brown's staff although Brown wasn't interested.

They moved to Chapman College, a Division II school where the coaches, at least, didn't have to sweep out the gym. They went 21–8 and 22–6. In a loss at Wright State, Hazzard got into an argument with a referee and pulled his team off the floor.

They were up for Farmer's staff again, this time as Peter Dalis's hand-picked candidates, whether Farmer wanted them or not.

Farmer, taking this as the handwriting on the wall, abdicated. Dalis offered Hazzard the job the same day.

Of course, what awaited them would have been formidable, even if they'd been better suited to it.

Hazzard was still ferocious after all these years. Jaleesa said his raspy voice sometimes scared babies. He was not one to smooth out the bumps in the road, and at UCLA the road was mined.

Up close, Hazzard was actually a warm man who liked to laugh, loved his kids, and treated his players like family. It was just his way, erupt, make up. He quarreled with a reporter from the podium at the post-game press conference after winning the NIT. He broke off negotiations for a shoe deal with Nike's Sonny Vacarro, then claimed Vacarro sabotaged his recruiting. Vacarro denied it, saying he'd have been glad to hire Hazzard but not at the John Thompson numbers Walt wanted.

Compared to Hirsch, Hazzard was as calm as John Wooden. It wasn't that Hirsch was thin-skinned; he didn't have a skin. "Jack," said Jaleesa, "always sees a disaster coming."

This time there really was a disaster coming. But this was the off-season and even the cocky Hirsch, who would later describe his second UCLA career as a "nightmare," was upbeat.

"Dues are overrated," said Hirsch before that season. "How many coaches can say they've swept rats out of the gym or who have played with bullet holes in their bags or who had players who didn't have enough money to buy jock straps? Who had to sweep the floor?

"That's paying dues."

By the time UCLA was done with them, those would look like the good old days.

They were in the big leagues again.

Hazzard was driving a Mercedes now, instead of a Mazda. Before the season started, a UCLA official asked if he preferred vans, station wagons, or busses. For what? asked Hazzard. To go to the airport on trips, he was told. Hazzard and Hirsch, conditioned to driving their teams themselves, looked at each other and laughed.

They sobered up quickly enough when they began to work with the little Farmer had left them.

Kenny Fields and Ralph Jackson were gone. Stuart Gray stayed just long enough to hear Hazzard tell him he'd have to win the job in competition with backup Brad Wright. Hazzard was hoping to fire him up but Stuart bolted into the NBA draft, instead, went on the second round and managed to get in seven seasons in which he averaged four-tenths of a point per game.

Hazzard didn't have a single returning player who had ever averaged double figures or an incoming freshman who ever would. Only forward Gary Maloncon had been a starter at the end of the previous season. Hazzard had to manufacture a point guard, switching Nigel Miguel, who'd had an undistinguished career on the wing.

Needing a body, they grabbed a raw 6-10 juco named Jack Haley, generally regarded as the biggest klutz to wear the uniform since Wooden arrived in Westwood in 1948. Bruin fans began referring snidely to "the Jack Haley era."

Haley was unusual, to say the least. The son of a well-off restaurant proprietor in the South Bay, he had spurned team sports and gone surfing instead. He had walked on at Golden West Junior College for the heck of it.

"I played one year there," Haley says, "and in all honesty, I was horrible. Beyond pathetic. I fouled out, I think, every game.

"My coach puts me in the L.A. summer league to learn how to play with better players. Stuart Gray goes hardship. UCLA's in a big bind. I'm playing with Reggie Miller and he sees that I'm a tough kid that bangs, sets picks. He tells Hazzard's third assistant, Kris Jason.

"Kris comes down, watches me play one game—where I get in a fistfight and don't even finish the game. About three days later, I get a call from Kris, says, 'We'd like to consider signing you. We'd like you and your family to come up.'

"I've never spoken to Walt Hazzard or Jack Hirsch. My mom, my dad, and I walk in the office and Jack Hirsch is sitting behind the desk. He's got his feet up on the desk. He says, 'Hey, how you doing? Come on in, sit down.'

"My father stands there in the doorway and holds me. He says, 'OK, I've changed my mind, my son won't come play here. My son will play nowhere where the man doesn't stand when a lady walks in the room.'

"So we got that settled. I never took a tour of campus. Jack Hirsch said, 'Look, here's the situation: You'll never play here. Stuart Gray's left, we need a backup body for practice. All we want you to do is work hard in practice. You have to get great grades and you round out our bench. We'll give you a scholarship.'

" 'Hey,' I said, 'free education at UCLA. I'll take it.'

"But I never met Walt Hazzard, never spoke to Walt Hazzard until the very first day of practice. Walked on the floor, Walt Hazzard's first words to me were, 'Hey, I had heard you were black.' "

Just to let them know where they were, they lost an exhibition game to Athletes in Action.

They lost a home game to Santa Clara. Then they embarked on what Hazzard called "the death march," road games at DePaul, Brigham Young, St. John's, and Memphis State, and lost them all, dropping to 2–5.

They were 9–11 before closing with a 7–1 run. Eighteen wins would have gotten them into the NCAA Tournament and 17 might have, but they were 16–12.

They accepted an NIT bid, not out of any enthusiasm but in the knowledge that their refusal the previous season had been used against them in recruiting—see, they're so snobby, they still have the same expectations, etc.

And they went out and won it.

Of course, the NIT made it as easy as possible for them. The schedule was set one round at a time, with the organizers making ad hoc decisions on who'd be home and who'd travel. The teams they wanted in Madison Square Garden—like UCLA—played their three preliminary games at home. Fairness had nothing to do with it; Fresno State, which had drawn better in the tournament, had to come to Westwood.

Fresno was an upstate power and, until then, beneath scorn to the Bruins who wouldn't play the Bulldogs. Fresno fans snapped up tickets for their dream matchup. They showed up wearing red; of the 12,200 in Pauley that night, about 8,000 were out-of-towners.

"It was unbelievable," says Hazzard. "The whole building was red. The players came in the locker room and said, 'Coach, I just can't believe all the redness out there. We don't have anyone at the game.'

"I said, 'So what? No big deal. What we're going to do is have a red evacuation at the end of the game.' And that's exactly what happened."

With Hazzard lashing them, the Bruins had developed into a tough defensive team. Miguel was a real stopper. Brash Reggie Miller had turned into a good rebounder for a 190-pound forward after Hazzard told him it was board or sit.

UCLA advanced to New York, beat Louisville and Indiana and won the tournament. A year later, the Cardinals would add Pervis Ellison and win the NCAA. Two years later, the Hoosiers would win it. It had been an impressive piece of coaching by Hazzard and persevering by his players, if it was celebrated minimally in Westwood.

"I was saying," says Miguel, "I just don't want to leave this university without accomplishing anything as a team. When we first started that season, they were saying that we were the worst team in UCLA history. Where we came from to what we ended up—that meant, personally, I know, so much to the seniors. We left our legacy there. They don't acknowledge it too much but every time I go in Pauley....

"They didn't want to put it [the NIT banner] up. I was surprised that they even put it up, to be honest with you....

"I know, I can remember Coach Wicks and Andre McCarter [two more assistants] and Hirsch telling us, 'Don't leave here without leaving your mark because once you do, you can't come back.' It was kind of tough listening to those guys because they had five banners between them sitting up there. And they were hard on us. They loved us but they kicked us every day.

"As the year went on, I grew not only to admire but to love Coach Hazzard. What he gave me, he gave me a start in life. From my viewpoint I have nothing but great things to say about him, and to this day still have a personal relationship with him.

"Not to say that it was all roses but man, what he did for me...."

So much for the good times.

Hazzard had pulled off a quick coup, signing Pooh Richardson, the nation's top-rated prep point guard, out of Philadelphia where Walt was still connected. But it wasn't going to save his second season.

Hazzard's second team would be even worse than his first. Jack Haley would be the center.

"Walt Hazzard told me," says Haley, " 'If you get an offensive rebound and you're wide open under the basket, still pass it to Reggie Miller.' I lived by that rule."

Hazzard needed a big recruiting class. He was hot on the trail of local stars Trevor Wilson and Kevin Walker, but there were no great young big men in L.A. Hazzard looked eastward, toward Virginia Beach, Virginia, home of J. R. Reid, rated the top player in his class, and Miami, home of Tito Horford. When daily routine interfered, Hazzard and Hirsch went recruiting, leaving Kris Jason and Andre McCarter to run practice.

"The year before," says Hazzard, "I had four seniors, no juniors, four sophomores and three freshmen. So we had to make up for some time and bring in a real dynamite couple of classes so that we had freshmen who could hit the floor and play and could help us turn it around because for that one year, we weren't going to have senior leadership.

"The year after Nigel and those guys left, I knew that Reggie had to lead the way. We had inexperienced Jack Haley. We needed one piece. That one piece could have been J. R. Reid. If we got J. R. Reid, that would have been a tremendous boost for our program, but it came down to him choosing North Carolina over us, and basically apologizing to us.

"He said, 'Coach, I loved you, I wanted to come but it's hard for me not to be a Tar Heel. I'm from this area, plus my parents will get to see me play.' "

Back in Westwood, the Bruin players, even the ones Hazzard had brought in, bristled at his absence.

"It was a rough year for me," says Haley, "because they tried to recruit some big-name centers, Tito Horford and some other guys, and they never got them. The knock on UCLA was we were a doughnut-hole team. Everything around the perimeter, nothing in the middle—that was me of course. Everybody pointed a lot of fingers at us.

"It was a rough year. The coaching staff kinda got full of themselves. They stopped doing the things that got 'em there. They started showing up late, especially Coach Hazzard. He irritated a lot of people because he started missing practices to go scout Trevor Wilson. He was looking for Kevin Walker.

"He was so hyped up on these future kids that he alienated Craig Jackson. Craig was going to quit. There were several guys talking about quitting."

The Bruins went 15–13 and accepted another NIT bid. The tournament organizers had them open at home, of course, against UC Irvine, a warm-up act.

Not that the Bruins cared. They were now a mutinous, divided team.

By all accounts, the unhappiest of the Bruins was Jackson, a sophomore forward. He had been recruited by Larry Farmer and, indeed, looked like the second coming of Farmer.

Jackson was also from Denver. He was a McDonald's All-American. He was good-looking and personable. UCLA officials remember him as quiet and introverted, not as much into basketball as he was into academics where he'd graduate with a major in economics. His basketball career wasn't as promising. Shunted off to a less gentle coach with no personal investment in him, Jackson hadn't played well and now, although he was starting, was playing briefly. Clearly he was only warming a seat for someone else.

"I tell you what," says Haley, "there were two team meetings the day before the [Irvine] game…. Jerald Jones and Craig Jackson, a lot of the guys, were really unhappy with Walt Hazzard…. The meeting was, 'Hey, let's stick it to him and not only lose this game but go get blown out.'

"It was almost fistfights in this meeting. Guys were, yelling, screaming 'cause a lot of us like myself and Reggie and Pooh, we didn't want to hear that. We wanted to win.

"That was the night before the game. Then the next morning before the game, we had the typical shootaround. We had another meeting that afternoon that was held by Kris Jason and Sidney Wicks because everybody basically liked Kris and Sidney.

"They basically said, 'Hey, if you guys are unhappy with Walt Hazzard, that's fine but you know you represent UCLA and you represent yourselves. We've got to go out there and play hard and win the game.'

Says Richardson: "It was crazy. It was crazy that we elected to go to the NIT and guys were like, 'No, I don't want to play.' And that was unbelievable. I never, ever heard of guys not wanting to play basketball....

"It was a lot of changes going on. Coach was bringing his guys in, making sure that his group was being taken care of, ready to play, prepared. And you've got guys who were playing a little when Coach Farmer was there who are now not playing at all, or very little and they were in the later years of their career. And it can be tough, especially when you have visions of being a professional and doing this and doing that. It can be tough on you and I understand that."

The Bruins played, badly. Before a desultory little crowd of 7,089, they lost, 80–74, to end an unhappy season.

"If you look back and watch the game," Haley says, "we wound up losing the game to UC Irvine. I mean, they had a good team and everything, but our team was so fragmented. It was horrible. I hated losing that way."

Hazzard says he never knew of the insurrection.

"I don't know about that," he says. "I'll just say that any player who calls himself a player, who ever walks out on the floor without the intention of winning, is not a player.

"If that's the case, then that's why we didn't win.... I mean, we had the Poohs and we had the Reggies and the Jack Haleys, but if you have some bad apples in the barrel, it makes it tough. And I would never make an accusation about a player playing for me and say he didn't play the best he could.

"I saw some players smiling when we lost my last game. I won't say who they were but I saw them smiling."

On the streets of Los Angeles, it was a wild new day.

Maybe it was modern basketball. Maybe it was the fact that far-away coaches no longer conceded the best players to UCLA but flew in to recruit as if it were a crossroads like Chicago.

157

It was a jungle out there. There was Sean Higgins of Fairfax, who signed a UCLA letter of intent, then claimed he never wanted to go there but was forced to do it by his stepfather who threatened him with a baseball bat. Coincidentally or not, Higgins's mother and stepfather had just bought a new house, after satisfying a tax lien of more than $5,000.

Higgins said Steve Antebi, a rich Century City broker who had Reggie Miller living in the chauffeur's quarters of his estate, had promised to give him a job and invest his money in the stock market. Released from his letter after a furor in the press, Higgins enrolled at Michigan and sneered at the Pac-10 as "soft, like Little Red Riding Hood."

There was Higgins's Fairfax teammate, Chris Mills, who became famous when an Emery Air Freight package from Kentucky assistant Dwane Casey to his father, Claud, tore open and $2,000 in cash was found in it.

But the feature act in this great circus was Crenshaw's John Williams, a 6-8, 250-pounder who was hyped as another Magic. In the eyes of Williams's friends and courtiers, a group that seemed to grow daily, dollar signs sprang up as if in cash registers.

One of Williams's friends was Kenny Miller, a young sports writer for the black-owned Los Angeles *Sentinel*. For Miller, it would prove to be one of life's sting operations.

For what it was worth, Williams wanted to go to Houston to play with Hakeem Olajuwon. However, his mother, Mabel, a high-strung single parent who saw danger lurking everywhere and often carried a pistol, would make the decision.

With only a vague idea of what she was doing, she was surrounded by advisers and street agents, like Kenny Fields' father, Don, who jumped into the picture, reportedly laying a string of demands on John's behalf to UNLV recruiters: $50,000 in cash, a Nissan 280ZX Turbo, $600 a month.

There is a question whether this came from Mabel or Don. Kenny Miller says Mabel didn't think much of Don because she thought he'd mishandled his own son's career.

Miller had covered John since he was a sophomore. He says he did little favors for Mabel like getting her floor passes at tournaments and she considered him a friend.

With access came opportunity. Miller says his boss at the Sentinel, Brad Pye, told him of a UCLA booster who wanted to talk to him about Williams. The booster offered Miller a car and the opportunity to attend classes at UCLA to put in a good word for the Bruins.

Miller told Williams it would be good P.R. to visit but Williams had long since eliminated UCLA.

The finalists were Houston, Louisville, UNLV, and LSU. Miller says he got a phone call from Jerry Tarkanian, offering to make him "the Main Man in Vegas" if he could deliver John.

He couldn't. Mabel didn't like the thought of that glitzy lifestyle for John.

"I go over to their house," says Miller. "The phone rings. Mabel answers the phone in one room, I'm in another room with John. We're just shooting the breeze. John's a very quiet kid, a very shy kid....

"Mabel asked me, 'Kenny, pick up the other phone. I don't want you to say anything, I just want you to listen.'

"And she's talking to Denny Crum. And Denny's saying, 'We really enjoyed your son.' John had just completed a visit there and he was really happy.

"She said, 'Well, where do you think John could play?'

"He says, 'Hey, we've got a senior that's going to be leaving out on the wing. We think he can come step right in and be a big-time player for us.'

"She says, 'Do you think John can play guard?

"He says, 'We don't see him as a guard.'

"She says, 'Hold on a second, Coach.' She puts the phone down and says, 'Kenny, do you think John can play guard in college?' I say I think he can play anywhere.

"So she says, 'OK, Coach, I think I've heard enough and we'll be in touch.'

"That was the end of Louisville and Denny Crum. Louisville died right there when Crum did not think that John could play guard.

"Following that, Mabel looks me in the eye and we start talking about schools. Houston was mentioned. She says, 'Houston is out of the picture because I think Joe Weakley [assistant coach at Crenshaw] has some deal worked out....' "

"Mabel says, 'Kenny, there's a lot going on, they're talking about killing you.... stuff you in the trunk of a car. Don't worry about it, I'm going to protect you but we got to get you out of here.

"She gets [LSU Coach] Dale Brown on the phone. She says, 'Dale, do you remember the reporter I told you about, the one that I really can trust?'

"I'm not on the phone so I assume that Dale says yes. She says, 'He's here with me right now. I want you to help him, I want you to get him out of here. Kenny's been good to us and he's the only one that I can trust.'

"I get on the phone with Coach Dale Brown: 'Kenny? Dale Brown here! You know, there's one woman who started the civil rights movement in this country—Rosa Parks! A little woman, sat on a bus! And I want you to know something, Kenny, I never met you a day in my life but I love you, Kenny! And if Mabel believes in you, Kenny, doggone it, I believe in you! How would you like to have a scholarship to Louisiana State University?'

"I said I'd love it very much.

"He said, 'All right, Kenny, I'm going to get you the papers, don't you worry about a thing! I just keynoted a district attorney's convention, I got a number of friends out there in L.A., we'll protect you Kenny! I'll give you around-the-clock protection, don't you worry about a thing, you're a good man!' "

Miller got an LSU application form in the mail, filled it out and began telling everyone he was going to LSU, until....

"I get a call from Coach Brown: 'Kenny? Dale Brown! Love ya, Kenny! Just want to know, did you get those papers?'

" 'Yes, I did, Coach, they're on their way back.'

" 'Great, Kenny! Now, I want you to know something, we're not going to bring you right in, but I'm going to bring you in and give you the opportunity to go to this fine university, Louisiana

State University! I want you to know that I believe in people like you!'

"Subsequently, he starts sending me poetry. When he was out of town, in Europe or wherever, he would call me: 'Kenny! Dale Brown! I love ya, Kenny!'

"And to be honest with you, I didn't know the guy was selling me BS. I mean, as far as I'm concerned, I'm talking to a prominent collegiate basketball coach at one of the finest universities in this great land of ours and perhaps there's an outstanding opportunity in it. That's all I knew. Because at that stage in my life, I wanted to believe something good was going to happen."

Miller says he got nothing but a LSU T-shirt from Brown. The young reporter was so shaken at the threat Mabel reported, he moved out of his apartment and hid out at his sister's place. Beset by fits of exhilaration and gloom, he had an accident in a company car and, in a dispute over his workman's compensation claim, was fired by the Sentinel.

Then came the cover-ups.

With the Los Angeles *Times* asking questions, Miller says he got another call from Tark.

"Tarkanian called me," he says, "and told me, he said, 'You call those people at the L.A. *Times* and you tell them that you never talked to me, that I never said anything to you, I never made any promises to you, I never said anything to you regarding the recruitment of John Williams. You call them, Kenny, and you let them know that. You do it right now.'

"Of course, I picked the phone up in 10 seconds and did it. It was petrifying."

Sports Illustrated approached him. Miller says he asked the writer for money just to get him off his back—and was paid $1,500 for an interview.

No one is sure what Williams got besides two years in Baton Rouge. Mabel moved there while he was in school. The manager of a local steakhouse told a Los Angeles *Times* reporter that he had hired her. The next day, Brown put the reporter on the phone with the manager, who recanted his story.

There were rumors of front money of $100,000 or more. At one point, Brown, ever the reformer, said he wanted to show Williams

$150,000 in a valise, ask if he was interested, then add $1 and declare himself to be the high bidder.

A few months later, Hazzard, in the process of noting Williams's freshman struggles ("Dale Brown has made him almost human"), recounted his own eleventh-hour attempts to recruit him.

Said Hazzard: "I talked to John. He was very receptive. My first statement to John was: 'No money. We're not going to pay you. I think it'll be worth money to you to stay in L.A. and play in Pauley Pavilion and be a local hero.'

"And that was the end of that."

No, it wasn't. Dale Brown called Peter Dalis. Mabel called Hazzard. Hazzard was obliged to apologize.

In the midst of it, however, Brown acknowledged that money had been offered by someone. "We all know it was," said Brown.

Williams left to enter the NBA draft after his sophomore season, which everyone knew was the plan all along.

"When John was at Crenshaw High School, you knew this guy was somebody special," says Kenny Miller. "He had girlfriends that were well beyond his age. People who never, ever wanted to befriend him were his friends. He never had to spend a dollar for three years because of who he was and the economical potential that he represented.

"And people want to share in the wealth of that economical potential. And I don't think that it's unfair. It's the American way."

It may not have been all he wanted but Hazzard brought in a fine recruiting class.

It had Trevor Wilson, a tough forward; Kevin Walker, a 6-11 outside shooter; and a coveted big man, 7-0 Greg Foster of Oakland Skyline.

Foster wasn't a moose like J. R. Reid or Tito Horford but he was athletic and promising. In a surprise, Jack Haley had improved. Pooh Richardson was coming. And Reggie Miller had arrived.

Miller had looked like a joke when he'd arrived, skinny as a strand of wheat, seemingly all ears and elbows. He was serenaded throughout the Pac-10 with "Cheryl! Cheryl!"—a reference to his more famous sister.

However, he'd caught everyone's attention, firing in a raft of shots from far behind the three-point line while Farmer gaped at him as a freshman. All he'd done under Hazzard was get better, not to mention more outrageous.

At BYU as a sophomore, he spit at a player. At Arizona as a junior, he staged a memorable scene with veteran referee Booker Turner.

"Booker is a very fair referee," Miller wrote in his book, *I Enjoy Being the Enemy*, "but I had so much bad history with Arizona Coach Lute Olson that it wouldn't have mattered who was officiating that day.

'If there was one coach that I could not stand, it was Lute Olson. Me and Lute to this day don't get along. I think he's a dick.... Anyway, this is my junior year and I went up to Booker after he made a call and said, 'Booker, you know what?'

"Now Booker and I usually got along so he said, 'No, what, Reg?'

"I said, 'This is the worst game I've ever seen you officiate in my life. You know what it seems like to me? Seems that all these motherfuckers in here paid you to referee a game like this.'

"Booker nearly fell to the floor in shock.

" 'I can't believe you'd say that, Reggie.'

"Then I turned to the crowd and started pinching my thumb and forefinger together, like I was feeling dollar bills.

" 'You were paid off, Booker.'

"Technical. Hazzard ran out, grabbed me and said, 'What the hell are you doing out here?'

" 'Coach, that motherfucker was paid off!' Hey, I was a psycho in college."

As a senior, Miller averaged 22 points and the Bruins went 25–7. They finished first in the Pac-10, then won the conference's post-season tournament. They won a game in the NCAA Tournament—their first since Larry Brown's march to the finals in 1980—but in the second round, were gunned down unexpectedly by a hot-shooting Wyoming forward named Fennis Dembo.

A year later, it all fell apart. Miller and Haley were gone. Greg Foster transferred after an argument with Hazzard.

"When the coach is not in charge, there's a problem," says Hazzard. "He made a decision, he was going to leave because I made a decision about his playing time. I didn't care. I still don't care. People say it may have cost you your job—I don't care. I really don't. There's no 18-year-old kid's going to control me. Period.

"When he was a freshman, I thought he was maybe the most talented athlete on our team but he couldn't match Jack Haley's toughness. That's why Jack played. That's why Jack's still playing. Jack is a great kid with character.

"The next year the job was his [Foster's]. Something happened, a situation happened and I decided to bench him....

"No, he didn't get in my face. None of them got in my face. If they tell you they did, none of them got in my face."

According to Keith Owens, then a freshman walk-on, it was a ten-word conversation that did it.

"Greg was starting," says Owens. "Kinda struggled a couple games and we lost a couple games. And Hazzard was trying to shake things up and made a lineup change.

"We had a practice the day before the game. I was shooting around. Greg was down at that basket. Hazzard came up and said, 'Greg, I'm gonna go with Kelvin [Butler].'

"Greg, all he said was, 'Whaaat? I'm outa here!'

"That was the extent of the conversation and he left. Walked right off the court then, didn't even practice. Went to the locker room, showered, whatever. Then ten minutes later, you saw him leaving.

"That was it. He never came back after that. I've heard when he was getting his paperwork and stuff together in the athletic department to transfer, they were trying to talk him into staying. Rumor was, one of the things they told him was, 'Well, we don't know how secure Walt's position is here.' "

The Bruins limped in 16–14, including a season-ending loss at Tucson in the Pac-10 tournament to Washington State, a team they'd beaten twice by a total of 22 points. Afterward, Hazzard told the players to decide if they wanted to accept an NIT—and the old rift opened up a last time.

"Coach told us in the locker room to decide if we wanted to go to the NIT or not," says Gerald Madkins, then a freshman.

"And those guys said, 'Why? 'Cause if we go, we're not going to play hard. So if you guys go, we'll go with you but don't count on us playing hard. Bottom line, we don't want to go. Why do we want to go to the NIT?'

"Well, shoot, to keep playing basketball, guys. It's not over. We can play five more games.

"I remember distinctly, there was a rap song out from LL Cool J, called 'Going Back to Cali.' I remember Craig Jackson in the back of the bus singing that at the top of his lungs, like he didn't give a shit. We just got beat by Washington State, whom we hammered twice in the regular season. We owned those guys in the regular season, we get beat in the season and it's like, we're going back to Cali— California. We're glad to be going home.

"I'm a freshman sitting in the front of the bus, thinking, 'Wow, is this what I have in store for the rest of my career here? I got to play with assholes like this?' "

The ground under Hazzard disappeared.

There had been a year-long NCAA investigation, checking out Miller's living arrangements on the Antebi estate, the Higgins allegations et al. UCLA had discovered and turned over two Sam Gilbert checks totaling $2,300—the NCAA called him a "well-known and highly identifiable representative of the institution's interests"—paying the rent of a Bruin recruit.

Because it had cooperated so fully, UCLA got a slap on the wrist: a loss of two scholarships. But the inquiry frightened the school; its lawyers' response looked like a telephone book.

Attendance in Pauley had fallen under 8,000 a game. Chancellor Charles Young had come to the last one, to check it out. The letter writers were mean as starved rats. UCLA, wrote one, now stood for, "Under Current Leadership, Apathy."

On top of that, Don MacLean, a 6-11 senior at Simi Valley High School, latest in the string of local "next Bill Waltons," was saying he was interested in UCLA but didn't want to play for Hazzard.

"Well," says MacLean, "that's pretty much what I just said, in a nice way."

Thus it was little surprise when Walt Hazzard, who loved UCLA so much, became the only basketball coach the Bruins ever fired.

The school deemed it prudent to honor his contract and Hirsch's. Hazzard is still employed by UCLA in community relations but his ties with the athletic department are severed.

"I lived with a certain amount of bitterness for a long time," says Hazzard, who now works as a Laker consultant and scout.

"I don't care about getting fired but don't assassinate me personally or my character and my contribution to that institution. Those people up in the stands are not God. The people that buy tickets to see UCLA play, they're not God. I'll be judged by God and not by them.

"I thought I deserved to be treated like one of their children. There were a few people at the university that did that.... It's cost me a lot of money over the last seven years, a lot of dollars. But my head is bloody but unbowed.

"My children would not go to school there. My oldest was in law school when I got fired. They lost a tremendous supporter in my wife who will have nothing to do with them. She was the first African-American song girl in the history of the school....

"I don't consider it a wringer. It was just a bump in life. My life is great. My children are doing well. My wife and I are flourishing with a grandson. All of my children are excelling. My oldest boy is an attorney, Stanford undergraduate, UCLA law. My second son is finishing up an MBA program at Tulane. My third son is an honor student at Morehouse College and my youngster's at George Washington."

In some romances, it goes like that.

CHAPTER TEN

THE MUTT THAT ROARED: THE HARRICK YEARS

Pete Dalis called me, he said, "Would you like to join me in the toughest basketball coaching job in America?" And little did I know what he meant.

—JIM HARRICK

As I'm sure you know, another disaster struck Los Angeles. But enough about UCLA basketball.

—JAY LENO, "THE TONIGHT SHOW"
AFTER THE 1994 LOSS TO TULSA

When Larry Brown began talking to J. D. Morgan about the UCLA job in 1979, Morgan asked him to consider keeping Larry Farmer as an assistant.

Brown's practice was to bring in his own assistants but Morgan pleaded Farmer's case: He'd been on UCLA teams that had gone 89–1; he'd been an assistant under Gene Bartow and Gary Cunningham.

Cunningham had two assistants but Morgan said he didn't care about the other one.

That was Jim Harrick.

It was obvious what the Bruins needed now: someone willing to take the job. They wanted a star, once more, but the stars weren't interested.

Mike Krzyzewski said he had a "four-minute conversation" with AD Peter Dalis but K wasn't interested.

Denny Crum.... Another brief phone call. Too late by ten years.

Jimmy Valvano.... He acted interested at least. He and his wife, Pam, flew out to interview. V's friends said he'd always wanted to live in L.A. A guy everyone called "V" would have to, wouldn't he? Of course, there was no way even an awakened UCLA could match V's North Carolina State package but his buddy, Sonny Vacarro of Nike, was willing to kick in $120,000 a year to get his client into this glamour position.

V's interest lasted until he and Pam checked out the housing prices in Beverly Hills, Bel Air and Brentwood (they didn't even mess with San Fernando Valley; V wasn't Gene Bartow). Let's see, a $300,000 house in Raleigh costs what in Beverly Hills? $3 million?

Or maybe V was never interested and was just working the boys back home. With him, you never knew.

Larry Brown.... Funny they should think of him.

He'd been thinking of them for the seven years he'd been gone. He had said over and over that leaving was "the biggest mistake of my life." There would be a problem getting Chancellor Charles Young, who now had to sign off on hires, to forget he had run off, but, as Brown had proven before and after UCLA, you might not like the tradeoff but he got you where you were going.

By 1988, he had coached the Denver Nuggets to the best record in franchise history; had taken the New Jersey Nets to their first NBA playoffs; and had taken UCLA to its only NCAA finals since John Wooden.

He had just won an NCAA title with a Kansas team that was 13–8 at mid-season and using football players to fill out an injury-depleted roster.

Young relented.

Brown swooned.

The day after Kansas had won its NCAA title, he flew to Los Angeles and announced he was returning to UCLA.

Then he flew back to Kansas and changed his mind. For Brown, whose personal life was fraying, and for the Bruins, whose program had pancaked, it was just how things were going.

"When I told 'em I was coming, I begged them to give me some time," Brown says. " 'Cause we had to meet the President, we had a big banquet at the university. There was a big parade. I wanted to go back and explain myself to the players.

"But UCLA wanted so badly to get on with it. The only thing they kept saying was, 'We're going to lose Don MacLean.'

"The only thing I kept saying was, 'You're not going to lose him but if you do, it's just one player. This program's going to flourish.'

"I accepted the job, but I kept begging them, 'Please, give me some time.' They kept insisting no, no, no.

"I flew back [to Kansas] by myself. I didn't have anyone there. And I was saying, 'How can I face everybody at this banquet, all the players, going to the President?'

"I was having marital problems. My wife [Barbara, his second] hated Kansas from Day 1. She wasn't even living in Kansas the final year. I thought going to L.A.—she liked L.A.—and going to UCLA would maybe make everything work out.' "

Two months later, Brown took the San Antonio Spurs job. He was an ex-Bruin forever. Even for him, it had been a busy summer.

By now, Dalis couldn't see for all the egg on his face.

Now he just needed a coach to pursue MacLean and, just as important, end this national embarrassment of a "selection process." If they couldn't find anyone to take the job, they'd have to drop the sport.

So they hired Jim Harrick.

Harrick was hardly a star but he was an ex-Bruin and he'd done a solid job at Pepperdine. He'd been conference coach of the year four times. Just as important, he wanted the job.

All they'd had was coaches who thought they wanted it. Harrick was prepared to suffer for it, even if he underestimated how much, and when the pain got worse than he'd imagined, he would suck it up. It wasn't that he didn't complain—he did—but he didn't back off. He never got that UCLA coaches' thousand-yard stare. It would take a while for him to prove it but he was the nut they couldn't crack.

In the beginning, however, Harrick was like any post-Wooden UCLA coach: up to his neck in problems, starting with the circumstances of his hiring.

"I didn't mind that," Harrick says. "It was a pleasure for me to be mentioned with the names of Valvano and Krzyzewski and Larry Brown, all national championship coaches. To have my name mentioned with those guys was an honor. There might have been some attitudes I didn't appreciate but that's all."

He was 50 and his whole life had been a warm-up for this. He'd had a nice career—a man could pick worse spots to finish than Pepperdine's Malibu campus—but he hungered for the glow of the lights downtown. In 1986, he finished second to George Raveling for the threadbare USC job.

Harrick had come from nowhere and arrived late. He was born in Charleston, West Virginia, of Lebanese ancestry, a little pepperpot whose playing career ended as a benchwarmer at Morris Harvey College. He wasn't thinking of coaching jobs when he and Sally got into their Chevy on their wedding night in 1960 and drove west. He wanted any job he could find.

"I was the same guy that Lasorda was," says Harrick. "How could the third-string guard from Morris Harvey College become the head coach at UCLA? Isn't that what Tommy says, how'd the third-string pitcher from Norristown High School become the manager of the Dodgers?

"I applied for a bunch of jobs, maybe 100 jobs, 50 in business, 50 in education. I got a job through a teachers' agency out of Boulder, Colorado, in Smith River, California.

"Our school district went to the Oregon border, right on the water. Rained 127 inches that year. We brought a U-Haul trailer full of gifts from our wedding and everything mildewed. People go now to the Oregon coast and talk about how beautiful it was. Little did we know at 22 years old it was beautiful and it had great scenery."

Get the drift? This wasn't going to be one of those trips to the moon on gossamer wings.

After a year in their Northern California rain forest, he got a job in Hawthorne, a Los Angeles suburb, and began a slow climb through the local school system, supplementing his income with night jobs like the one at Mattel where he put water rifles together.

"It was four years before I got a high school job," he says. "I was teaching all subjects in a self-contained classroom in the seventh grade. I've always used this statement—the Lord has never put me in a situation I could not handle. That's why He started me in the seventh grade.

"You know what I learned? How... to... teach!"

The high school was Morningside in Inglewood. It was integrated when Harrick got there, all black nine years later as whites fled the neighborhood. He started as a jayvee coach and, in five years, moved up to the varsity. At 32, he first began to think of himself as a basketball coach.

"Only thing that ever crossed my mind before was the thirtieth of the month," he says. "That motivated me, got me along.

"I got married, we came west, the first year my wife worked a little bit. Then we moved down here and the second year, we had a baby. Then I moved to high school and the first year in high school,

I had another baby. The year I got my head coaching job, I had my third baby. So my land sakes alive, all you care about is the thirtieth of the month. I started making $4,700 a year. My first take-home pay was $291 a month."

In 1973, Morningside was ranked No. 1 in the nation by *Basketball Weekly*. Harrick was coach, athletic director, refereed football, basketball and baseball and taught driver training.

He coached some stars like Stan Love and met the college assistants who came to recruit. Frank Arnold, then at Oregon, recommended him to the new Utah State coach, Dutch Belknap, who wanted someone who could recruit Southern California.

Belknap offered Harrick, now 37, an assistant's job and an $11,000 pay cut.

Harrick didn't know what to do until he mentioned it to a friend at Morningside, a language teacher whom he had watched grow old on the job. The man now walked with the aid of a cane. He had taught Latin. Now they were an inner-city school and he taught remedial English.

"The bell rings," says Harrick, "we're going back to class. Here we go, he and I." (Harrick walks his fingers across his desk in his UCLA office to illustrate.)

"I said, 'You know, I've got a chance to go to Utah State, but I've got to take an $11,000 cut in pay.'

"He says, 'You know, Jim, I had a chance to go to junior college one time and I had to take a $2,000 cut and I didn't go.'

"And immediately, I stopped in my tracks and I watched him walk and I said," (Harrick claps his hands to the sides of his head and mouths the words), 'Oh my God! That's me!'

"I went right back, called Dutch Belknap and told him I'd come to Utah State. That's exactly how I made my decision."

Two years later, Gary Cunningham, whom Harrick had met while at Morningside, brought him to UCLA. Two years after that, after Cunningham had tipped him to his own departure, Harrick took the Pepperdine job.

At 50, he returned to UCLA, the sixth coach to succeed Wooden and the oldest.

Harrick met the troops. The troops weren't sure what to think.

He couldn't have been more different from Hazzard. Hazzard had been a star player. Harrick was a little guy who talked a mile a minute in a West Virginia twang the players would soon be imitating and punctuated his remarks with dramatic pauses for emphasis.

Guard Gerald Madkins remembers their first meeting, the upbeat new coach asking if he knew Oscar Robertson had once averaged triple-doubles, telling Madkins he thought Gerald could do that at UCLA. Madkins says he went home shaking his head.

"At first I was very skeptical," says Keith Owens. "It was like, What's this guy talking about?

"His delivery and everything, his whole tone. It was very odd. I remember that first meeting. I remember everybody looking around at each other, like, What the hell? Who is this guy? Because it was so different than the year before."

The problem wasn't so much Harrick's style as his predicament. Thirteen years after Wooden's retirement one Bruin, Kelvin Butler (signed by Walt Hazzard just before his first season), had played four years for the head coach who'd recruited him. Players were handed from one coach to another. They could make the best of it or transfer and sit out a year.

Once again, eras were changing fast.

Harrick quickly signed MacLean, to the relief of the administration and the joy of Bruin fans. MacLean didn't want to play for Hazzard but had known Harrick since attending his camp at age 11.

MacLean, as the next four years were about to prove, was a fine player but a mixed blessing. On one hand, Don could play. On the other, he was Don.

He was the archetype of the modern young star, meaning he'd been hyped to the heavens since he was a pre-teen and looked at everything in terms of his NBA career. He was a no-conscience scorer with an unshakable belief in himself. He was tougher than he looked, which was fortunate because he infuriated opponents. Friends had to figure him out, too.

"The thing I always say about Don," says Owens, his roommate for two years, "people ask me what's he like? I say that, first off he's going to rub you the wrong way. He's very self-centered and into himself and all that.

"But laying that aside and dealing with him with those things as a given, he's a great guy to get along with. I actually got to be real good friends with Don.

"I don't remember noticing it as much the beginning of his freshman year but I think there was a game he had like 41 that season and after that, he was like another guy. The sun didn't rise until he woke up and it set when he went to sleep at night."

At least the top local players were turning back toward Westwood. Recruiting turned around. The Bruins became deep and athletic. By Harrick's fourth season, he had eight players on the team who would play in the NBA.

Harrick would later tell friends he thought he'd done a good, not great, job all along, one that would have been well received at most schools. He was, in fact, a professional who worked hard and knew how to teach.

However, he was prone to blowups at referees and his teams to late-game stumbles, late-season slides and tournament pratfalls. The Bruins were strong offensively, suspect defensively. Somehow, Harrick always seemed to be serving himself up to his critics, like a pig with an apple in its mouth.

It was UCLA; it was the times, too. If expectations had slowly diminished in Westwood, the tenor of college basketball had changed. Gary Cunningham says the pressure on his old assistant, Harrick, dwarfs anything he ever faced.

Of course, the modern salaries dwarfed what Cunningham made, too.

"Coaches are being paid more than CEOs of companies," says Cunningham. "So they should perform for what they're being paid. They're being paid more than anybody at their universities. Much more."

Harrick would grow into the job, but it would take time. There was a history of unchecked temperament at UCLA. The volatile Reggie Miller had given way to Trevor Wilson, a wild horse whom opposing players baited into outbursts. Ticking Trevor broke in Demanding Don MacLean. Harrick would later rue the fact that he had given Wilson so much license, but at the time he had more immediate concerns, like keeping his job.

Tracy Murray, a silky-smooth gunner, arrived a year after MacLean but the so-called M & M Boys had little in common except a uniform, the first letter of their last names and a rivalry. There was speculation that each kept his own running total and the other's, too.

The Bruins won 20 games annually but not even they were happy with that. Bill Walton, returning to do TV commentary on their games, went on ESPN's "Up Close" and said Harrick's teams "peaked against the Little Sisters of the Poor."

It wasn't just the alumni, the press, letters to the editor or talk radio. The players were disappointed, too. Some—like MacLean—would even acknowledge their own contribution to the problem.

"Maybe if we had been a little more cohesive and a little tighter we may have been able to carry it over the hump," MacLean says.

"And I've since figured that it was me first because I was probably leading the charge in that regard. I was on my own agenda."

"Well, I mean, Coach gave him that leeway," says Gerald Madkins, a two-year captain.

"It was Don's team, basically. When Don came in as a freshman, Don got a starting spot. Don really didn't have to earn it.

"The tone was set from day one when Don stepped on campus, that it was going to be his team. By his sophomore year, it was his team. They say the top guy sets the tone so, I guess, if he wants to take the blame for it, I guess he's right. It starts from the top down. I would even go farther and say the head coach, the very top, it started from him.

"I just felt that guys who tried to do the dirty work were never appreciated by Coach Harrick. He said he did appreciate it but I've always been told actions speak louder than words....

"If Don does something, kick his ass out of practice. He would let Don go off and basically cuss him when we wouldn't do it, not because of our respect of Coach Harrick, just the position of coach. It didn't matter to Don.

"Tracy would pout, wouldn't play, he'd still be stuck out there, pouting like he was seven, eight years old, not playing hard. Hell, if he's not going to play hard, put him on the bench and let somebody else play. If we lose, so what? Say, 'I'm not going to run my program like that.'

"He [Harrick] would say, 'Well, Madkins, I can't do that. If you go to Syracuse, they're like that. You go to Vegas—you're not going to go anywhere in this country and it's not like that.'

"It was really a dysfunctional team and I talked about it constantly. I was always harping on it, to coaches, to other players. We had three or four closed-door me-'n'-him meetings [with Harrick] about this stuff....

"I think he was probably more afraid of the media and the administration: 'These are the guys that were brought in to win a championship, why aren't you using them?'

"That job has so much pressure. Until you, I guess, sit in someone else's chair, walk in his shoes, you can't honestly say what was going on."

Amazingly enough, Harrick had a honeymoon, two seasons worth.

He hit the ground running. He landed MacLean. He went to Philadelphia to see Pooh Richardson's parents, to see where Pooh's head was, to make sure the point guard who'd been so close to Hazzard wasn't thinking about transferring. Richardson says it never crossed his mind but after that, he and Harrick were close.

There was nothing Harrick wouldn't do for his players. When Madkins broke his hip in a scooter accident, Harrick invited him to stay in his home. One of his sons gave up his room for two weeks. Madkins remembers the night Harrick and his son, Monty, lugged him upstairs in his wheelchair, just so he could watch the big-screen TV with everyone else instead of the regular TV downstairs.

"I still feel indebted to him," says Madkins, "that side of him, away from basketball. He was just unbelievable."

Their first team, with only seven scholarship players returning, went 21–10, won a game in the NCAA tournament and lost, respectably, to North Carolina in the second round.

A year later, the Bruins went 22–11, upset No. 2–seeded Kansas in the second round of the NCAA and lost a close game to Duke in the Sweet 16.

A year later, the curtain dropped on the honeymoon phase of Harrick's career. The Bruins started 14–1 but finished 9–8, then were upended in their NCAA opener by lowly Penn State, a No. 13 seed.

"That was an up-and-down season," says Keith Owens. "I think we were ranked as high as like fourth and we had that January spin where we lost four in a row and the team started questioning its abilities. You know, were we really that good? 'Cause UCLA'd always been a good front-runner but when things got tough, especially in the recent past, they had a tendency to kind of fold and play like a team that's tight and we definitely did that.

"I remember the night before at the hotel, we watched Syracuse lose in the first round and they were in our bracket. At the end of the game, guys came out in the hallway and we were like high-fiving: 'We're in the Sweet 16, Final Four, North Carolina's the only team we gotta beat!'

"So we were already chalking ourselves up, three rounds deep, before we even played a game. We came into that game and guys just weren't there. Just like, four guys were out there missing in action, going through the motions, not really playing the game....

"After that game, I kinda remember thinking, 'Why am I not pissed off that I just went out as a senior in my last college game, to the No. 13 seed, in the first round?'

"I wasn't pissed off. I just could laugh because that one game epitomized everything. I think I was the Chevrolet player of the game that game. I went out there playing hard. It was like, tournament time, UCLA gets a lot of attention, I'm going to try do to something and make myself known. So I was playing hard but I felt like I was out there by myself."

Back home, Ed O'Bannon, sitting out his freshman year with a knee injury, watched in disbelief.

"I was at my friend's house," he says. "We sat up and threw stuff at the TV. It was really unbelievable. The game was over, I went outside, people were just saying, 'UCLA got beat by Penn State?' That was the feeling. During the game, I remember having the feeling, I'm glad I'm not out there."

"It was the worst loss we ever had at UCLA," says Mitchell Butler, then a sophomore.

"I think that was the most heat we ever felt at UCLA on any loss. I didn't know if Harrick would survive that. I thought that would be something that people just really couldn't let him live down."

A few weeks later, Owens, who'd play a season with the Lakers, went to see Harrick about getting into a pre-draft camp. They talked over old times.

"He was like, 'I could see it coming, the downfall of this team,' " says Owens.

"He said it was hard for him to run a tight ship when you've got parents coming in and pressuring you and threatening you with having their kid transfer.... I know Tracy threatened to transfer a lot if he didn't get X number of shots. He did or his dad did, the same thing.

"Don and Tracy would at times play games against themselves, against each other within the game, like who was going to be the leading scorer tonight?

"That happened a lot in the second part of the season. And then you had Darrick [Martin, the point guard] who was going for stats and assists and he knew Don and Tracy were going to shoot so he was passing to Don and he was passing to Tracy and he kinda had tunnel vision to those players. Other players might be wide open. He was just trying to get it to somebody who was going to shoot without dribbling.

"That pretty much would epitomize my career at UCLA, a disjointed team, guys claiming that they wanted to win but it seemed like they had their own personal agendas higher on the list of priorities than team success."

If leadership had been a problem, Gerald Madkins decided it would be so no longer.

Madkins was a hard-nosed, blunt-spoken young man, determined to leave his mark at UCLA. He'd just been appointed captain, and that was all the invitation he required.

Before the start of practice, he gathered the players in a room at a mall in Culver City for 90 minutes of paint-peeling straight talk.

"My first year back," says Madkins, "I was just trying to blend in and see if I was going to be capable of playing on this level again. My second year, Coach named four of us captains—me, Keith, Darrick and Don—so it wasn't my place to say, 'Look guys, this is how it's going to be.'

"But that last year, it was my team. I was the team captain and I was going to speak my mind—to players, coaches, administrators, I didn't care who it was. We had the talent to be one of the top three or four teams in the country and it was my last year, I wanted to do everything I could to put a banner up because that's all UCLA was about. You slip into obscurity if you don't put a banner up there and it's the truth. It'll be that way until, I guess, that school burns down. Hell, Reggie Miller—nobody ever thinks about Reggie's years! Nobody!

"I think after losing to Penn State and having a whole summer to think about it, even the most confident people on that team wanted to make sure where everybody's head was.

"Don was a senior now, the NBA draft was coming up, he was an All-American and he didn't want anything to go wrong. Tracy was thinking about leaving and he eventually did. Darrick was a senior. Everyone had their own agenda.

"I think that was the most honest we ever were. Guys didn't hold their tongues. People said stuff about me I didn't agree with but I listened. I thought it was good. I thought it was therapeutic. I thought guys came back with a new focus. Coaches didn't. I remember one, I'm not going to say which one, he called it 'lip service—you'll see, they'll go back to their old ways. When the shit hits the fan, we'll see.'

"And eventually it did but for a while, we were happy."

Harrick had his own meeting with MacLean, to suggest that Don's NBA stock would be higher if he averaged 18 points on a champion than 25 on an also-ran. MacLean resolved to pass more. He let Murray outscore him (it was close, though, 706–661) and the Bruins went 28–5.

It was a heady trip. They opened the season, demolishing Indiana in the Hall of Fame Game in Springfield, Massachusetts. They won at Louisville and Arizona. They started 21–1 and rose as high as No. 2 in the polls.

It was too heady. At mid-season, Harrick disclosed his frustrations at his pay to the Los Angeles *Daily News'* Ron Rappaport, who published them in a column that would haunt Harrick for years.

"I think they were a little desperate looking for a high-profile coach," Harrick told Rappaport.

"When Larry took the job, they hadn't interviewed anybody but me. So when he says no, what were they going to do—open it up again?

"I know they offered Brown this kind of money," (holding his hand up above his head). "And I know they offered me this kind of money." (lowering his hand to his waist)....

"I need to know the philosophy here. Don't you think they have some responsibility to step up? They sure think about firing you when you don't do well.

"I've beaten Bobby Knight, Lute Olson and Denny Crum this year. You want me to beat these guys? Of course you do. But you don't want to pay me what these guys are getting."

Harrick had initially signed for $200,000 ($100,000 in salary, a $25,000 "appearance fee" for doing media interviews plus the right to keep the first $75,000 provided by a sneaker company). After each of his first two seasons, the contract had been extended and sweetened. He was now up to about $300,000. Of course, the big guys' scale started at $500,000 or more.

The reaction to Harrick's complaint was incredulity, not sympathy. However, a Pac-10 title (their first in five seasons) and a No. 8 rating in the final poll kept everyone at bay, for the moment.

The NCAA seeded the Bruins No. 1 in the West. They won two games and marched into the regional finals at Albuquerque, their deepest penetration in twelve years.

Waiting for them was ... oops ... Indiana.

Knight was no Bruin fan, no man to overlook any slight, and no one to irritate in any event. He must have been fascinated to hear Harrick had based his request for a raise on beating him. Unwittingly, Harrick had tweaked the nose of one of the profession's primal forces.

Thus, it may not have been a coincidence that the Hoosiers not only trashed the Bruins but ran up a 106–79 score, too.

Knight had his players deny the entry passes that started the UCLA offense, pushing them far out on the floor. With Indiana pressuring, there should have been back-doors available but the Hoosiers proved better at covering secondary options than the Bruins did running them.

Instead, said Madkins, the Bruins whimpered and died.

"You've got to go to your fifth or sixth option to get into a play," Madkins says. We weren't used to doing that.

"We just broke down. They turned up the intensity and we didn't match it. I remember Don saying something about being tired and Tracy said the same thing, he felt lethargic. In the biggest game of our lives, our two big guns, quote, unquote, were nowhere to be found. And that's not to blame them solely, but hell, you've got to produce in the big games."

Afterward, Madkins went off on the team's stars and the double standard he perceived to the press, angering the coaches, among others.

"I've never been a guy to hold my tongue," Madkins says. "I've always been a man. I wasn't hurting anybody. I was telling it like it was.

"I know Mr. Murray and Tracy, they were upset with me for a minute. Don's mom was upset with me for a minute. But I remember distinctly Don coming up to me at the banquet and saying, 'I know you, that's how you feel, I know you weren't personally trying to attack Tracy or me.'

"And that was the end of it."

Maybe not.

The young Ed O'Bannon, who'd just spent his comeback season as a No. 3 forward, watched Madkins that day with slack-jawed admiration.

"We're losing to Indiana," O'Bannon would say later, "we're just getting blasted and he was yelling at everybody, 'Don't lay down and die! We won't lay down and die!'

"Here's a man who's getting his brains beat in and his pride would not allow him to quit—if they're going to beat me, they're going to beat me but I'm not going to lay down.

"I mean, his whole game, everything about it, I admired. The leadership, the speeches after games. He was a man who didn't take any BS. When guys were taking too many shots and complaining about it, he'd get pissed off and yell, 'Man you're getting all the shots, why are you complaining?'

"I liked that. If you're shooting all the time, don't be complaining."

Years later, when O'Bannon would feel the need to take over, it would be Madkins he would remember. He'd often find himself wondering what Gerald would have done.

So, Gerald Madkins left his mark at UCLA, after all.

Of course, it didn't show for a while. MacLean left with his class. Murray went, too, entering the NBA draft as a junior. Harrick reportedly pleaded with Tracy's father, Bob, to call Laker GM Jerry West to check out his prospects. Murray went eighteenth and was waived twice within three seasons.

Ready or not, it was the O'Bannon era.

Ed O'Bannon had been a prospect to make a coach's mouth water, not only talented but nice, with a solid family background and a father, Big Ed, who was supportive but didn't push. Big Ed had played football at UCLA. The Bruins recruited Little Ed from the time he was in grade school. When he left high school, he was regarded as the area's best prospect since John Williams.

To show how things were going, Ed chose UNLV, switching only after the Rebels went on probation.

"I think," he says, "if you ask any player being recruited at that time in '88, '89, what school would they have gone to—Vegas had just won the championship, they had all their players coming back.... LJ [Larry Johnson] was there, Stacey Augmon.

"The knock on UCLA was the players weren't playing together. It was just tough, saying all right. It was almost like I was just set-tling. It was like, 'Oh, OK, I'll take UCLA.' It was almost like that."

It got worse. In a pickup game before his freshman year, O'Bannon tore up his left knee, devastating his families, real and Bruin. The O'Bannons selected a surgeon who, in a new technique, replaced Ed's anterior cruciate ligament with a cadaver's but his first year back was tentative, to say the least. Coming off the bench, he averaged four points.

As a starter a year later he averaged 17 as the Bruins went 22–11. Seeded No. 9 in the NCAA's Western regional, they won their first game, then startled everyone by taking a 19-point first-half lead on Michigan's celebrated, talkative Fab Five.

Ed went for 30 that day, a sign he was on his way back. The Wolverines rallied to tie it. At the end of regulation, sophomore point guard Tyus Edney drove into the lane passed a shot and tried to make a pass but Michigan's Jimmy King stole it. Michigan won in overtime.

"The first half," O'Bannon says, "that's something I'll never forget. Coming out at the beginning of the game and seeing them as cocky as they were and sure they were just going to kill us and then us having them on the ropes.

"It was like a fight, you're just beating somebody up and they're looking at you like, when are you going to stop? Please, relax for a minute. That's how if felt to me that whole first half. We were just killing them. It felt great.

"The crowd, before the game when they were warming up, all of the kids and everybody were on their side, watching them warm up. To us, we were warming up to win. And for them, they were warming up for the crowd, doing acrobatic layups and all that.

"They introduced Chris Webber, the crowd would go crazy. Then they introduced Ed O'Bannon and it was like, all right, whatever. Juwan Howard and the crowd would go crazy, and so on. It was a great feeling.

"We hung with the Fab Five. At that time, from where we were at, that was a huge thing."

For Harrick, in Bruin limbo, a finishing flourish was well-timed. A long-promised extension came through, but it suggested an internal debate about keeping him.

He didn't get a raise. His guarantees were cut. Instead of 100 percent as in his old contract, it was 75 percent, 50 percent and 25 percent of the remaining years.

A new clause said he could be fired "without cause."

Needing some good news, Harrick landed another O'Bannon.

It was close, again. The 6-5 Charles was the effervescent brother, a spectacular runner and dunker who'd been recruited by all the biggies. Kentucky's Rick Pitino spoke at the Artesia High banquet. Charles was going to UK but at the last moment, found himself unable to turn his back on his family. He was doubly valuble because other players liked him so much. A year later, Marques Johnson said his son, Kris, an all-city forward, chose UCLA because Charles was there.

Charles started right away and his presence seemed to electrify everyone. The Bruins went 14–0.

They made it to No. 1 in late January ... before unraveling again. They finished 7–6 and lost their share of the Pac-10 title in their final game, at Oregon. Ed O'Bannon, who had started well, fell off. His girlfriend, Rosa Bravo, was pregnant. Her parents were upset.

"I've always been the type of person, I didn't care what people thought," Ed said later. "But that, I think that one kind of got under my skin.

"People would be like, 'You're not married, how come you're having a kid?' Everyone makes mistakes, I'm human. I'm not perfect. My reputation kind of came into question and that also kind of made me lose focus."

They headed back into the NCAA, on a downer.

"We had just lost to Oregon," says Ed, "and that hadn't happened in fifty years [UCLA had won 16 of the last 17]. I think that right there I just said, you guys might as well not even enter the tournament.

"I would rather have just stayed home, watched it on TV. That's how I felt. Because we weren't ready to play. We didn't practice well, we weren't together. We weren't having fun at all. That team, it was just ready for us."

"That team" was Tulsa. When the matchup was announced, with the Bruins seeded fifth and the Golden Hurricane twelfth, O'Bannon told the press, "To tell the truth, I didn't even know Tulsa was in Oklahoma."

This was no compliment to the UCLA history department, in which Ed was pursuing a major, or the Golden Hurricane, which ran up a 29-point lead and coasted to a 112–102 victory over the limp Bruins.

"It was just a horrible experience," says Ed O'Bannon. "The whole game, the whole time we were in town, the whole feeling.

"To be honest, if we would've won that game, I don't know that we would've won the next one. Now that I think about it, I'm glad we lost. It just put us out of our misery."

Not everyone's misery was over. Peter Dalis called Harrick after the game and told him he wanted the staff in his office the next day to explain what had happened.

Said assistant Mark Gottfried to a reporter: "I wonder if we'll still have jobs."

They did but they had to accept a stern lecture from Dalis.

"He called," says Harrick. "He wanted to talk to all of us, wanted to know what happened. That's all. He just wanted to know what happened to our team from mid-year on and if I was the AD I'd want to know that, too, because he has to answer to a lot of people."

After the meeting a somber Dalis announced, "I don't think there's anyone who is associated with UCLA who was happy with anything the last half of the year and in the tournament. I was deeply disappointed. I think we all are."

Dalis said the Bruins were weak on fundamentals. He told the coaches they'd have to do a better job of teaching them. He added, in what didn't even sound as good as the dread vote of confidence:

"They'll need to demonstrate they can do that."

There was no joy around the UCLA basketball offices that summer.

CHAPTER ELEVEN

IN THE BELLY OF THE BEAST: NEW JACK-IT-UP CITY AND THE WARM-UP SUIT CAPITAL OF THE WORLD

As John Calipari said his first year at UMass, "If I'm recruiting a kid and he tells me, 'My dream's not to play in the NBA,' I don't want him." He doesn't want some guy who wants a scholarship to be an accountant or a doctor or a lawyer. Very few guys reach that goal but the coaches want someone with fire in their eyes.

—CRAIG FRANCIS, PUBLISHER, *HoopScoop*

Rich Goldberg, founder of the American Roundball Corp., has discovered a nine-year-old basketball player he thinks has a bright future. Harrison Schaen is already 5-foot-5 and projects to be 6-8 or taller. "He's going to be an outrageous player," Goldberg said.

—LOS ANGELES *DAILY NEWS*, SPRING 1995

At adidas 1995 summer camp for the nation's top high school players, a veteran prep writer looks down from the press section at 1,000 gym rats with 1,000 agendas.

"There's a lot of weird people here," he says.

He's got that right.

There are 230 high school players; as many coaches; about ten "recruiting gurus"; a few demented fans; some dropouts from the scene like Manny Goldstein, the goniff who led the NCAA a merry chase in his days as an assistant at New Mexico State and Southwest Louisiana when he and his friend Ben Franklin (the face on $100 bills) went on recruiting trips together; Bob Minnix, an NCAA enforcement guy and one of the posse that hunted Manny....

This is the mother of all camps, hosted by Sonny Vacarro, who invented the form back in the '60s. There are four games going at Fairleigh Dickinson in Hackensack, New Jersey, but as much action in the bleachers where Utah Coach Rick Majerus pulls out the business cards people have pressed on him.

"This guy wants to take my team to Australia," he says. "This guy [a Manhattan hotel rep] wants my business. That guy there is a runner for an agent, hitting me up for Van Horn."

Keith Van Horn will be a senior at Utah and, Majerus says, "a lotto next year." An NBA lottery pick. The pot of gold at the end of the rainbow. The twinkle in the eye of everyone here.

Even with the NBA's new rookie cap, the last lottery pick will be worth a three-year, $2.6 million contract, of which an agent will get about $100,000 for some perfunctory negotiating—assuming he can sign Van Horn, himself. The runner's name is Dana Pump. He's a summer league promoter from Los Angeles. He is telling people he works for Arn Tellem, a big-time agent for NBA players who's based in Los Angeles; Tellem says he's only considering hiring Pump. This is what basketball has evolved into in the '90s: a bazaar.

At its center are the kids, ages 15 to 18. The oldest are going into their senior year. The youngest are "rising sophomores"; some are coming out of junior high and haven't even set foot in a high school yet.

So much for an age of innocence. If "professional" means someone dedicated to a craft which he pursues year-round in a continuing attempt to improve, these kids are already pros. Poorly compensated for the moment, to be sure; paid off by shoe companies in "product"—sneakers, sweat suits, bags; covertly subsidized by street agents and shadow sponsors, but professionals just the same.

A kid would have to be an idiot if he didn't understand what brought him here, and it isn't education.

They can do that "Stay in School" song and dance all they want, they can make them go to those morning SAT classes, they can show "Hoop Dreams" every day as they're doing at the Nike camp. The kids can still tell what this is about: business. The coaches need players, the gurus are getting $20 for the latest scoop on their 900 lines, newspaper guys need stories, people writing books need local color. Everyone here is hustling. Everyone is making a living or, in the kids' case, wants to.

The kids have been flown in from all corners of the nation. Vacarro, who was fired by Nike, has set this camp up directly opposite Nike's in the Indiana Hoosierdome.

At Nike, kids stay in hotels. Sonny has his kids in the Fairleigh Dickinson dorms but he has a hundred more and most of the top players. As these things go, he's won.

Attesting to his acumen, a Who's Who of college coaches watches from the bleachers—Dean Smith, John Thompson, John Calipari, Jim Calhoun, Gene Keady, Lute Olson, Gary Williams, Dr. Tom Davis, Lefty Driesell—eyeballing the young blood.

The young blood shows off in typical camp fashion (get it, shoot it, welcome to New Jack-It-Up City) and dreams of circumventing the process, altogether.

All these players dream of making the NBA. (If this turns out to be a good year and an incredible camp, twenty or thirty might.) Most have their hearts set on the lottery. The more audacious, or naive, hope to be in it after a year or two. The stars are wondering if they can skip college entirely.

Everyone is still knocked out by Kevin Garnett's move.... No. 5 pick in the NBA draft right out of high school! Couldn't get his SAT score so he jumped right to The League!

Pro scouts called Garnett a once-in-a-generation prospect but in the kids' eyes there's a new generation each year and here comes theirs.

"I think he opened things up for a lot of players," says Lester Earl, a high-jumping 6-8 center from Baton Rouge, Louisiana.

Tim Thomas, a 6-10 center from Paterson, New Jersey, rated the top player among the rising seniors, has decided not to choose a school early. He'll wait until the last moment for maximum leverage.

"There are too many coaching changes, too many players going pro," says Thomas's cousin, Jimmy Salmon, who coaches his summer-league team. "Let's face it, he's not going to be in college that long."

A newsletter headline reports: "Thomas Trims List of Schools to 13."

By one of those quaint rules with which the NCAA tries to regulate this free-for-all, the courting process here is silent. Coaches are not allowed to talk to players and are segregated from them. In the absence of conversation, eye contact means everything, assuring the player the coach cared enough to follow him here, there, everywhere.

Accidental meetings or "bumps" are OK, according to the NCAA. Coaches joke about "getting some bump."

"The bad thing," says a Rutgers assistant, edging nearer the doorway as players stream into the gym, "is they can't see you."

Basketball, like the capitalism which permeates it ever deeper, runs on enterprise and at Fairleigh Dickinson this July, it's running very hard, indeed.

Skeptics say Sonny Vacarro doesn't care about camps any more but stays in for access, fronting for Arn Tellem.

Tellem says they're just friends but Sonny's a good friend to have. Tellem is big at UCLA, having just landed Ed O'Bannon and Tyus

Edney. UCLA has a Reebok contract but Charles O'Bannon and Toby Bailey have jobs as counselors here this summer.

Anyone who knows Sonny knows better than to discount the possibility he's working more than one angle but this isn't just business. His wife, Pam, is on the staff, working in an upstairs office where she can keep an eye on Jared, their three-month-old son, snoozing in a stroller. Pam, a pretty blonde, is Sonny's second wife. They met when she was in high school in Pittsburgh, helping out at his Dapper Dan tournament.

Skepticism rules this twilight world where people cross the line back and forth from newsletter publisher to tournament promoter, camp director, marketing rep, agent and coach. George Raveling, the former USC coach, goes back to the '60s with Sonny, slept over at his house in Pittsburgh as an assistant at Villanova and Maryland, was best man at Sonny and Pam's wedding. Now they're feuding. Raveling thinks the NCAA should limit the sneaker companies' involvement; Vacarro says Raveling took a lot of the companies' money before he got so high and mighty.

In the '80s, when Vacarro was, as he puts it, "Sonny Nike," insiders joked that this gnome with the perpetually worried look ran college basketball.

If that was a hype he encouraged, he certainly knew it from top to bottom, with a special emphasis on where the bodies were buried. He had a special relationship with coaches from sea to shining sea, including such as hard-to-get-next-to John Thompson.

The rise of this "little Italian kid from Pittsburgh," another of Sonny's descriptions of himself (or "fat little dago from Trafford High"), is also the story of the rise of Nike, for whom he worked, and the sneaker revolution in general.

Like Sonny, the companies were outsiders, marginal players until their breakout in the '80s that changed sports forever. Entire sports rose and fell because of them. Their promotional budgets fueled basketball's ascent, turning hand-picked stars into game-transcending celebrities. Baseball lost out for one simple reason—kids didn't wear spikes on the street.

Nike made a demigod of Michael Jordan, who'd been turned down early in his career for a McDonald's campaign because the

Micky D folks were afraid to put a black man out front. Nike made a legend of withdrawn, none-too-friendly Bo Jackson, who was only a curiosity who happened to play two sports before his TV commercials.

Basketball was very, very good to Nike, and Sonny Vacarro moved Nike into basketball. If you're looking for the ant who moved the world, here he is.

Vacarro had been a star athlete at Trafford but got no farther up the main stream than a baseball scholarship to Youngstown State and a graduate assistantship in basketball under Ralph Miller at Wichita State. He was trying out careers as a basketball agent and rock promoter while living with his mother when he staged the first Dapper Dan Roundball Classic in 1965.

Until then, high school kids played loosely organized basketball locally and sporadically in summer. The Dapper Dan was the first national event matching good players. It packed the Pittsburgh Civic Center and turned into the inaugural of an annual event. Coaches, then allowed to recruit 365 days a year, arrived in force.

Years passed while Vacarro tried to think of a way of to make a living the other 51 weeks of the year. He moved to Las Vegas and tried becoming a gambler. Never at a loss for ideas, he tried to interest a new sneaker company based in Portland, Oregon, in a basketball shoe that he and a Pittsburgh craftsman had devised.

"I brought them, actually, in an old burlap sack," Vacarro says. "And I went up to Nike and Phil Knight. At that time, it was a very young company and I just said I had some ideas about basketball shoes.

"Just for the record, they never gave me my prototypes back and today, those same types and style are being used.

"So that's how I got my introduction to Nike. They didn't take my styles, but eventually I worked with them. They had no ideas and this is something that's verified. They weren't doing anything at all in basketball. They were a very small running company at that time.

"All my connections were in the east in the '70s. And I went to them and said, 'You're doing it all wrong. You've got to get involved with college teams and high school players because they're the real life of this game.'

"I got close to everyone because of the Dapper Dan game. Because the game was so big and there were no rules, everyone came to the game and since I was the man who picked the teams, I had this entree to the kids. So I watched these kids grow up. George Karl went to my high school camp, played in my game. I had Jimmy Lynam—I could go on all day—Chuck Daly. All the guys worked my camps and came to the all-star games."

Sonny had a sure-fire way to get college players to wear Nikes, too: hire their coaches.

His "connections" were young, hungry guys like Jim Valvano of Iona College, rather than the older, more famous ones. But he was starting from the bottom and inventing the game as he went along so who was going to complain?

"Picture this," Valvano later told *Sports Illustrated*'s Curry Kirkpatrick. "Two guys named Vacarro and Valvano meeting at La Guardia Airport. Vacarro reaches into his briefcase. Puts a check on the table.

"I look at it and say, 'What's this for?'

"He pulls a sneaker out and puts it on the table. Like we were putting a contract out on somebody. He says, 'I would like your team to wear this shoe.'

"I say, 'How much?'

"He says, 'No, I'll give you the shoes.'

"You got to remember, I was at Iona. We wore a lot of seconds. They didn't even have labels on them. I say, 'This certainly can't be anything legal.'

In basketball, it was an idea comparable to the invention of the printing press. If the players were supposed to be amateurs, the coaches assuredly were not and they chose their teams' equipment. Converse had long ruled the field just by offering free product.

Now Nike offered product plus a fee for coaches, who became "consultants." Their players became Nike models wearing the trademark "swoosh."

At his zenith, Vacarro estimates he had about ninety coaches, including mainstays Thompson, whose predominantly black teams were greatly admired by young blacks across the nation; Valvano, the merchandiser's dream who'd do anything for the company (remember when he dressed his Wolfpack players in those spandex body stockings?); and Jerry Tarkanian, who brought more of that wonderful outlaw chic.

In the '80s, six of Vacarro's schools—N.C. State, Georgetown, Villanova, Kansas, UNLV, Michigan—won the NCAA title, a run he compares to UCLA's.

If it was a coup for Sonny, it was a problem for the universities. It was blatantly commercial, like giving coaches the right to sell billboard space courtside. However, it put money in the coaches' pockets, eased their salary demands—and cost the schools nothing.

The schools went along, to their shame. By the '90s, when Nike was reported to have paid Mike Krzyzewski a one-million dollar signing bonus, the practice had become institutionalized.

Nike's sales of basketball shoes went from $7 million when Vacarro arrived in 1978 to $300 million in 1987, aided in no small way by another Sonny coup: signing Michael Jordan.

In 1984, when Jordan left North Carolina, there was minimal marketing of athletes but Nike boldly signed him to a $1 million endorsement contract and designed an entire "Air Jordan" line— before Michael played an NBA game. In comparison, young stars like Magic Johnson and Larry Bird had small-potatoes hookups with Converse. When Jordan turned up for All-Star weekend decked out head to foot in his designer gear, a group of resentful veterans, led by Johnson's buddy, Isiah Thomas, tried to freeze him out during the game.

Air Jordan made Nike preeminent in the industry but it had only settled on Jordan after an in-house debate, and at Vacarro's recommendation.

"We had X hundreds of thousands of dollars to spend that year, 1984," says Vacarro. "And you have to remember, in 1984 this is still not a big company.

"They did not want him. Howard Slusher [an acerbic attorney and agent who served on Nike's board]—quote this if you use nothing else in your book—Howard Slusher was and still is a main person at

Nike and he came to me and said, 'OK, who do we pick to sign?' That class was Charles Barkley, Sam Bowie, Hakeem Olajuwon.

"Howard said to me, 'Which ones do you want?'

"Basically I said give it all to Jordan.

"So then Slusher said to me, 'Well, will you bet your job on it?'

"I mean, that was the quote that lived forever up there. They didn't want Michael at the expense of not having any other players. We rolled the dice with Michael.

"The irony was, I didn't know Michael. But he had the rarest of things, he had that ability to transcend basketball. He had a good healthy look. He was the right story. I don't know, I don't profess to know inner things here but I guessed right."

Unfortunately, Vacarro wound up betting his job, after all. He started his own marketing company. Nike thought he was taking players to other shoe companies and, in a surprising development, fired him.

Vacarro moved to Converse, then adidas when the German company revived its dormant North American operation. He has brought his friend, Dick Vitale, to adidas. He has a summer camp opposite Nike's and a tournament in Las Vegas opposite Nike's.

"C'mon," Vacarro says, laughing, "I'm a pimple on Nike's ass! They're one of the greatest companies in the world, there's no question about it.

"I'm much more limited than they are but it gives me great satisfaction that this year I have the five top players in America at this camp. No matter how they evaluate these camps, no matter where it's right, wrong or indifferent, the same five names come off everyone's lists. As they say on Broadway, the reviews will be in about a month and we'll kick their butt and it'll make them shuffle their lineup....

"The irony of Nike and I falling apart was that I was starting my own marketing company. The lunacy of it all is, they are now the biggest agents in the world, this multibillion-dollar conglomerate. They're agents! You know that, don't you? They've got Alonzo Mourning, they've got Harold Miner, they've got Rick Mirer.

"Why is it that they're different? They're agents! I know for a fact, they sat in Dean Smith's office with Jerry Stackhouse. They made him a presentation to represent him in a shoe deal, to represent him in an all-encompassing agency deal. They did the same thing with Grant Hill. I know that for a fact!

"What if David Falk was running this camp and flew everybody in? I mean, the FBI would be here!"

The end result is two super-camps instead of one and more competition for players. That's basketball in the '90s.

On Court 4, Keith Bean struggles through his first game.

Keith will be a sophomore at Fontana High in Riverside, California, in the fall, which makes him one of the youngest players here. A power forward, he's listed as 6-6 and moves with an easy grace but he's lost. Either he's intimidated, which he has vowed not to be, or can't get the ball, a distinct possibility since the guards aren't giving it up, particularly to younger guys.

Keith has the bad luck to be matched against Mikey Robinson from Peoria, Ill., Richwoods, a senior already on his way to distinguishing himself as the fastest trigger in this shot-happy camp. Mikey means to impress; he has signed with Purdue, although he denies it, or would if he was talking to the press, which he isn't. People think he just wants to take more recruiting visits.

Anyway, Mikey hits a bunch of long shots over Keith, who has never seen anything like him before.

Keith, meanwhile, gets one shot off all game and misses it.

"It was like, if you've got a name, then you don't really want to give the ball up," he says afterward. "You just try to make your moves. Some people do pass but like, it's hard trying to get the ball.

"I didn't do too good. The man I guarded, I wasn't guarding him very well. I understood why he [his coach, Elvert Perry] took me out because I wasn't playing any defense."

Perry, upset at seeing Keith being interviewed, breaks it up. Protocol is important at camps where no one is sure who anyone is and would be skeptical of their motives in any event.

Perry is Keith's summer-league coach in Riverside. In Perry's day job, he works with sexually abused kids. He coaches as a hobby and has a reputation for being optimistic about his kids' ability and fiercely protective.

"I'm just trying to get his feet wet at the camp so he can learn some things," Perry says. "He's going to be a big-time talent. Next year he'll probably dominate the camp but there's a lot of things he's got to learn. Like today he didn't play hard. He's got to learn how to play hard and play well all the time. He has all the talent in the world.

"But he's learning. He's a great kid, got about a 3.5 in school. He's going to be a big-time kid. I just love him.... He's 6-8, about 220. He should be about 6-10. He's going to be a hell of a player."

On Court 2, Tim Thomas is a no-show.

The 6-10 senior from Paterson, N.J., Catholic is rated the top player in the country but he sprained an ankle the first day, blew off the morning SAT seminar the next and has been suspended for a session.

The formal name for Vacarro's camp is ABCD, Academic Betterment and Career Development, an attempt to deal with the charge it's a meat market. Of course, not everyone is as worried about P.R. or delicate sensitivities.

"It is a meat market," says Bobby Kortsen, a Columbus, Ohio, youth coach and Vacarro's right-hand man, cheerfully.

"If you want steak for dinner and you want the best steak, you go to a good meat market. I mean, there's nothing wrong with taking a bunch of good players and putting them together and letting them play against one another for the colleges to come and evaluate. We're saving them thousands and thousands of dollars and hours and hours of time so they should pay for that." (They do. The press gets a free program with campers' names and uniform numbers. The coaches' program, with heights, weights, high school statistics and most important, home telephone numbers, costs $50.)

"For the kids, it's a great experience because growing up, they're wondering, 'Well, how do I compare?'

"This guy from Albany, Georgia, he wonders, can I do it against Tim Thomas? That's good and that's healthy. I don't see a negative to a meat market."

Of course, the super-camps aren't the only events of their kind, just the biggest. Many of these players will travel from event to event all July, returning home for only two or three days. There are 40 more camps from June–July 5th.

Here's the schedule for the week after this camp:

July 11–14	West Coast All-Star, Dominguez Hills, Calif.
July 11–14	Metro Index Camp, California, Pa.
July 11–15	Dave Krider Camp, Cincinnati
July 14–21	Five Star Camp, Pittsburgh
July 15–20	Slam'N'Jam, Long Beach, Calif.
July 15–22	AAU 17-Under Tourney, Winston–Salem, N.C.
July 15–22	Las Vegas National Prep

These days, a top player will start leading the Basketball Life at age 11: traveling to tournaments, staying in hotels, etc. By the time he's 17, he'll have seen a lot of this country and played abroad, too. Summer-league teams all over the nation will have wooed him and flown him around. Schea Cotton, a Southern California kid, will play for Riverside Church, a New York City team.

John Wooden used to tell his Bruins they were basketball players and only basketball players for two hours a day, at practice, but after that, they were to study and otherwise lead their lives. In the light of everything that has happened since, it feels like he's been gone longer than twenty years.

On Court 1, Kobe Bryant is knocking them dead.

The son of a former NBA player, Joe (Jellybean) Bryant, Kobe was named after the city in Japan. Explains his father, a grown-up free spirit: "It was the '60s. We weren't naming kids John or Joe."

Kobe is a 6-6 swing man who'll win the camp's most valuable player award. A slashing player who was born overseas when Jellybean was playing in Europe, he now lives on the toney Main

Line outside Philadelphia but has a downtown game and, as they say, can shoot it, too.

Enthusiasm does not run in short supply in these circles. By the end of summer, HoopScoops's Craig Francis will say of Kobe, "...The Grant Hill comparisons are in order."

Joe is now a LaSalle assistant coach. Kobe supposedly wants to stay with his dad so Joe is hearing some interesting speculation about what head jobs might open up by next summer.

Twenty-five years ago, he was in Kobe's shoes but it wasn't like this.

"No doubt about it," Joe says. "I get calls. People come up and talk to me all the time. I mean, I don't go anywhere without someone mentioning Kobe in some form or fashion, whether it's what school he's going to, whether he's going to get an agent, whether he's going to go right to the pros.

"I want him to play the game for fun. I think what I try to do as a parent, I try to keep all the pressure off him. I try to intercept all the calls, all the meetings. I make him aware of what other people might say to him. So when people do say those things, he's not carried away by it. He says, 'My dad said you were going to say that.'

"He's not like a normal kid where you got a lot of people coming up to you, selling you lollipops and you're loving it all. He understands the situation."

In the bleachers behind Court 1, Rick Majerus looks for the Utah players. They're not hard to tell, he jokes. They're the white guys getting their shots blocked.

Majerus competes marginally for out-of-state talent since it's so hard to convince a black youngster to come to faraway Utah and live among Mormons. In addition, he came up as an assistant to the great gadfly, Al McGuire, and has similarly mixed feelings about the rat race.

"I talked with Dean Smith for 20 minutes," says Majerus. "Dean Smith's here. Dean Smith will have a whole wall in the Hall of Fame. He's probably one of the greatest coaches in the game and one of the greatest people and you know, he's here. If Dean's here, I should be here...."

"But this is a sad field of dreams. Of 230 kids here, for approximately 200, this could be the zenith of their career. They'll be playground warriors, playing at Venice Beach and the YMCA and the rec leagues across the country, saying, 'You know, back when I was at the adidas camp or the Nike camp....'

"We've seen a lot of guys peak out. Antoine Joubert comes to mind. Remember him? They called him the Judge, out of Michigan? He was legendary. People ask me all the time, who's the best high school player you've ever seen? I can definitively say that the greatest talent I ever saw was a kid at [Los Angeles] Verbum Dei, Raymond Lewis. Now the sad thing is, I signed a kid from Verbum Dei two years ago. My assistant, Donnie Daniels, and I, we're in the parking lot and a guy comes up to Donnie and asks for money. It was Raymond Lewis....

"Maybe I'm in a Pollyanna attitude, too. Adidas runs this because it's good business. Adidas has their agenda, we have our agenda, that kid has his agenda, the guy writing the scouting report—there's a lot of money going down here and a lot of big decisions relative to money are being made.

"There's a kid out there ripping on his teammates. There's a kid ripping on the referee. There's a kid with an earring your wife wouldn't wear. This is where Derrick Coleman starts."

Coleman, a talented Philadelphia 76er forward, is also considered the leading boor of his generation. None of these kids may approach his genius but they're all aspiring stylists.

There are about twenty kids playing with snips of adhesive tape over the studs in their ears. Earrings are dangerous in games but the kids have just had their ears pierced and don't want the holes to close.

That's the thing everybody wants to forget about kids. They're so... young.

Keith Bean, whose struggles continue through the camp, is asked about his goals in basketball.

"I'm going to go two years of college," he says, "hopefully get drafted.

"And then if I can, come back and finish my years and get a college degree. And be a high school All-American, for three years at least."

The thing about the coaches, they're so ambitious.

They have an annual in-group networking opportunity, too, the National Association of Basketball Coaches convention held each Final Four weekend.

Hundreds of them in uniform—sneakers and warm-ups with school logo on the breast—swarm over each other in a hotel lobby, vigorous young men in primary colors, grateful for the opportunity to wear free gear all their lives, hoping to get higher on the totem pole where the big perks are.

"Hi, Coach!"

"Wassup, Coach?" (Players' slang for "What's up?" Can also be shortened to "Sup?")

"This is Coach ___."

Within the profession, "Coach" is an honorific, like knighthood. A coach will never call another coach, employed or not, anything but "Coach". It's applied to assistants, too, and suggests a complex of common hopes, privileges, attributes and burdens.

The profession runs on a spirit of enterprise that dovetails nicely with forays into the private sector. Careers like those of such aces as Valvano and Rollie Massimino are said to have been derailed by an infatuation with side deals. Victor Neil, the proprietor of SportsBooks in Los Angeles, remembers Valvano doing a signing for him, writing best wishes on the flyleaves and joking with the customers, all the while talking into his cellular phone—to someone at Nike, to his agent, to someone booking his appearances,—"and, I think, to his stockbroker."

College coaches, like athletes, have a keen sense of their professional mortality and a fear they'll leave a nickel out there unspoken for before they pass from the scene. Actually, the coaches are relatively secure, compared to their cousins, pro coaches. A 1994 survey showed that season's Top 20 coaches had an average tenure of 11.7 years; the coaches of the 16 NBA playoff teams averaged 2.8.

In college, mentors are merely tortured. The new hot diagnosis is "exhaustion" which just waylaid Duke's Mike Krzyzewski, the hottest name in the business; Maryland's intense Gary Williams and UNLV's overmatched Tim Grgurich.

Pressure manifests itself in a variety of ways. Bobby Knight, perhaps the best, brightest, and certainly the outstanding *enfant terrible* of his time, can be counted on to embarrass himself periodically. The most recent example came after his first-round loss to Missouri at Boise in 1995, when he went on an inopportune tirade (it was televised) at an NCAA moderator who reported, incorrectly, Knight wouldn't attend the press conference.

Knight: We only got two people that are gonna tell you I'm not gonna be here. One is our SID [sports information director] and the other is me. Who the hell told you I wasn't going to be here? I'd like to know, do you have any idea who it was?

Moderator: Yeah, I do, coach.

Knight: Who?

Moderator: I'll point him out to you in a while.

Knight: They were from Indiana, right?

Moderator: No, they're not—

Knight: No, weren't from Indiana and you didn't get it from anybody at Indiana, did you?

Moderator: Could we please go on?

Knight: No, I, I'll handle this the way I want to handle it, now that I'm here. You fucked it up to begin with. Now just sit here or leave, I don't give a shit what you do.

No action was taken against Knight but the NCAA fined Indiana $30,000.

No one has yet reined in Knight after a career dotted by chair throwing and grabbing, pushing or kicking players. When IU tried to object to his flip joke about rape to CBS's Connie Chung, Knight flew to New Mexico to suggest he might take the job there and brought the school to its knees.

There's only one Knight but many wannabes. At the adidas camp, two coaches vehemently defended his Boise tirade. They said they'd felt like that after an emotional loss, etc. What it suggested is how embattled the whole profession feels.

In practice, however, a precarious balance of power exists between university president and coach. The prexy may tinker with the rules but asserts his primacy at his own peril. President David Roselle, who cleaned out Kentucky's program after the Chris Mills–Shawn Kemp et al. scandals, was hounded out of office and went to Delaware. UNLV's Robert Maxson, who took on Jerry Tarkanian and dreamed of turning his school into a desert Duke, didn't survive Tark by much and wound up, ironically, moving down the ladder to Tark's old school, Long Beach State.

The modern college coach complains endlessly about his press coverage, his ivory-tower president, the insensitive rules that won't allow him to bring in deserving players, whatever....

At the 1994 NCAA tournament, Cal's Todd Bozeman said the press tried to "tear our family apart," speculating Jason Kidd and Lamond Murray would leave early (both did). Missouri's Norm Stewart, who once told a writer he knew where his family lived, was so offended at mentions of his six first-round losses in eight appearances, he read a list of every school Mizzou had beaten in NCAA openers since 1944.

"Stress?" says Connecticut's Jim Calhoun, twitching one eye theatrically.

"You know, I think what started out to be a game is being made more than ten kids in shorts running up and down the court. What we all started out to do, all of us, isn't quite the same game maybe we started with....

"March Madness has become so super big for all of us, everybody, kids included, that it's almost beyond the game. It's become a way of life, a culture, a subculture of its own. For this month, people who don't know anything at all about basketball are involved in pools— 'Hey, UConn with Calhoun coaching against Cincinnati'—and they know things that they normally wouldn't know.

"I just think there's no question, it's changed a great deal from what we all started with, which was a tournament to find out who's the best team in the country. It's become a happening for America.

"By the way, it's one of the great things that has greatly promoted our sport. The only thing it's done is take an edge where only one guy can win and as you get to a particular point, it becomes a lot of losers. Well, you can't win 26 games and be a loser. You can't be Lute Olson and win 24, 25 games and be a loser.

"That's why I think football coaches are so smart. Why they won't have a playoff."

Schea Cotton is at the Nike camp and it's not working out great.

Schea began this summer as the top-rated player in his class. He has been the young prince of L.A. since he was discovered—at age 11—by Pat Barrett, a summer coach and year-round influence peddler of note. Barrett was coaching against Schea's summer league team and there was no missing him.

"I thought the other team was trying to cheat and had brought a ringer," Barrett says. "I thought he was two, three years older than he was. I said, 'Hey, this kid's way too old.' I mean, the things he could do....

"Schea's one of a kind. I mean, not too many players come along like Schea, once in a lifetime. I mean, he had a man's body when he was 12 years old. He came with us in the fifth grade. We're playing 100 games a year and we've won a couple national [AAU] championships with him and we've been everywhere through the country with him."

Schea—no one could handle his given name, Vernon Chevalier—dunked at 12.

When he was 16, going into his sophomore year and one of only five invitees from his class, he was rated one of the 10 best players at the Nike camp by the respected Bob Gibbons, publisher of *All-Star Sports* and, as the man who selected the campers, the event's semi-official spokesman.

Now, at 17, there are whispers Schea's overrated. Another newsletter publisher has a two-word scouting report: "He's peaked."

Scouting players so young is difficult. Stars often mature early and fade as their age group catches up. Others blossom later, like Jordan, who was cut from his high school team as a sophomore. It's tricky to project where a 16-year-old will be in three or four years; NBA scouts have enough trouble guessing where a 21-year-old will be in one.

Nevertheless, it's the lingua franca of college coaches, whose careers depend on such judgments. The mainstream press covers recruiting lightly and gives the summer circuit a pass altogether, trying to hold the line on decorum, leaving a hungry market open to the newsletter publishers. The latest scoop has Schea failing to "dominate" this summer's Nike camp, as a player with his billing is expected to. Bob Gibbons says Schea was handed his lunch by 6-6 Corey Benjamin from Fontana High in Riverside.

"If you had to single out one kid who had the best week," Gibbons tells the Los Angeles *Times*, "it was Corey Benjamin. He was phenomenal. He hit three-pointers. He dunked. He played with an absolute fire that was something to behold. He went out to prove he was better than Schea Cotton, and he was."

More skepticism attaches itself to Schea's recent transfer, the latest in a series of maneuvers as his parents, James and Gaynell, look for the right schools for their sons.

Schea repeated the sixth grade, a common tactic to give a child an edge against his age group.

His older brother, James Jr., now a promising player at Long Beach State, started at Artesia High School but transferred to St. John Bosco—out of the shadow of Artesia stars Avondre Jones and Charles O'Bannon.

Schea enrolled at St. John Bosco but never played, transferring after a battle of wills with Coach Gary Breslin. Breslin said he was trying to teach Schea defensive fundamentals. James Sr. told *Sports Illustrated*'s Austin Murphy, "He was trying to break Schea. He wanted to tear him down and start from scratch, and we've got too much time and money invested in him for that."

Schea enrolled at Mater Dei in Orange County. James and Gaynell moved to Huntington Beach with him.

Two years later, Schea has just transferred back to St. John Bosco. There are reports he missed more than 50 days of school at Mater Dei.

Back from Nike, Schea is playing on a local AAU team in the Slam'N'Jam tournament at Long Beach State. James Sr. is in the bleachers, a lean man in a cowboy hat and boots. Born in rural Louisiana, he's easy-going and friendly. He says he believes in education first and makes sure Schea approaches it that way. James finds this scene scary and won't let Schea go anywhere alone.

"We have to be there to draw the line and say, 'Hey, this is a 17-year-old kid,' " says James.

"It does get scary. Because you see everybody coming at him and you just have to talk to him, tell him, 'You can't take anything from anybody, don't give out any interviews unless they talk to your mother or myself.'

"He wants to be just a kid. That's kind of hard to do, with all the publicity."

The Cottons are trying to figure out how to raise a prodigy, trying to strike a balance between protecting and promoting him. They let him talk for the *SI* piece but Gaynell, the confrontational parent, has tried to prevent other interviews or insisted on sitting in. Now, after Schea's transfer back to St. John Bosco, they have cut off the newspaper people.

Personable and relaxed, Schea seems remarkably unaffected. At this level, he's so overpowering he can play any position on the floor, but he's a decent ball handler and a good shooter. This will come in handy. Unless he grows, and he hasn't recently, he looks like a small forward in college and a big guard, should he make it to the NBA.

In summer leagues, where stars are allowed to roam free, he scores at will. Tonight, he gets elbowed in the nose, leaves, returns to find his team has blown a 10-point lead and scores three points in the final minute to win the game.

"It's a lot of fun," he says. "You have to keep it fun right now because it turns into a job later on so you got to have fun while you can."

Schea saw "Hoop Dreams" at Nike and before that. He says it put everything in perspective.

"You realize that basketball isn't everything," he says, "so you have to go to school and try and do your work as best to get a degree, if possible, and then go from there.... It's kind of scary 'cause you see the surgery on his [William Gates, the movie's sidetracked young basketball star] knee and everything and you start thinking about yourself, kind of put yourself in his place. That's why I thank God for my health and just take it day by day.

"Somebody can undercut you. Like, having a name is kind of good and kind of bad because they have people aiming for you. Like today. People that basically want to make a name for themselves if they get a key block on you, or maybe run up under you and stop you from dunking."

Later James says Gaynell is "a little upset" that he has allowed himself to be interviewed.

Gaynell says she has nothing to say.

"It's real quiet and peaceful," she says. "We're going to leave it the way it is....

"It's not an easy situation, living with a kid that can play basketball or, I guess, any other sport. Basketball season's over. We're out of the papers and the press and we'd like to keep it that way. I'm not speaking to anyone. I don't intend to give any more interviews."

There is speculation the Cottons have broken with Barrett, a former Mater Dei assistant who recommended the Orange County school. Schea just left Barrett's summer team but Barrett denies there's a rift.

"Things just didn't work out for him in Mater Dei," says Barrett, "but they were successful and he just wanted to move on. It's unfortunate but Mater Dei will go on and Schea will go on. Everybody would have liked to see him stay but he didn't.

"But Schea is Schea. Schea's a great player. His brother's a good support system for him. I mean, James [Junior] is a very levelheaded person. I always said if you put James's mind in Schea's body, you'd have another Michael Jordan. James is having a great summer. At first, I thought Schea was going the furthest between the two. Now it may be James."

Schea, 17 years old, a public figure who wears braces, is still trying to be a kid but it's getting harder.

CHAPTER TWELVE

SEATTLE '95:
TY AND ED'S INCREDIBLE
ADVENTURE

*This group of people— Edney, Zidek, Ed O'Bannon—
they'd taken their lumps. They'd been beaten by the
Fab Five in overtime. And then we lost to Tulsa. We
had lost some games over the years so, you know, they
understood.*

—JIM HARRICK

*I'd watch SportsCenter every night, just to get a feel
of how much respect or how much lack of respect
people had for our team. I wanted to let the guys know,
no matter how big you think you are, people don't see
it that way, and it's up to you to make them feel
that way. You have to earn your respect. You won't get
respect by sweeping Arizona, because no one really
cares about Arizona. People care about winning a
championship....*

—ED O'BANNON

Tulsa.

Tulsa, Tulsa, Tulsa, Tulsa, Tulsa, Tulsa, Tulsa, Tulsa, Tulsa, Tulsa, Tulsa, Tulsa.

That was all that was on anybody's mind. When UCLA basketball came up, somebody said, "What about Tulsa?" When they won a game, the anchors on ESPN's "SportsCenter" did Tulsa lines. They might as well have renamed the school UCLA-T, the University of California at Los Angeles-Tulsa.

Actually, UCLA-T was loaded. In an era in which top players turned pro early, UCLA was a rarity, with three senior starters including 22-year-old Ed O'Bannon. They had four starters back from a team that won 21 games and a hot freshman class.

They were ranked sixth in the pre-season Associated Press poll. *Sports Illustrated* picked them first while calling them "underachieving beachcombers from the underachieving Pac-10, a team that was last seen falling behind Tulsa, 46–17."

Jim Harrick, asked for a reaction to the pick by *SI*, called it "stupid" and "ludicrous."

Arkansas, bringing back most of its championship squad, was an overwhelming favorite. Experts wondered if the Bruins could forget Tulsa and what would happen to Harrick if they couldn't.

Nobody was ready for what happened.

This season would have several turning points: the reality-check against Kentucky, the grisly loss at Oregon, the great Mizzou finish.

But the first wasn't readily apparent, since it had already happened, at half-time of the Tulsa game, with no immediate impact. The Bruins trailed at the time, 63–38, and if they cut it to 112–102, it looked like the vagaries of extended garbage time.

Someone had taken charge. In an upset, it was Ed O'Bannon.

O'Bannon had many attributes. He was a nice young man and a good player but as a leader, he'd been strictly follow-my-example. He seemed to lack the confidence or the desperation to put himself on the line. By half-time of the Tulsa game, desperation wasn't a problem any more.

"I never had this feeling where I wanted to take off my uniform and just quit," he said of that moment, "because I felt like I didn't deserve to wear the UCLA uniform.

"We were in the locker room, we were all kind of sitting in there, no one was really being emotional or anything and it was kind of frustrating to me because I've been brought up in a competitive atmosphere and a family where you just don't accept whippings like that. And that's what we was getting.

"Basically, what I said to the team was, either you show some heart, show some pride or go out there with your tail between your legs and have them continue to kick your butt."

The melody may not have counted as much as the volume. Harrick, on his way in after conferring with his assistants, could feel the vibrations through the walls.

"Ed's the kind of guy that will defer everything to the older players," Harrick says. "He's so nice and polite, even though I always felt he was our leader. He would always let the other guys do it because I named them captain because they were seniors.

"At half-time of the Tulsa game, before I got into the locker room, I heard him just screaming and yelling, after 'em all. And I felt at that point, and I really didn't know it at the moment, but I felt that as I look back now, that was the moment he said, 'OK, I'm going to take over this team.'

"And he certainly did."

The story of the O'Bannons' personal growth at UCLA is also the story of the UCLA renaissance, and all three were precarious. Ed had arrived by accident after UNLV went on probation. Charles was going to Kentucky.

Ed thought he'd play two years of college and go to the NBA. Instead, he blew out his knee and if it wasn't a career-ender, it was the next worst thing. Going into his final season, he still wasn't all

209

the way back. The NBA teams knew about him but he hadn't excited them yet.

The nice thing about Ed, once he figured out what he had to do, he went after it. A month after the Tulsa game, before the semester ended and everyone scattered for the summer, the Bruins were working out and talking among themselves and vowing next year would be different.

Ed's personal life came together. A month after the Tulsa game, his girlfriend Rosa gave birth to a son, Aaron. If Ed had been numb before, he was now your standard blissed-out first-time Dad. He brought Aaron to games. He bragged about him. Sometimes, it seemed as if he didn't want to talk about anything but Aaron.

"At first," he said later, "I wouldn't say I was ashamed but I had mixed emotions about being a father out of wedlock.

"He showed me. He's a person, he's growing every day. His life depends on his mother and I. That to me is more important than anything. It taught me that basketball is just a game, basically.

"We went on a trip, it was about three or four days. I came back and he was at the baby-sitter's and he was out in the front yard in his walker. He had his back to me. He turned around and he almost jumped out of his walker, he was so excited, jumping around and stuff. That to me, that was the best part of the trip.

"My parents talk about Charles and me. I used to think why are they bragging? All these people aren't interested in what they have to say about us. But I found myself being a parent, you want to talk about your kid all the time. I never understood that....

"I wanted the world to see that I had a son and how beautiful he is to me."

The season took shape in a hurry.

The second game was against powerful Kentucky at the Anaheim Pond. The Wildcats led by 10 points but the Bruins came back to win, 82–81, when freshman J. R. Henderson made two free throws with :00.6 left.

Meanwhile, Henderson's classmate, Toby Bailey, played briefly and sulked about it.

Bailey was an explosive player and anything but shy. He dated Koa Warren, Mike's daughter. Like many of his peers, he couldn't imagine a pecking order based on experience. This wasn't the start he'd envisioned.

"I've grown up with different players who are freshmen around the nation like Ricky Price [Duke] and Jelani Gardner [Cal]," he said later.

"That day before the game, I was watching Ricky and I think he got player of the game against Illinois. He's like one of my best friends. I was just happy for him. That's great for him. And I went out there and I wasn't starting and I didn't get that much playing time and I wasn't really performing." (He played 10 minutes and scored one point.) "I was just a little disappointed and a little angry. I think that just showed I wasn't really that mature at the beginning of the season."

Here came the loud voice of experience, Ed O'Bannon. Harrick, watching, was thrilled.

"Boy," Harrick said later, "Ed just jumped right up into him— 'Get up here and enjoy this with your teammates.' And boy, I'll tell you, his attitude has been picture perfect ever since."

The Bruins started 6–0 and were ranked No. 1 when they went on their annual Oregon swing.

In Eugene, where they'd lost a one-point game the season before on a rebound basket, costing them a share of the conference title, they gave up 25 offensive rebounds and fell, 82–72.

Harrick was ejected with :37 left. The Ducks made both technical fouls to break open a four-point game. There was a mob scene on the floor afterward and Bruin players had to fight their way off.

The whole thing looked like a familiar loss of poise. A day later, the Los Angeles *Times* ran a follow-up under the headline, "Harrick: Always a Question."

Nor did UCLA fans yet sense a bandwagon that needed jumping on.

Playing in their cozy 12,800-seat arena, the Bruins would sell out two home games all season. On February 1, the days before they lost to Cal, 100–93, at Pauley, the Los Angeles *Times* carried this:

Think college basketball is a big deal? The Saturday telecast of the Cal–UCLA game drew a 3.6 rating in a five-county Southland area. Four other programs shown at the same time drew higher ratings: a rerun of "Three's Company," two reruns of "Family Ties," and a "Baywatch" rerun.

Ed O'Bannon, channel surfing and reading everything he could to find motivational material, never had to stretch a point.

"Leading up to the first Oregon game," he says, "we hadn't lost and there were a couple teams that were undefeated around then. And we lost, and the next day the papers were 'Here they go, Harrick gets a tech, what is he thinking, the team folded under pressure.'

"And then we barely beat Oregon State and it was unbelievable. It was, 'This team, they might as well just mail it in.' "

For years Bruin teams had turned whiney when they lost in the little gyms at Cal, Stanford, the Oregons and Washingtons, to say nothing of playing before Lute Olson's red-clad rowdies, but this one was different. With only an occasional lapse, the players worked at the defensive end. They didn't complain about their press, the calls, the breaks, the burden of being a Bruin.

Two weeks after the loss at Oregon, they headed for Arizona, where Harrick had beaten the Wildcats once in six seasons while taking beatings by 19, 24, and 38 points. This time, they were coming ready as he could get them.

"I told 'em, 'I'm not going with you, Edney, you and O'Bannon, Zidek.' " Harrick says. "As my opening talk Monday, I said, 'I'm not going.'

"You know, they kinda look at you. I said, 'I don't want to be out there, getting my butt beat by 24 and 19. I'm not going down there unless you guys bring your attitude and go down there and compete. We don't talk about winning and losing. I'm talking about not getting beat by 19 or 24!'

"We kind of tried to set the tone that way and Tyus Edney dominated the game at Arizona. He scored the first four points, took Damon Stoudamire right to the basket and scored on him and set the tone for the whole game. He got 22 or something like that."

Edney had 19 points, nine rebounds and five assists. The Bruins won, 71–61. When they won at Arizona State, Coach Bill Frieder, who assembled Michigan's 1989 champions, said they were "better than any team I ever coached."

They kept getting better, too. Bailey became a starter in February. The Bruins won their last 13 games. They steamrolled their last six opponents by an average of 19 points.

"We started kind of dominating games," says O'Bannon. "The guys were healthy, and we were together, no one was bickering about anything. Usually in the middle of the season towards the end, you can tell whether or not if you're going to win just by the bickering that goes on, if there is any.

"It's funny because we had cliques on the team but they were good cliques. We had one group called 'Crew' and another one. And they battled each other. But it wasn't a bad thing.

"One side of the bench was one and they all sat in certain areas. It was fun, and it kept everyone loose. It was just great."

O'Bannon was the most fortunate of young men, able to appreciate the moment and to seize it. He began bringing his video camera to games and taping everything. On Seniors Night, his last game in Pauley, he hoisted Aaron over his head in pre-game ceremonies, scored 24 points in a romp over Oregon, then bent down and kissed center court. Then he told his teammates, who were about to put on "Pac-10 Champions" baseball caps, to take them off since they weren't interested in a mere conference title.

"Me and him was sitting on the bench," said the effervescent Cameron Dollar, "and he was like, 'Man, we haven't done anything yet.'

"I was like, 'I know, man.'

"He said we should take 'em off, tell everybody to take 'em off.'

'So I get up and I'm the vocal guy: 'Take em off!' And then if anybody gives me any problems, I say, 'Hey! *Ed* said it!'

"And that's how it gets done."

If you draw little Florida International in the first round of the NCAA tournament, what don't you say?

Correct. Even if you've never heard of such a school and have no idea where it is (Miami), you don't volunteer that to the media.

It wasn't easy. FIU was 11–18, the worst record for an NCAA tournament team in 39 years. Coach Bob Weltich had announced he wouldn't return as far back as January when his team was 3–10.

The FIU center was 6-5. At home, they played before an average of 539. When they upset Mercer to win the Trans-America Athletic Conference tournament, the players laughingly chanted, "We want UCLA."

To which assistant coach Clarence Flournory said he responded: "No, you don't! No, you don't!"

Said the other assistant, Ed Riggan: "The biggest thing is that people will finally know where FIU is. It should make it easier to recruit for whoever gets the job."

People had to look quick. The Bruins set upon these human hors-d'oeuvres and cruised to a 92–56 victory.

For once, they missed Indiana.

From the moment the pairings were announced, Bruin coaches were grumbling about having to face IU in the second round when the national top seed should still be facing cream puffs. The experts noticed the bracket; Dick Vitale said UCLA was ripe to be beaten. But in a mild upset, the Hoosiers lost in the first round to Missouri.

The Bruins had another problem: Edney's left ankle, sprained in the opener.

An adventurous player, the 5-10, 152-pound Edney had had his share of injuries: a bad back, tendinitis in his knees, etc. Battered, he was still a fine player and had been since he arrived, a large-eyed tyke (he said girls he didn't know gave him hugs) who looked eight years old.

Appearances notwithstanding, he wasn't the team mascot, more like the eye of the storm: quiet, confident, a little withdrawn around strangers. By the end of his freshman year, he'd made Darrick

Martin, a two-year starter, into a reserve and had been a fixture ever since. The Bruins called him Scary Boy.

He was all point guard. He liked having the ball, telling everyone where to go, taking it to bigger guys, which, in his case, meant everyone. For months Ed O 'Bannon had been insisting to everyone he was the best player on the team.

"We had taken Tyus to a couple doctors and got his tendinitis straightened out," Harrick says. "I'd always told his dad, 'He's playing about 85 percent, in my opinion.' Because I'd seen him in his sophomore year, he was magnificent. Mag-nificent!

"All through his junior year, he had nagging injuries, nothing serious but his tendinitis in his left knee—that makes you play 90 percent instead of 100 percent.

"We got him straightened out a little bit and about the last couple weeks of the season, he got to feeling really good and in the tournament, he played like Tyus Edney. That's the way he plays. He plays like that in practice all the time.

"Have you ever seen anybody block his shot? It's amazing to me. I keep telling him, 'Don't go in there, don't go in there.' He goes in there."

If there was one thing Edney knew, it was how to play hurt so when they tipped it off against Mizzou, he was out there, as everyone knew he'd be.

It was a struggle from the get-go. Norm Stewart's Tigers were deep and scrappy and in this game, red-hot. They hit 64 percent of their three-pointers. The Bruins couldn't turn them off and tried to keep up.

"It was funny," says Ed O'Bannon, "because all the other teams had already played, like, a serious game. We didn't really get much out of our first game. Missouri, they'd already played Indiana so they were already into it. And we already had a week off. So it was kind of hard to get into it. I think that's basically why we came out flat.

"They kept making all of their shots. It was like us against Michigan that time. They had us on the ropes. Every time we would make a run, they would hit like two three-pointers in a row that would just crush us.

"We did all we could as far as playing without intensity. And they played a great game. That's what I remember, how well they played. They made all their shots. Man, big fellas, 6-9, stepping out—it was unbelievable. I'm glad they didn't have a chance to shoot like a half-court shot at the end. They would've made it."

In the closing seconds, with UCLA leading by a point, Mizzou freshman Kendrick Moore drove into the lane and hit Julian Winfield open underneath.

Winfield laid it up with 4.8 left to make it Missouri 74, UCLA 73.

Was there more time than that left in Harrick's UCLA career? Harrick says he never thought about that, never worried about the game for an instant.

OK, maybe for an instant.

"I will say this," he says, "I believe that coaching and teaching is communicating your ideas effectively to others. *Never* have I ever been tested in my life more than when the ball went through the basket and Missouri scored and I had five players turn and rivet 10 eyes right at me.

"It was like they're stuck in a foxhole with a gun at their head, saying, 'Help me Coach, we're desperate.'

"At that moment, that was a desperate basketball team. Only time I saw them all year shrug their shoulders and put their head down. Because we just kept coming back and they kept hitting threes. And when they scored right there, I reached back for everything I'd ever known about basketball.

"I knew Tyus could go the length of the floor because I watched Jerry West do it and I had my teams practice it for years and years. I got a drill from Don Nelson, a six-second drill, where you give the ball to a guy under the basket and he's got to face the defender, go the length of the floor and try to score in six seconds. And we work on that six, seven times a year.

"I had seen Edney do that. He had won four games like that as a sophomore so there was no question in my mind, he could go the length of the floor in 4.8 seconds. No question in my mind they're not going to foul him. No question in my mind he's going to take the ball to the rim.

"One of my assistants says, 'We've got to throw the long pass.'

"I said, 'No, we're not doing that. That's my decision.'

"We got up out of the huddle and I put my arm around him, knowing the Michigan game [in the '93 tournament]. I said, 'Edney, you... shoot... the ball! Make... sure... *you*... shoot the ball!' "

On the other bench, Stewart sat his foul-prone 7-foot shot-blocking freshman, Sammie Haley, and went with dependable, low-jumping 6-9 Derek Grimm. Stewart didn't want to take any chances. He had the lead; the Bruins had four-point-eight to see if they could take it off him.

Edney caught the in-bounds pass uncontested and started up the floor.

Missouri's Jason Sutherland, shadowing him cautiously, tried to steer him toward one sideline or the other. Edney found himself headed for the left boundary and, at full stride, went behind his back left-handed and cut back into the middle.

Sutherland was behind, out of the play as Edney approached the top of the circle. Grimm came out, cautiously, intent on getting in the way without fouling.

Edney, far quicker, drove him back, veered to the right a smidgin, enough to get off a running five-footer that banked high off the board....

And, as the buzzer went off, fell in.

OK, what used to be the most famous play in UCLA history? The Bruins went crazy. Back home in L.A., fans cheered out windows and honked horns.

"It was a good thing we didn't lose," O'Bannon says. "That was the feeling. And thank you, Tyus. He saved us. The first time he could've saved us, he didn't. But this time, he did."

"I know if we had lost," said Harrick after that game, rolling his eyes upward, "... well, I don't want to answer that."

Let's just say there would have been some second guessing. Maybe a groundswell big enough to get him fired? Pete Dalis had been insisting Harrick was secure but this would have been a major firestorm. L.A. was on the bandwagon now and Harrick's decision not to throw the long pass had been a daring one.

After the season, Harrick would write a book, *Embracing the Legend*. In it, he said of that play:

"It was like standing in front of a firing squad, ready for that final moment, and all 12 guns fail to go off."

You didn't want to mess with the Bruins now.

The West regional was at Oakland, an hour's plane ride from home. They played Mississippi State and Connecticut and routed both.

Before the Mississippi State game, Harrick lit his players up for real, warning them against any future letdowns. O'Bannon said it was the maddest he'd ever seen his coach. Mississippi State had a fine sophomore center, 6-11 Erick Dampier, but Edney canceled him out with two early trips down the lane, drawing two fouls on him and turning him into an afterthought. The Bruins ran up a 36-point lead and won, 86–67.

UConn's Huskies were supposed to be tougher. Ask them if they weren't.

They had been ranked No. 1 much of the season but a late fade had sent them west, away from their frenetic fans, for which they were actually thankful.

UConn was a very modern power, with starters from Israel, California, South Carolina, Utah, and Washington, everywhere, in fact except Connecticut. The Huskies were, nevertheless, the pride of their adopted state and were covered by a 19-newspaper press corps nicknamed "The Horde." They had all the stardom they could handle and then some.

"You can't walk through a mall," said Coach Jim Calhoun, trying to explain his players' delight at being so far from home. "There's a great many parts to that. I know when you're a freshman, you think it's wonderful. When you're a sophomore, you think it's pretty good. When you're a junior, you don't go to the mall."

The pride of the Big East, they embodied the new snobbery. Once players went west for sunshine; now they went east to get on ESPN in prime time.

Calhoun said Edney wasn't as fast as hotshot Georgetown freshman Allan Iverson, which the Bruins took as a challenge, coming as it did in the pre-game bouquet-toss. Unfortunately, Calhoun would get to see just how fast Tyus was. He played a full-court press; if the Bruins could run it, they'd be in the open court.

The Bruins led by four points with :03.6 left in the half when they called time-out. Edney then came back and hit a running 26-foot three-pointer and, uncharacteristically, struck a hands-on-hips pose as teammates mobbed him.

UCLA ran up a 23-point lead as Toby Bailey, a force in an open game, dunked his way to 26 points. They won, 102–96, and they were in the Final Four. On the sideline, Harrick and assistant Mark Gottfried cried.

"I had the game when Jim Harrick, God bless him, called the time-out with 3.6 in the half," says Al McGuire, now doing color commentary for CBS.

"I say, which no one else is gonna say on TV, I guarantee you no one's gonna say it—and I love Jim Harrick, we're all brothers—so I say, 'I mean, that's the craziest time-out I've ever seen called in my life.'

"And this guy, Edney, comes and makes the Hail Mary. You say, they can't lose. I don't care what Arkansas does, they can ... not ... lose."

Actually, Charles O'Bannon had called the time-out. By now, it didn't seem to matter.

"It was a lot of fun," says Ed O'Bannon. "The funnest thing about it, though, was the day before the game we kept hearing about how they were going to run us into the ground. I didn't want to say anything at that time but I couldn't believe that these guys thought they were going to outrun us. It was, what are they saying?

"I know our games are on late on the East Coast but you had to have seen one game. Oh well."

A 50-foot inflated basketball with "NCAA" on it, sitting atop the Space Needle....

The Bud Light "ladies"—four bow-legged guys with hairy calves in dresses and high heels—walking down the street, en route to a press conference....

Downtown streets cordoned off for a new mall, lined by tents sponsored by Nike, Foot Locker, et al....

The annual Dick Vitale Sound-Alike National Finals....

Music all day long in the parks: At Occidental Park, the Boogie Brown Band, followed by Stampede Pass, Guitar Slim and the Caribbean Superstars Steel Drums....

Fan Jam at the Convention Center (10 A.M. Rick Barnes, Clemson; Tom Davis, Iowa: Noon clinic with Bill Packer, Steve Lappas, Villanova). Fans can dunk on low hoops, shoot at 10-foot hoops, play on virtual-reality hoops....

Licensed merchandise—caps, T-shirts, how about a $1,400 hand-stitched leather jacket? The NCAA says it expects $750,000 worth of this stuff will move here....

Sixteen corporate partners who have bought "exclusive" marketing rights to the name "Final Four," including American Airlines, Coca-Cola, Frito-Lay, Pizza Hut, Rawlings, Hershey and Double-tree Hotels....

It's a good thing, as promotions director Alfred White says, the NCAA is so "conservative about the commercialization of its championships." You'd hate to see what this would turn into, otherwise.

This is Final Four weekend, the culmination of March Madness, now second in sheer impact only to the Super Bowl, spilling into Monday prime time and early April—and it has dollar signs coming out of its ears. "Trust us," writes the Seattle *Times*' Ron Judd, addressing the tourists, "we relish the mere sight of your $miling face$."

Top hotels like the Four Seasons sold out a year ago. The good restaurants stopped taking reservations weeks ago although, for a good friend or a valued customer, one can find something, as Mick McHugh, owner of the steakhouse F.X. McCrory, did for some senior officials of Key Bank in Cleveland who begged him for a table and game tickets. McHugh tells the Wall Street Journal he only charged them "a grand apiece."

The NCAA does all right itself. In 1964 when UCLA won its first title, gross receipts were under $500,000. In 1975 when John Wooden won his last title, they were $4 million.

In 1994 gross receipts—*not* including those from TV—were $154 million. CBS paid an additional $143 million.

It was a humbler affair when it started in 1939, the NCAA's answer to the established NIT, which was held annually in Madison Square Garden. In 1943, after the NCAA championship drew an announced 6,500 in Kansas City, it moved to the Garden, too, and stayed there six years.

The NIT was still the big ticket. In 1944, Utah accepted an NIT bid (it offered the bigger guarantee), lost, got into the NCAA and won. As late as 1950, the NCAA championship was a rematch of the NIT's, Bradley vs. CCNY. City College won both games and titles.

As the game's popularity increased, top players began going to big state schools rather than the NIT's independents. In the '50s, Bill Russell, Wilt Chamberlain, Jerry West and Oscar Robertson appeared in NCAA Tournaments and the spotlight swung.

In 1964, the Bruins won their first title before 10,864 in Kansas City's musty old Municipal Arena. The NCAA liked the place because it was close to home (the organization's offices were there). Sports Network paid $140,000 for TV rights. The final game wasn't shown in many small towns.

Five years later, when Kareem Abdul-Jabbar and his teammates won the Bruins' fifth title, NBC arrived with a rights fee of $547,000.

In 1973, when Bill Walton went 21 for 22, the finals, which NBC had just moved to Monday night, set a ratings record. It lasted until 1979 when the Magic Johnson–Larry Bird game set the basketball record, pro, college, or Olympic, that still stands.

As entertainment, the tournament was as good as it gets, awakening a nation's fans to the excitement the game could offer. One classic followed another: North Carolina's victory over Georgetown on freshman Michael Jordan's jumper in 1982; N.C. State's last-second upset of Houston's mighty Phi Slama Jama in 1983; little Villanova's "perfect game" that toppled Georgetown in 1985; Indiana's victory over Syracuse on Keith Smart's last-second jumper in 1987; Duke's upset of "unbeatable" UNLV in the '91 semifinals; the fabled 104–103 Duke–Kentucky shootout in the '92 Eastern regionals with five lead changes in overtime, Christian Laettner hitting a game-winning corkscrew jumper at the buzzer and teammate Thomas Hill putting his head in his hands and weeping on the floor; Carolina's victory over Michigan's Fab Five in '93 when Chris Webber called a time-out he didn't have.

In 1982, a surprise bid by CBS stole the tournament. In 1991, the network put up a blockbuster $1 billion for seven years to keep it.

Then, with three years left on the deal, CBS extended it by another five—for $750 million more—making the NCAA's annual take $219 million. CBS vice president Len DeLuca called it "our foundation event."

Innocence fled along with intimacy. The '95 venue was the Kingdome, which seated 38,646, some of them hundreds of yards away from the floor. Only 9,640 tickets went on public sale, the prizes in the lottery which drew almost 100,000 entries. The rest were set aside beforehand for the schools, coaches, NCAA big shots and corporate sponsors.

The '96 game is set for the Meadowlands but after that, it's all domes: Hoosier, Alamo, Thunder, Hoosier again, Hump, Georgia...

Welcome back, UCLA, even if it looks a little different to you.

The Bruins had already checked out the Kingdome. On their annual Washington trip, Harrick brought them over for a look at the promised land. The promised land had an RV show on it but they thought it was inspiring, anyway.

Their semifinal matchup was Oklahoma State, unglamorous but dangerous. The OSU coach was Eddie Sutton, the refugee from the Kentucky scandals, an old-line teacher of fundamentals. His game plans were simple and his teams executed them. If Sutton didn't want the Bruins to run, they wouldn't run.

The Seattle *Post-Intelligencer*, in its matchup comparison gave Sutton the nod over Harrick. Sutton had a droll 7-0, 290-pound center named Bryant "Big Country" Reeves with a lot of moves and a feathery touch for a farm boy. Otherwise, the Cowboys were short of firepower. Theyt would have to beat the Bruins with defense and might have, except for Scary Boy.

Midway through the second half, with Oklahoma State within 50–49 after an 8–0 run, Harrick turned the game over to Edney.

Edney was rolling for real. He had hit another highlight-reel special, a blind, flip over his head with his back to the basket in the first half. He had sprained his right wrist taking a charge and was having trouble shooting jumpers but the Cowboys couldn't keep him out of the lane. He had greased the OSU point, Andre Owens, and Sutton was auditioning his reserves for the role.

Harrick was Wooden disciple enough to resist one-on-one basketball. In the '93 loss to Michigan, Shon Tarver had turned into a monster but Harrick had stopped short of running every play for him. He had wondered about it since.

"About the eight-minute mark," Harrick says, "I finally realized that Owens could not stop Edney. So with eight minutes to go, I'm up yelling 'T-a-a-ke him! T-a-a-ke him! T-a-a-ke him!'

"But Owens had three fouls, then he got the fourth and then he was tenuous and Edney just ... poof!

"So he made four big, big, big-time plays and the last one was bigger than all of them."

Edney's last one was a drive into the chest of Big Country, himself. Tyus got the shot off, made it, was fouled and made the free throw. UCLA won, 74–61. Jack Nicholson, the new Bruin fan, walked off the court with them.

Edney went to the hospital the next day to have his wrist X-rayed. It was put into a temporary cast as a precaution.

The only way to be the best was beat the best. The Bruins would play Arkansas in the finals.

The experts lined right up with Arkansas. Of 23 coaches and commentators polled by the *Post-Intelligencer*, 18 picked the Hogs, including ESPN's Digger Phelps and Dick Vitale.

"I'm going with the Razorbacks," announced Vitale. "I've gone with the Hogs all the way, and I can't change now. Hog fans should be going bananas."

Arkansas had had a difficult season, trying to defend its championship, but the Hogs were on a roll now. Their semifinal victory over North Carolina had been typical; the game turned when Dwight Stewart, a chubby 6-9 center, hit a half-court shot just before half-time.

They were bigger and deeper than the Bruins. Coach Nolan Richardson played 10 players and pressed; he called it "40 minutes of hell."

Richardson was a little bear of a man with a bass voice that filled a room like a stereo speaker. A college football player, he had grown up poor and black amid all the prejudice El Paso, Texas, could muster in the '40s and '50s. He burned with a righteous anger and wasted no opportunity to preach to a captive audience, to complain about the lack of respect accorded him, his program, athletes.

This was college basketball in the '90s. Deliberately or not, coaches united their teams with a siege mentality, us against the world. There was so much complaining, the interview sessions before the NCAA finals were unofficially known as "No Respect Day."

Few could match Rollin' Nolan. When his string of disrepects was interrupted by the sound of a freight train passing the press pavilion outside the Kingdome, Richardson murmured into the mike, "Even the train doesn't like me."

Respect was coming, in one matchup anyway. The *Post Intelligencer* gave the nod to Richardson over Harrick.

By contrast, the Bruins were relaxed and carefree. Harrick, who had every reason and probably some temptation to gloat, didn't. His players, asked about the burden of being a Bruin, etc., were remarkably upbeat.

Harrick said Edney wouldn't practice but didn't sound overly concerned about it.

By that evening, Harrick was getting more concerned by the minute.

By the next day, he was numb. Edney's wrist wasn't responding. He'd wrap it and try to play but what would he be able to do against the Razorback press and Richardson's rotating, ball-hawking guard corps?

"By the time we left from the hotel for the game, I knew he wasn't going to play," says Harrick. "I was devastated. I didn't even want to get on the bus.

"I went out there and [UCLA football coach] Terry Donahue and his wife were there, they're with our boosters, they're having a good time. They've been out on a boat, toured the harbor, went up on the Space Needle. Oh, he's having a great time!

"So he's laughing and joking. I'm getting on the bus, I'm just devastated. *Devastated!* He comes over, gives me a little pat, says 'Hey....'

"I say, 'Terry, he can't play. I don't know what I'm going to do.'

"He says, 'Listen, if I can beat SC with John Barnes, anything in sports can happen.'

"We get to the game and I'm really sniveling. They [his assistants] are saying, 'Hey, remember Willis Reed in '70, came out on one leg'—you know, they were giving me all that crap.

"I said, 'Hey, fellas, this is the real deal. This is Arkansas, we're in the Final Four and they're defending national champions.' "

Harrick's pre-game speech was different, too. A man who prides himself on not cursing in front of his players, he concluded his remarks yelling, "Fuck Arkansas!"

Hoping against hope, Harrick started Edney. He was a senior, he'd gotten them there, maybe the adrenaline would kick in, maybe there'd be a miracle, maybe he could do something inspirational, like Willis Reed.

In the time it took the Arkansas guards to sniff out that sore wrist, take the ball from Edney and run off eight points in a row and a 10–5 lead, Harrick knew that wasn't happening. Edney was going to have to come out.

"Never even looked at him," says Harrick. "Wouldn't look at him. I refused to look at him.

"I didn't want him to change my mind so I wouldn't look at him. Sometimes, you look and see the hurt in their eyes—he's not to ever question anything but it *is* the last game."

Indeed, Edney cast a plaintive look at Harrick's back, told assistant coach Steve Lavin, "It's not right, it's not fair," and came out for the last time as a collegian.

In went Cameron Dollar.

Dollar had been alerted he might be needed by Edney but he didn't need that. Dollar had been born ready.

He was a brash young man, one of the contingent of born-again Christians on the Bruins. He had made his original visit to UCLA, wearing a suit and tie and had asked to see Peter Dalis, the only recruit Dalis could remember making such a request. When Dollar played, he'd bawl out everyone, up to and including O'Bannon.

The first time he touched the ball, the Razorbacks' Clint McDaniels stripped it, scored on a lay-up and it was 12–5.

Dollar had two more turnovers the rest of the night. The Bruins dusted the press and turned the game into a layup line. O'Bannon was soaring. Toby Bailey was showing off his repertoire, standard dunks, reverse dunks, tip dunks. Corliss (Big Nasty) Williamson was trying to knock bigger George Zidek out of the way and it wasn't working. Corliss was on his way to 3-for-16 and a new nickname: Scoreless.

The Bruins tied it by half-time. They took the lead. They put the Razorbacks away.

"As I look back," says Harrick, "Cameron's turnover might have been the best thing that ever happened to us because they kinda thought they were going to come in for the kill. They really came after us then and it opened the floor and that's when Cameron's really good, when they open the floor."

"It was a weird feeling," said Bannon, "because the man who carried us, basically, you can say all you want to say, but you've got your top dog sitting on the bench.

"It was a devastating feeling. How could we get all this way and then get to a certain point and not be able to get over the hump? It was like climbing a hill and getting to the top and then there's a huge pit that you can't climb over. How come you didn't tell us about this when we were climbing up the hill?

"But we got some rope and climbed over that, too. The rope was named Cameron Dollar."

O'Bannon scored 31 points, the most in the finals in 17 years. When the game ended, he sank to his knees on the court and put his hands over his eyes.

"I thought about how hard it was to get there," he said later. "All I could think about was how people said we had no heart, we had no courage, that we couldn't do it. And when we had our chance, it was against the No. 1 team...."

The post-game ceremony went according to the schedule that had been passed out to the media:

• Winning team will remain on the floor for spontaneous celebration while staging is set up at center court.

• FIVE MINUTES (approximately) after conclusion of the game, CBS will go to a two-minute commercial. On that cue, winning team and chair of NCAA Men's Basketball Committee will be escorted to the awards platform.

There was one departure. Presented with the outstanding player trophy, O'Bannon called Edney up to the platform. "There's the real MVP right here" he said. "Right here, man. Give it up."

Someone mentioned the tournament exploits of another freshman, Michael Jordan, to Bailey, who'd scored 26 points.

"I was thinking of Michael the other day," said Toby. "I was thinking, 'This is where stars are made, in the finals.' "

Months later, Harrick was back in his office, with a smile that wouldn't die and a season he'd never forget.

"I thought more than anything, we had great leadership," says Harrick. "I thought that was the key.

"They led by their leadership, they led by example and certainly all three of the seniors were unbelievably unselfish. And I don't know that I'll ever coach in my career and have three guys like them again."

On the other hand, he'd paid enough dues waiting for them to come along.

AND THEY ALL LIVED HAPPILY
EVER AFTER

Sure they did.

This was still UCLA, after all, where they don't like disappointment and treasure their rights of expression. A few days after winning the title, when the Bruins raised their eleventh championship banner in a ceremony in Pauley and Los Angeles Mayor Richard Riordan told the capacity crowd, "Next year No. 12 will go up!" Jim Harrick almost tackled him.

"I voted for you," Harrick said, seizing the microphone. "Don't go talking about next year. I've got enough problems."

On the other hand, the Bruins never celebrated a championship the way they celebrated this one.

Ed O'Bannon won the John Wooden Award, became the eighth pick in the NBA draft and got a three-year, $3.9 million contract.

George Zidek went on the first round, to Charlotte.

In the lone disappointment of the spring, Tyus Edney, who had suffered another injury, breaking a bone in his hand at a pre-draft camp, fell to Sacramento on the second round. One month into his first season he was the King's starting point guard.

Harrick got another extension, this time with a raise in it. His contract now runs through 2000 and his salary has been boosted to $420,000. He was named Coach of the Year by the Pac-10, the Naismith Committee, and the National Association of Basketball Coaches.

Bruin fans almost buried the Los Angeles *Times* with letters, many savaging college basketball writer Gene Wojciechowski, who'd picked Arkansas along with most of the big-name experts.

> Ordinarily, I would defend Gene Wojciechowski in his right to be witless, vapid, senseless, obtuse, moronic, inane, inferior, foolish, feebleminded, dumb, dull, dense, brainless, or asinine but this time he has abused the privilege.
>
> —JAY S. LOWY, TARZANA

Or they pilloried the unfaithful among their own ranks:

> I guess the bashers will have to settle for hanging another national championship banner from Pauley Pavilion's rafters instead of Jim Harrick.
>
> —STEPHEN DUE, INGLEWOOD

Or in one case, a Bruin fan even hinted he might have been a tad fickle, himself.

> On this day of Passover, let us give thanks to Jim Harrick and his Bruins who, without Tyus' mighty right hand but with Ed's outstretched arm, brought us from sorrow to joy, from mourning to festivity, from darkness to great light, and from bondage to redemption. I would eat crow but it's not kosher. Next year in the Meadowlands.
>
> —RABBI RONALD LEVINE RESEDA

Let the good times roll.

By the end of the summer, Harrick had been to Washington, D.C. and Las Vegas twice; to Lisbon, Portugal, and Nagoya, Japan. He and Sally had vacationed in Maui and the Portuguese Riviera and had been to the Academy Awards. He'd gone to the final round of the Masters.

In July, he pulled out his appointment calendar in his Westwood office to see where he'd been.

March 27, 1995: The Harricks attend the Academy Awards as guests of "Forrest Gump" co-producer Wendy Finerman, daughter of UCLA team physician Gerald Finerman.

"They hosted Sally and I to the Academy Awards, took us to the Governor's Ball," said Harrick. "That was the Monday night after the regionals, before the Final Four. I would probably normally not go but it was a once-in-a-lifetime opportunity for my wife to go see that and it was exciting.

"Everything in the world, you go around and say, 'Well, that's big time.' That is a good definition of big time....

"You're standing beside Clint Eastwood. I mean, you're right beside Clint Eastwood! And Jodie Foster. And [Sylvester] Stallone and Dustin Hoffman and Robert DeNiro. I mean, Paul Newman.... Those guys, you're just kind of, 'There they are!' My wife and I, we just kind of walked by, we never said anything, we just kind of walked by.

"They've got eight lanes of limos—you've got to go in a limo, now. So we went with Chancellor Charles Young and his wife, Sue. We're out in row eight. You get out and you walk on the No. 8 row carpet. The No. 1 carpet has the participants. And there's a stand with all the cameramen, they're taking pictures. So we're just walking way on the outside, I mean, it's not really a big deal. But somebody up in the stands recognized me and it was on ESPN, my wife and I.

"At the Governor's Ball afterwards, Wendy Finerman walked up to me, slapped that Oscar right in my hand and she said, 'Next

Monday night it's your turn!'

"Darned if Wendy wasn't right, after which the merry-go-round started spinning in earnest.

> April 4:   The night after the championship game, the Bruins do Jay Leno's show. (After their '94 loss to Tulsa, Leno zinged them in his monologue but life is about forgiveness.)
>
> April 5:   The Bruins get a parade down Disneyland's Main Street. Back on campus that afternoon, 13,000 students jam Pauley Pavilion to watch the championship banner raised.
>
> April 7:   Black-tie dinner downtown as O'Bannon gets the John Wooden Award.
>
> April 8:   Harrick flies to Dallas to speak at Billy Packer's clinic.
>
> April 9:   Harrick goes on to Atlanta with side trip to Augusta for the final round of the Masters. CBS helps get him in. A member has to extend an invitation so the network gets Frank Broyles, the Arkansas athletic director, to do it.
>
> April 10: Back in his tuxedo, Harrick receives the Naismith Coach of the Year Award in Atlanta.
>
> April 12: Harrick flies to Boston for breakfast at Reebok, which outfits Bruins and employs him as a consultant. O'Bannon flies in, too, as the company tries to sign him as an endorser (Ed later signs with Nike). They fly back to Los Angeles for a *Sports Illustrated* reception to announce its commemorative issue.
>
> April 20: Harrick, O'Bannon, Cameron Dollar and Chancellor Young go to Sacramento as guests of the legislature.

"Probably the week or two after, the most popular person in the state of California was Ed O'Bannon," says Harrick. "He's got about fifty people following him, kids and even workers there in the Capitol. We're going from the Senate to the House of Representatives. There's probably about five people kind of wanting my this-and-that and the Chancellor is walking, he's got nobody with him.

"I'm saying, 'Oh, that's a good deal, here's a guy who's our boss.' "

April 25–26: In Tampa, Harrick appears on the Home Shopping Network, selling Michael Jordan cards for Upper Deck.

April 29: Harrick and the Bruins throw out the first ball at the Dodger opener.

May 2: They throw out the first ball at the Angel opener.

May 19–22: Harrick flies to Chicago for the National Restaurant Show. He speaks to Sun-Kist distributors at Michael Jordan's Restaurant and signs autographs at the show.

May 25: Harrick flies to Washington, D.C., to see Zidek honored at the GTE Academic All-American banquet.

June 1–2: The Bruins fly back to Washington, D.C., to visit the White House. Side trips to the Treasury to see the money being printed (with many jokes about lottery-pick-to-be Ed's batch) and the Pentagon. They meet General John Shalikashvili, chairman of the Joint Chiefs. Defense Secretary William Perry shows them a picture of a since-dismantled Ukrainian ICBM with seven warheads.

He told us they had had 100 of those intercontinental ballistic missiles with seven on each one of them," says Harrick. "Seven on each one of them. Seven hundred warheads, all pointed at American cities. Now that was about three or four years ago. I tell you, the eyeballs of our players were just bulging. Me, too. I mean, this is serious business. This is no basketball game. I mean, this is the real deal."

That afternoon, they meet President Clinton. High points include assistant coach Steve Lavin getting the President to drop into a defensive crouch.

The reception is held in a ballroom but an FBI man takes Harrick to see the Oval Office. "Most beautiful thing I've ever seen in my life," says Harrick. "The lighting was magnificent. It was just perfect."

June 5: The Harricks stop in Las Vegas on the way home, stay at the Mirage, see Siegfried and Roy.

June 9–16: They fly to Portugal as guests of local coaches, whose clinic Jim addresses. Side trip to the Algarve, the Portuguese Riviera.

June 18: The Harricks are back home to see son Glen graduate from UCLA.

"One of the great days of our life," says Dad. "I'll go back to the twenty-eighth of July a year ago. We had our first granddaughter. So from our granddaughter to the Academy Awards to the National Championship to the Masters to our son graduating, it has been a magical, magical year."

He still had to go to Japan where he would advise the Mitsubishi basketball team; to Las Vegas to address a convention at Gold's Gym; to Greenbriar to address a group of bankers from West Virginia (yes, his speaking fee, which was once nothing, is going up); to Rancho Cucamonga to throw out the first ball for the minor-league Quakes.

If the world has gone nuts, what can a basketball coach do about it? By fall, Harrick would have covered fifteen time zones and even a UCLA season would seem like a relief.

In a sobering development, CBS's ratings for the '95 finals fell 12 percent from the year before. Critics noted the long commercials (eight three-minute TV time-outs in addition to the teams' regular ones).

Anyway, all the Bruins enjoyed it hugely.

Bill Walton, zealous as ever, is taking it a little lighter on the Bruins these days. Now an NBC commentator on its NBA package, Walton also does Clipper games where the organization has begged him to consider the positive. He occasionally can be found in Michigan or somewhere, doing a Continental League game.

Roy Hamilton is a producer for CBS Sports.

Michael Holton played in the NBA for parts of six seasons. He is now assistant coach at Oregon State.

Nigel Miguel has become an actor, appearing in such films as "White Men Can't Jump" and "The Air Up There." He is still active in UCLA activities, which he finds interesting, to say the least.

"I'm happy for Coach Harrick," says Miguel, "but as you well know, what have you done for me lately? Being part of the Alumni Association and the Chancellor's Associates now, I'm on the other side of the ball. So now I hear what used to be said about us, ten years later. It's brutal in there, man."

Keith Owens played for the Lakers for a year, played in Europe and is now deciding whether to apply for UCLA business or law.

Gerald Madkins worked his way up from the CBA to play in the NBA for two seasons.

Jack Haley is entering his seventh NBA season.

Marques Johnson acts ("White Men Can't Jump," "Blue Chip," et al.) and does commentary of Sonic games as well as UCLA games. His "Yeah, baby!" call of Tyus Edney's game-winning lay-up against Missouri was so popular in Westwood, they made up "Yeah, Baby!" T-shirts. Johnson presented one to President Clinton during the visit to the White House.

Larry Brown took the Indiana Pacers, who had never won an NBA playoff series, to the Eastern finals in his first two seasons there. He still says he wants to be a college coach.

And John Wooden finally got to say a few words to the Bruins.

Contrary to reports, it didn't happen at Seattle, where he was determined to stay out of the way, but at Pauley Pavilion before the banner-raising.

"I like this basketball team very much," Wooden says. "I got to know some of the players a little better over a period of years.

"Zidek, for example, I have great respect for him. Outstanding student, knew why he was there and I like that. I like the fact that all three of the seniors they had there, he and O'Bannon and Edney were all graduating. That pleased me. I got to know Toby Bailey. His girlfriend is Mike Warren's daughter.

"I just liked the players on this club off the floor as well as on the floor. And on the floor, I thought we played about as unselfish as I've seen a UCLA team play in many, many years. And also, they seemed to realize, and my own contention was that defense usually wins championships....

"To see them tuck it in when they lost Edney and play so well, that was most gratifying to me and I know how gratifying it must have been to Coach Harrick.

"Jim took some criticism, not so much criticism for his coaching. Jim made some inadvisable statements, which he said, that his mouth was his biggest enemy. I think he's shown he was a good coach from the very beginning. He just didn't become a good coach this year. He's paid his dues, high school, assistant at Utah State, assistant UCLA, head coach Pepperdine. I think he did well every place he's been.

"I think a lot of the criticism was never of his coaching as much as being underpaid or statements of that sort. And then he said 'I' instead of 'we' when he referred to the team and he got some criticism along that line but those are just, perhaps, slips of the tongue. I never felt—do you?—that there's been that much criticism of his coaching."

When you're 84, a phone that rings all the time, as Wooden's did after the championship game, is a nuisance. For a while, the man who always calls back didn't.

But things were back to normal by the summer when Wooden made an appearance in Watts where former President Jimmy Carter and his wife, Rosalyn, had come to build houses for Habitat for Humanity.

"I took his book of poetry that a friend had sent me," says Wooden. "At the luncheon, the first day I was down there, I sat right beside his wife and she noticed the book and she said, 'You've read my husband's book.'

"I said I was hoping, I didn't want to intrude in any way but I thought there might be a possibility that I might get him to autograph it. I said, 'Would you autograph it for me?'

"And she said, 'Certainly, I will and I'll do more. I'll go get Jimmy!'

"There's a President's wife, running over to get the President!"

So Wooden met a president, too, and got an autograph and his picture taken.

The next day, one of Wooden's sons-in-law, a grade school teacher, visited the project with three of his students. So it goes, each one teaching one, and this wonderful spirit will never die.